TOKYO

Classic dancer in Edo-period costume

TOKYO

A CULTURAL HISTORY

Stephen Mansfield

OXFORD
UNIVERSITY PRESS

2009

OXFORD
UNIVERSITY PRESS

Oxford University Press, Inc., publishes works that further
Oxford University's objective of excellence
in research, scholarship, and education.

Oxford   New York
Auckland   Cape Town   Dar es Salaam   Hong Kong   Karachi
Kuala Lumpur   Madrid   Melbourne   Mexico City   Nairobi
New Delhi   Shanghai   Taipei   Toronto

With offices in
Argentina   Austria   Brazil   Chile   Czech Republic   France   Greece
Guatemala   Hungary   Italy   Japan   Poland   Portugal   Singapore
South Korea   Switzerland   Thailand   Turkey   Ukraine   Vietnam

Published by Oxford University Press, Inc.
198 Madison Avenue, New York, NY 10016

www.oup.com

Oxford is a registered trademark of Oxford University Press

Co-published in Great Britain by Signal Books

Library of Congress Cataloging-in-Publication Data
Mansfield, Stephen
Tokyo : a cultural history / Stephen Mansfield.
    p. cm—(Cityscapes)
Includes bibliographical references and index.
ISBN 978-0-19-538634-9; 978-0-19-538633-2 (pbk.)
1. Tokyo (Japan)—Civilization.   2. Tokyo (Japan)—History.   I. Title.
DS896.5.M37 2009
952'.135—dc22   2008052679

9 8 7 6 5 4 3 2 1

Printed in United States of America
on acid-free paper

Contents

Foreword
by Paul Waley

Of all the clichés that help to define life in the world's largest city none is more persistent than that of the city of constant destruction and rebirth, the destruction inflicted both by natural forces and by the human desire to wring as much money as possible out of urban land. The Tokyo we see today has changed radically from the city of the 1970s, which in turn bears no resemblance at all to the city of the 1920s, and even less to Edo, the capital city of the Tokugawa shoguns. But what does it mean to live in a city where the landscape changes with such frequency and such totality? What is the effect on its residents of living in a city that is so plastic and pliable, where so often it is impossible to find the buildings one remembers from one's youth?

Tokyo has none of the monuments of the national capitals of Europe, nor of its Asian neighbours. None of its buildings conveys the sense of pride and pomposity of the Invalides in Paris or the monument to Vittorio Emanuele in Rome. You will not find in Tokyo a great open space like Tiananmen or a national monument like the one in Jakarta. There are no palaces—apart from the Imperial Palace, which is, famously, invisible—and the temples and shrines are a far cry from the Sacré-Coeur or Westminster Abbey. Japan's modern history has involved an uncomfortable relationship with the past. Much of the period has been spent trying to forget the past and to ensure that as few reminders as possible are retained in the urban landscape. No wonder perhaps that the one significant exception is the most controversial site in the city, the Yasukuni Shrine, where the souls of the Japanese war-dead are commemorated.

Lacking this visible aura of a capital city, Tokyo appears to many who visit it as missing a sense of unity and coherence. There is no sense of where the city starts or ends, no centre and no edge. There is no gravitas to the city, and no civitas. Lacking this authoritative script of its own history and without a commemorative urban landscape, Tokyo has no generally accepted aesthetic standards. A landscape law was passed a few years ago, but it has made little difference. Controls on building heights exist, but these are complex and have been vastly relaxed. This is a city where you can build more or less what you like wherever you want to build it.

Tokyo is, in other words, a city that allows you strange freedoms. And the most fundamental of these is perhaps the freedom to read what you will into or onto the city. Everyone makes their own map of the city, creates their own centres and their own peripheries. Because no one imposes a vision of Tokyo on you, you make what you will of the city. And if there are few buildings around to kindle memories of the past, of one's personal past as well as the city's past, then the memory gravitates around people more than places. Tokyo is a city about people, ebbing and flooding, great waves of people washing around the buildings, rushing through the channels, and pouring back out again.

Tokyo is not just a city about great numbers of people moving around. It is a city composed of the maps and the memories and the struggles and strategies of its many million inhabitants, as they meet with colleagues, with friends, with soul-mates, with former classmates, and then break off and move on and meet with others. As they do so, they create their own routes around the city, marking here a favourite restaurant, there a bar for a water-cut whiskey. And in the end each individual ends up giving Tokyo the shape that suits and accords with their own lives.

Tokyo is a city, then, where you draw your own map and make your own spaces. And so the spaces of the city are unorthodox, interstitial, hidden away in neglected corners, down stairways, up elevators, and nearly always extremely difficult to find the second time round. They lie round behind the *sakaya*, the liquor shop, and past the soba noodle restaurant, or down a flight of steps at the bottom of a short, sharp slope. These, not the privileged eyries on the top of its skyscrapers, are the real spaces of the city.

And the stories of Tokyo are just as personal, off-beat, and anecdotal as the spaces. Many of them revolve around the common people of the city and their encounters with ghosts and animals, or they are stories of patience and fortitude in the face of adversity. Some of them have even left their mark on the urban landscape. In what other city of the world does the most celebrated statue represent a dog, Hachikō, who came every day to Shibuya Station to wait for his master? These are the stories that Stephen Mansfield introduces us to here in the pages of this book.

It is a further cliché of the city that places of historical interest are disappearing, destroyed, crushed, swept away. The past is constantly receding. But this has been the pattern for well over a hundred years. Visitors to the city in the 1880s and 1890s were already complaining that the Japanese were westernizing their capital city and in the process destroying their own precious culture. And the plaint has been heard ever since.

We are particularly fortunate therefore to have such a perspicacious guide as Stephen Mansfield. Having lived in Tokyo and written about it for many years, he is able expertly to reflect in these pages the quirky, unpredictable, and multifaceted stories that go to make up the narrative of the city. He interleaves his tale with references to and quotations from both, Japanese writers and non-Japanese visitors to the city. In doing all this, he also conveys a sense of the changing tide of national history.

Preface & Acknowledgments

Henry James once summed up London in just a few words, calling it "the biggest aggregation of human life—the most complete compendium of the world." The definition could just as easily apply to contemporary Tokyo, the world's largest, most convulsively changing megalopolis. The city's writers, artists and designers may be better qualified to interpret Tokyo than its legions of town planners or bureaucrats. Architect Maki Fumihiko, for example, has observed, "The aesthetic that this cityscape generates is one that favors fluctuations, fluidity, and lightness; it suggests the discovery of a new perceptual order."

If Europeans are overawed by the architecture of the past, convinced that nothing as visionary or accomplished can ever be built again, this is where Tokyo, having none of these convictions or inhibitions, radically deviates, believing that it can improve on the past and produce something more outstanding, or at least more apropos the times. A city so utterly fixated on the present would seem incapable of producing a culture deeper than the neon script and signage that ripples across its surfaces; yet Tokyo, westernized but insistently Japanese, provides the setting for a culture that is simultaneously ancient and brand new. In an exciting city, full of stories about itself, you can feel a kind of fermentation beneath your feet as you walk its streets, something its writers and artists, eager to see the city's nooks, crannies and mutations for themselves, have always done. There are few cities where emotional responses to transformations in the urban landscape have been so scrupulously recorded by writers, where literary themes and styles have evolved so directly from memory and observation.

From the very onset, Tokyo was destined to be a city of transformations. A city transfixed on the moment, its unflagging cycles of change have acquired the regularity of tradition. So great is the intensity of change that the city seems at times to be completely severed from its own history. Yet irrespective of the reality that assails the eye, the past is deeply engraved into the fabric of the city. It is these lines of historical continuity, connecting Edo and Tokyo, that this book explores.

*

In order to make structural sense of Tokyo's relationship to its past, I have chosen to track its cultural and historical development chronologically rather than thematically, though themes continually highlight the text. Japanese names appear throughout this book in their native order, surnames preceding given names. Thus, Kawabata first, rather than Yasunari. In the case of Japanese works of fiction, I have opted in most instances for the ones used in the standard English translations where they exist. Hence, Kafu's *Bokuto Kidan* is rendered as *A Strange Tale from East of the River*. Photographs throughout are my own. Photographs throughout are my own. I have also used images from my collection of Tokyo postcards from the Taisho to early Showa periods. I have tried to be as accurate as possible in the placement of historical events, spellings and dates, where conflicting facts arose during the research for this book. Where matters of literary and historical interpretation are concerned, however, I have only myself to blame.

The imprimatur of several writers marks this work. I have been privileged to read about and hear first-hand Donald Richie's recollections of a city he has known intimately for more than six decades, to have access to his private photo collection and permission to examine his journals before they were finally published. I am indebted to conversations with the author and journalist Henry Scott-Stokes, another long-time Tokyo resident. Possessed of an infallible memory, Henry was both friend and biographer of Mishima Yukio, one of Japanese literature's most complex figures.

I would also like to express my gratitude to translators like Donald Keene, Alisa Freedman, Lawrence Rogers, Jay Rubin, Shogo Oketani and Leza Lowitz, who have brought Japanese literature into the English reading realm, and to writers like Paul Waley, who have undertaken translations for their own books. Burritt Sabin, formerly of *The East* magazine, was an indulgent and generous editor who allowed me to explore Tokyo subjects at will. Alex Hendy at the *Japan Journal* suggested a long series on Tokyo districts and writers some years ago, which fired up my engines on this subject. I am also indebted to the wonderfully idiosyncratic and detailed Tokyo histories of the late, much missed Edward Seidensticker. Where else could you read that during a pet owning fad introduced in the Meiji era by an enterprising Englishman and his American partner, a person in the Tokyo district of Shitaya "was fined and jailed for staining a white rabbit with persimmon juice"? The two Tokyo books and countless research papers of Paul Waley, great-nephew of that eminent translator of Japanese literature, Arthur Waley, have been invaluable as models of cultural geography. The echoes of Paul's work reverberate along the walls of this one.

This book is for Kazuko, without whom I would not have lived in Japan long enough to write a book about it.

Introduction

Few people living in the great capitals of Europe in the eighteenth century had any notion that there stood at the other end of the world a city vastly larger in population than any of their own. The fact would doubtless have prompted a similar mockery and incredulity to that with which Venetians greeted Marco Polo's accounts of imperial China. But such a place existed. This was Edo, the city that foreshadowed Tokyo.

Edo was divided into the Low City areas known as the *shitamachi*, and the *yamanote*, or High City. The Low City occupied reclaimed land to the east and south of Edo Castle, a flat river delta of canals and water-courses where merchants, craftsmen, fishermen, actors, and members of the so-called "naked trades"—palanquin carriers, labourers and other lowly occupations—were obliged to live. The warrior class took the elevated ground, the variegated landscapes of the High City, with its natural springs and well-watered gardens.

What the shitamachi lacked in space and comfort it more than made up for as the stage for an expansive cultural life. A source of immense pride to the townspeople, the Low City enjoyed an unrivalled degree of cultural hegemony until the city of Edo became the capital, Tokyo, in 1868. All roads led to Edo. Traffic between the city and the imperial capital of Kyoto passed along the *Tokaido*, or Eastern Sea Road. Other trunk roads connected the city with the northern, western and southern provinces, vectors along which increasing amounts of goods and skilled workers flowed.

The city underwent great developments at this time, including the rise of a merchant class, who were beginning, to the outrage and stupefaction of the authorities, to express a cautious but nevertheless fractious disrespect for the social hierarchy and the still dangerously unpredictable samurai. The transgression of social codes could result in brutal punishment, but as the city became wealthier and more ostentatious in its tastes, so its people, even the most impoverished, became bolder in their pursuit of pleasure and independence. Although Kyoto remained Japan's capital until the end of the nineteenth century, Edo was its *de facto* political centre, the incubator of a vibrant new culture. As such, its self-confidence grew as gifted artists and writers were drawn to the city.

Tokyo today occupies a generous swath of the alluvial Kanto plain in Honshu, the largest and most populous island in the Japanese archipelago.

Situated on the eastern Pacific coast, its main geographic features are its undulating hills to the west, the flatlands to the east and its main watercourse, the Sumida river, running from the north-eastern reaches of the city into Tokyo Bay. The easternmost of the great Asian capitals, it stands alone on the edge of the continent. Sitting above the world's most geologically unstable terrain, it hangs perilously over an ocean that quickly plunges to depths of 30,000 feet. Almost a quarter of the nation's population, in excess of thirty million people, live in and around the city, a demographic fact that squarely places Tokyo, the largest capital in the developed world, at the centre of Japan's political, economic and cultural life.

Infinite and chaotic, its tangled infrastructure and curious spatial combinations apparently impenetrable, its buildings covered in advertisements, ideograms and electronic messaging, the physical setting is immensely complex. In submitting itself to repeated sessions of radical urban surgery and implanting, allowing the scalpel to slice away and dispose of loose tissue, Tokyo's remodelled surfaces always seem youthful, to have somehow escaped the rigor mortis of older capitals. This is not to say that the contemporary city is without the graduated shading of history. There exists, below the colossal conflation of shapes, a remarkably intact structural core dating from the original city of Edo. A city apparently incapable of producing a culture any deeper than the ripple of neon script that animates its building surfaces is, it turns out, all about depth.

For all its rapacious development, its tireless reinvention of self, Tokyo has a surprising number of green and pleasant places. Thousands of city parks, some spacious, others barely large enough to support a children's swing, sandpit and bench, grace the city. Edo-period gardens, some almost intact, others greatly reduced in scale, remain immensely impressive. Adding to the greenery are sacred groves located in the grounds of shrines, and rows of potted plants outside small wooden houses in the lanes of the city's older quarters. Flower and plant festivals, many with their roots in the days of Edo, are periodically held in the grounds of temples and parks, which come to life with plum, peony, ground cherry, morning glory and chrysanthemum fairs. Many streets are planted with avenues of gingko and Zelkova, and there are rules requiring residents of new apartment blocks to create rooftop gardens. There is even talk of creating a vast forest along Tokyo Bay. The city's flora benefits in no small measure from a regular abundance of rain, clear autumn skies, a relatively mild winter and very pleasant spring temperatures, when cherry blossom viewing is succeeded by a keen appreciation of flowering azaleas and wisteria. Tokyo's sub-tropical summers are quite a different thing. Extreme humidity descends on the city, turning Tokyo nights into steamy nocturnes akin to those of Bangkok or Shanghai.

It is *pro forma* in introductions to important world cities to describe them as unique or as anomalies. In the case of Tokyo, where the normal standards used to judge cities are largely absent, those terms do seem singularly apposite. With only the scantest traces of a visible past, Tokyo offers little physical evidence of its origins. Its history is in the distillation of its own narrative. Writers who wish to describe the city have to engage in a process of historical reconstruction, relying on prints, paintings, photographs and the accounts of writers and early foreign visitors. Great cities are invariably associated with the work of literary figures that have lived or put in long sabbaticals there. Mary McCarthy is remembered for her boarding days in Venice, Gerald Brenan is associated with Granada, Henry Miller with Paris. With the exception of the American author Donald Richie, who will surely be recalled as Tokyo's pre-eminent muse, the man who took on the task of cultural interpreter for a megalopolis that defiantly resists such categorization, few foreign writers or artists of note have taken up permanent residence in Tokyo. Many have lingered beyond their intended stays, however, allowing the city to exert its influence on them.

There are, of course, as many Tokyos as there are visitors. If a common perspective is missing, this is a tribute to the diversity and complexity of a city that can generate so many different interpretations. This present interpretation of Tokyo was not conceived as a guidebook, though in a very real sense it can be read as a guide to a cross-section of the city's cultural life. I have not attempted a district-by-district description, but to evoke the atmosphere of the city, its sensuality (a word rarely associated with Tokyo), and to indicate areas of creative fermentation past and present by focusing on elements of the city's culture, in particular the extraordinary richness of its literature. Rather than divide the book by subject, I have detailed the historical development of the city from its pre-Edo origins to the present day, allowing themes to surface and dominate the text as they arise naturally in the course of the city's evolution.

Important subjects touched upon here are the establishment of the castle town of Edo as paradigm for a national power structure, the rise of the merchant class, collapse of the shogunate, relocation of the emperor to Tokyo, the rapid modernization programmes and arrival of foreign experts and visitors that followed, the conflict between western ideas and a deeply rooted isolationism. As with the formative Edo period, I have devoted considerable text space to the subsequent Meiji era, the so-called Age of Civilization and Enlightenment, and the hybridization that affected the appearance of Tokyo. The latter part of the book places the growth of popular culture and the first yearnings of democracy alongside the traumas of the great Kanto Earthquake of 1923, the rise of militarism and the devastation of Tokyo in the Second World War. The final two chapters describe the rebirth of the city and its remarkable transition to the present day.

While the book tracks a chronology of events, of formative dates that have in some way shaped the city, the main themes form a commentary on people and culture: Tokyo's persistent craving for the new, its urge to replace outmoded forms, aspects of contemporary Japan that are by no means recent phenomena. Takao Yoshii, in his book *The Electric Geisha*, describes how even in the Edo period, the rapid dissemination of information among the townspeople hastened the replacement of old values and tastes. "In the urban setting," he notes, "social and cultural phenomena would arise one after another and each new value thus generated might soon be overturned by the next." If change in Japan is essentially culture and technology driven, then Tokyo, the laboratory for this experimentation, is in both the real and fictive sense, the global imagination's proxy setting for the future, as the science fiction novels of William Gibson illustrate.

It would be easy enough to conclude that Tokyo today is poised in a transition between past and future upheaval, but the truth is that Tokyo is a city of perpetual transitions. There are few cities in the world as well schooled in the concept of destruction as part of the cycle of rebirth. Earthquakes, volcanic eruptions, typhoons, epidemics, floods, the eerily beautiful fires known as the "flowers of Edo", the bombing of tightly compacted civilian areas in the war—these and many other calamities have been periodically visited upon it. Whether as Edo or Tokyo, the city has faced these and other cataclysmic strokes and endured, a testament to its granite heart. Tokyo's insecurities, its impermanence, the conviction that it could all be gone at any given moment, lend this city of dark premonitions and bright lights an intensity unlike any other capital in the modern world.

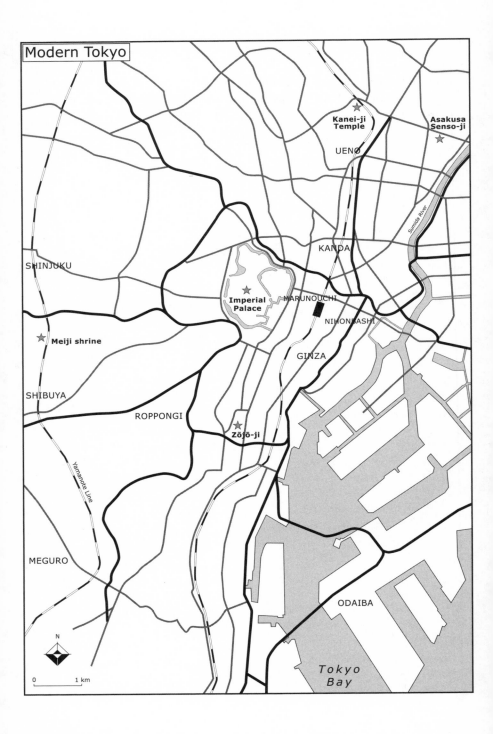

Chapter One

THE SHELL MOUND
EARLY HUMAN SETTLEMENT TO MILITARY CAPITAL
8000 BC?-1590

Even by American standards of individualism, Edward Sylvester Morse was a strange bird. Where other western visitors to Meiji-period Japan (1868-1912) attempted to establish trade agreements, amass valuable art collections, convert the Japanese through missionary endeavours or write accounts of the exotic capital of a lotus land at the extremity of the earth, the New England zoologist had come to Japan to further his studies of brachiopods, Western Pacific shellfish.

Insatiably curious and with a passion for detail, Morse had travelled to Japan at his own expense, setting himself up temporarily in the port city of Yokohama. The morning after his arrival on 18 June 1877, he boarded the newly inaugurated Tokaido railway line from Yokohama to Tokyo. Six miles from the terminal at Shimbashi the train passed through the village of Omori, moving slowly enough for passengers to take in the details. Glancing out of the window of his carriage at the sunlit embankment, Morse's trained eye fell on an object of little interest to his fellow travellers: a five thousand-year-old cockleshell, *Arca granosa*, something he recognized from his walks along the coast of Maine.

What everyone had seen, but only Morse had noticed, was an ancient kitchen heap, a prehistoric midden alongside the railway tracks. Conscious of its significance, Morse returned to the site a few days later with a group of students from the recently founded Tokyo Imperial University. "Frantic with delight," as he put it in one of his beautifully written accounts, "we dug with our hands and examined the detritus that had rolled down and got a large collection of unique forms of pottery, three worked bones, and a curious baked-clay tablet." The pre-Bronze Age site, known as the Omori Shell Midden, marked the birth of Japanese archaeology and provided an immeasurably valuable key to human settlement in the Tokyo Bay area.

More discoveries followed. On 2 March 1884, three students digging into the shell heaps near present-day Nezu station unearthed quantities of pottery shards. Older than anything previously found, the discovery pushed back the date of the earliest agriculturalists, communities that gave up nomadic existences to settle in the region. More Neolithic remains have been found in the Tokyo area than in any other region of Japan.

As the sea advanced, deep encroachments into the valleys and plains of this area forced inhabitants up onto the ridges and bluffs, vantage points from which plentiful supplies of fish and shellfish could still be gathered. An important part of the diet of the Stone Age dwellers of the Jumon period (8000-300BC) who lived along the ridge of the wave-lapped Yamanote hills, the shells were dumped onto middens. As the waters of the bay gradually retreated, brackish pools and swamps were left behind at spots like present-day Koishikawa, Shinobazu Pond in Ueno and at Tameike near Toranomon. Primitive settlements existed at the head of the bay. From the remains of stone tools unearthed in strata excavations along the upper banks of rivers, we know that the region was the home of late Palaeolithic inhabitants, hunter-gatherers in a biologically diverse area. During the Meiji period fifth-century burial mounds containing swords, armour, gems and totemic clay sculptured vessels known as *haniwa* were discovered in Tokyo's Setagaya ward.

A Goddess in the Nets

On 18 March 628, two fishermen hauling their catch from the Sumida river found a golden image trapped in the nets. The Hinokuma brothers, credited with finding the statue of Kannon, goddess of mercy, are remembered in Asakusa Shrine, next to the present Asakusa Kannon temple, also known as Senso-ji. Built to house the statue and dedicated in 635, it is the oldest Kannon temple in Japan.

The establishment of the temple on the edge of the desolate Musashino Plain probably represents the arrival of Buddhism in this area. The remains of stone pillar bases in Kokubunji in west Tokyo mark the spot where another temple was erected after Emperor Shomu's 737 decree that each province should have its place of worship and a monastery. At the same time, an official road was opened, connecting the plain with Kozuke in present-day Gunma prefecture. This allowed hunters access to the game-rich area and opened the plain to the breeding of horses. The same century saw the arrival of groups of naturalized Koreans who settled on the plain.

The name of the deep, eroded valleys and diluvial swampland appears in the poems of the eighth-century anthology, the *Manyoshu*. The desolate wilderness of reeds, pampas and wetlands inspired educated and privileged travellers who, in the manner of the age, kept detailed literary diaries. Visitors on imperial business passed through the region via ancient routes that radiated from Kyoto, the capital. A very basic ferry system existed for crossing the Sumida. The poet Ariwara-no Narihira used it in 880. His verse about seagulls flying over the river seems to have inspired the adoption of the bird as one of the symbols of present-day Tokyo.

Crossing the river one windy autumn night in 1020, the twelve-year-old Lady Sarashina, returning to Kyoto after her father's recall from the provinces, found little to admire in the desolation she recorded the next day. The pampered members of Kyoto's Heian court, where the aristocracy resided, were easily vexed when expectations of profound and mystic landscapes raised by reading literature, failed to correspond with reality. "On the beach the sand was not white but a sort of muddy colour," she writes; "in the fields, there were none of the murasaki plants I had heard about."

Close to the volcanic sands of the bay noted in the *Sarashina Diaries* mention is made of the ruins of what might have been either a temple or early dwelling called Takeshiba. The number of inhabitants in the area, however, remained small. The Musashino Plain was still a lonely place, an expanse of reeds and tall grasses, the moon turning the tall vegetation into a sea of silver plumes. The melancholic cry of the plover could be heard near the banks of the Sumida, where a few wretched huts stood. Even in daylight Lady Sarashina found that the reeds were so high "the tips of our horsemen's bows were invisible."

Two centuries later, Lady Nijo, determined to see the eleven-faced Kannon statue at Senso-ji temple in Asakusa, crossed the plain in autumn. To reach the goddess she had to go through vast fields so densely covered with bush clover, reeds and pampas grass that no other plants were able to grow there. The height of the grasses was such that a man on horseback could pass through unseen.

Desolate though it may have been, the plain was not completely uninhabited. Several pre-Edo residences have since been unearthed in the area. In Akasaka's Hitotsugi-machi district, traces of the home of the twelfth-century lord Imai Kanchira have been identified as the coastal dwelling of Edo Shiro Shigetsugu, a local chieftain who seems to have taken his name from the area where he established a clan power base. Armed bands passed across the plain during this period of clan rivalry, engaging in vicious but forgotten battles and leaving disease and famine in the wake of their bloodbaths. The plain could still inspire moments of inspired literature, even entire works like the poet Motomasa's *The River Sumida*, written in 1432. The *Noh* play, centring on a woman who, driven insane with grief, is comforted by the ghost of her child, was adapted by the composer Benjamin Britten after he visited Japan in 1956. The libretto for the work, *Curlew River*, was written by the English poet and novelist William Plomer, who lived in Japan in the late 1920s.

THE WARRIOR POET

This wild and scattered grassland, destined to become the largest urban development in the world, was organized into a martial entity, a domain of sorts, with the arrival of Ota Dokan in 1456. Ota, a minor feudal lord, belonged to a cadet branch of the Uesugi family. Its patriarch, Uesugi Sadamasa, served the Kyoto-based Ashikaga shogun. The clansman settled on a location called Chiyoda, connected to a primitive road leading north. Despite the bleakness noted by poets and diarists, the site had some obvious advantages. Situated in the largest of Japan's alluvial plains on well-irrigated rice land—the farthest position from a potential continental invader—it provided good grazing and exercise for the breeding of horses, an important factor in the rise of the warriors of the eastern seaboard. The tributaries and watercourses of the Tone river, the largest in the east, served as important transportation channels and were conveniently close.

Villagers were removed and work on the building of a castle began. Its earthen embankments, palisades, bamboo poles, shrubs, thatched buildings, wells and ditches gave it the appearance of a military camp rather than a fortress, but as the plain was dominated the settlement grew in scale. Though the castle was still surrounded by insalubrious marsh land, rice fields were cultivated in place of the tall reeds.

Great men were expected to be versed in the classics. By all accounts Ota was an untutored rustic more interested in subjugating rival clansmen until an encounter while out hunting in the area where Takadanobaba station now stands turned him into a man of culture and good taste. The

Statue of Ota Dokan, the "warrior poet", in the Tokyo International Forum

story was no doubt liberally embellished over the years, but a kernel of truth remains. Waiting out a heavy shower, Ota asked a peasant girl emerging from a hut to provide him with a *mino* (straw raincoat). To his dismay, the girl presented him with a single wild flower, a yellow rose, before silently withdrawing. Baffled by the gesture, Ota asked his fellow hunters the meaning of the girl's action. An ancient poem, he was told, describes the simple dignity of a yellow rose that, though blooming abundantly, produces no seed.

Sad indeed am I
That I have not one straw raincoat
Like the seven-petalled, eight-petalled
Blossom of a yellow rose.

The characters for the flower in Japanese, *mino hitotsu*, can also be read as "one straw raincoat". Humbled by his ignorance of the language of poetry, Ota determined to apply himself to the study of literature. The story illustrates the point that rulers were expected to be men of culture, and how historical events are often subsumed into literary accounts. Ota subsequently became known by the title of the "warrior poet" on account of his devotion to literature and works of Chinese philosophy.

The fortified castle of Ota Dokan, built in 1457 and equidistant between the fiefdoms of northern and southern Honshu, was on rich farmland endowed with plentiful land and water access. The ancient site name, Edo, meaning "mouth of the estuary", was retained. Ota administered the settlement that grew around his military fortification for thirty years, turning the town into one of the key shipping and trading centres of the Kanto region. Boats anchored at its gates offloaded iron and copper weapons, fish, tea, rice, even rare medicines imported from China. Ota's fortress also provided an unintended shelter for monks, poets, artists and aristocrats who had abandoned the imperial city of Kyoto during the catastrophic Onin civil war of 1467-77, a feud that destroyed much of the capital.

As a highly able administrator and military strategist, a man of sensibility and good taste, Ota attracted the envy and suspicion of his own lord, who ordered his assassination in 1486. With Ota's death the settlement passed into the hands of weaker descendants who were swiftly overcome by the predatory Hojo clan. Warriors in the purest sense, unwilling to contaminate themselves with trade, they allowed Edo's thriving commerce to languish, finally abandoning the stronghold to the elements. Made almost entirely from wooden materials, the castle, merchant houses, lowly hovels and salt-encrusted port structures facing the bay were subjected to damp and decay during Japan's sub-tropical summers, turning a dynamic trading entrepot into a worm-ridden, termite-infested ghost town. Edo fell into a trance state lasting a full century.

In 1573 effective rule over the whole of Japan fell into the hands of one man, the warrior and military general Oda Nobunaga. A Machiavellian figure whose passion for unifying the country was matched by his ruthlessness in quelling enemies—including on one occasion an entire monastic complex of fractious monks—Nobunaga was also a sensitive devotee of the arts. A close link between official power and the arts was always strong in Japan. When, in 1582, he was assassinated by a general he had insulted, it was, in a strangely fitting choreography of death, while he was in a temple dancing a scene from a Noh play.

VISIONS OF A CITY

Nobunaga's second-in-command Toyotomi Hideyoshi appointed Tokugawa Ieyasu as chief commander of his forces. Anxious to remove Ieyasu from the centre of political power in Kyoto, he offered the warlord large land holdings in eastern Japan in exchange for his territory near the imperial capital. To the consternation of his followers, Ieyasu readily accepted. As *daimyo* (feudal lord) of the eight provinces of the Kanto, Ieyasu's audacious private vision was to create from the insignificant village of Edo a military capital from which he and his heirs would control the entire country.

With Toyotomi's death in 1598, Ieyasu moved a step closer to realizing his ambitions. Daimyo were resolutely divided into two factions: those supporting Toyotomi's son Hideyori, and those who gave their backing to Ieyasu. In the ensuing power struggle among contesting daimyo, culminating in the decisive battle of Sekigahara in 1603, Ieyasu prevailed. The emperor formally appointed the general as shogun, or military governor, an ancient title abbreviated from the longer "Commander-in-Chief for quelling the barbarians".

Ieyasu, now effectively the country's military dictator, immediately transferred the seat of the *bakufu*, the military government, to Edo though Kyoto remained the imperial capital. Moving the centre of civil and military power from the weak aristocratic court in Kyoto to Edo Bay, he ruled over Japan in the name of an emperor so powerless that many Japanese today would be hard pressed to even recall his name.

Despite the coastal swamps and lack of natural spring water, Ieyasu saw much promise in a flat, easily defensible, sea-facing settlement standing at the point where an important trunk road to the mountain province of Kai, the Koshu Kaido, also branched off in the direction of imperial Kyoto. An official entry into Edo was made on 1 August 1590. Ieyasu's first night in the town was spent in the rooms of a Buddhist temple, common hostelries at the time for honoured visitors. The first foreign diplomats to arrive in Edo in the nineteenth century would find themselves similarly accommodated.

Shinto shrines were places of worship for a religion concerned with customs and rituals useful to earthly existence, a faith predisposed towards encouraging benevolent fortune. They demanded courtesy calls, something Ieyasu quickly set about doing. The first pace of worship he came across was a shrine dedicated to the deity Tenjin. Ieyasu remarked, "Ota was a poet? It was surely natural that he should build a shrine to the god of literature!" The temple, out on the marshes of Asakusa, was duly visited in the following days.

The deserted castle that Ieyasu inspected was in a deplorable state. Three wooden steps made from the beams of old ships led to the main gate, a rickety portal conveying little sense of even diminished grandeur. The outlines of the main building, the Honmaru, flanked by two smaller buildings, the Ninomaru and San-no-maru, could still be made out. Other structures, the outbuildings and kitchens were thatched, the ceilings made of narrow boards, the walls blackened by smoke. Underfoot the straw matting was damaged and sodden from leaking roofs made from crude wooden shingles.

The citadel would have to be completely rebuilt. It cannot have taken much effort clearing away the fungus-stained buildings. When the time came to erect a new city, nature had already done most of the demolition work.

Chapter Two

THE CITADEL
1590-1638

Three days of *Noh* and *Kyogen* followed Ieyasu's self-appointment as shogun, a measure of the importance the performing arts would have on the new city. In his younger years Ieyasu, a contemporary of Shakespeare and Marlowe who went on to earn a reputation as a drama critic, had performed Noh himself. Throughout his office he continued, as Hideyoshi had done, to support the four main schools of Noh with estate rights and generous rice stipends, a practice continued by his successors until the overthrow of the Tokugawa shogunate in 1868.

Kyoto, where the emperor, the Heavenly Sovereign resided, remained the nominal capital of the realm. A new city for a new century, Edo was not yet the national capital but its status as the *de facto* military and political capital, and its potential as an engine for wealth creation, foreshadowed its later domination of the entire country.

In selecting Edo as a site for this new political machinery, certain requirements of Chinese geomancy would have to be met; symbols and coordinates, correctly chosen, would endorse and secure the power of the new city. The east, the direction of the Cyan Dragon, required a major watercourse. The Sumida served this end. The west, provenance of the White Tiger, demanded a major road. The Tokaido trunk road was already in place. The domain of the Vermilion Bird to the south required a pond. With a little imaginative interpretation, Edo Bay might substitute for such a pond. The north, the lair of the Dark Warrior, was more problematic. This direction demanded a mountain. Mount Fuji was the obvious choice, but its orientation lay to the west. The problem was solved by repositioning the castle's main gate, the Ote-mon, from its traditional place in the south to the east. Using the new castle layout as a compass, the mountain's coordinate could hence be read as north. Traces of these considerations survive today in Tokyo place names such as Tatsunokuchi (Dragon Mouth) and Toranomon (Tiger Gate).

As an extra precaution against ill fortune, Zojo-ji temple, dating from 1596, was moved to Shiba, an undeveloped area to the south of Edo. A special place of worship for the Tokugawa dynasty, experts in geomancy were consulted to ensure that the temple was correctly appointed to protect the city from infiltration by evil spirits. A grand gate, the San-mon, was erected in 1605. Classified as a national treasure, it still stands today, a rare survivor of earthquakes, fires and man-made catastrophes. Temples, shrines and monasteries lent the new city some much needed cultural credentials. For the first time, Ieyasu had the Chinese classics printed on paper and brought the renowned library of the Kanazawa Bunko to Edo.

The building that ultimately proclaimed the ascendance of a new *realpolitik*, and which served as the lodestone of Edo's structure and protective force fields, was the Tokugawa citadel itself. The construction of this supposedly unassailable fortress was a titanic undertaking. The remains of Ota's old fortification, its rotting mats, collapsing earth walls and termite-infested rafters were soon cleared away. Carpenters set about replacing the putrescence with sweet-smelling freshly planed timber. Following the tastes of Kyoto aristocrats who treasured the flower as an aesthetic adjunct to the tea ceremony, Ieyasu even had a camellia garden created at the centre of the castle.

The area, now the Imperial Palace East Gardens, formed the nucleus of the complex, with a five-storey donjon at the core. In order to make the castle grounds impregnable, a system of river-connected moats and canals, closer to a series of whorls than precision circles, was dug. These disgorged at two points into the Sumida. The channels were breached by bridges and fortified gates. The shape was something akin to a logarithmic spiral, a mystical form in Shinto deriving from the ancient, Chinese-based *yin-yang* scheme by which the universe functions. The spiralling moats and height of the buildings within emphasized centrality, a single, unassailable political organism. The view of the castle from the congested alleys, low-rise homes and stores of the townspeople who depended on the citadel and its needs for their livelihoods must have been impressive. A green, watery void surrounded by a human termite nest, the working parts of this precision machine were designed to ensure that they would not rebel against each other.

Recent advances in engineering meant that certain natural disadvantages of location could be overcome. Ieyasu's priority was to develop recla-

Townspeople crossing the original Ryogoku Bridge

mation projects along Edo Bay that would secure major coastal roads and provide quays for ships. Shipping was the lifeblood of the trade that supported the city; one early visitor observed that the vessels moored in the bay were "as thick as the scales upon the back of a fish, while the masts presented the appearance of a dense forest." As more space was consumed, the bay was forced back, land reclaimed, hills levelled. Beginning the remoulding of the city that continues relentlessly up to today, earth was taken from the higher bluffs to fill in the Hibiya Inlet, a watercourse that flowed from the bay to the feet of the castle site. Edo's water-courses were adapted into more geometric, rectilinear forms, the inner moats and canals containing the castle, the intermediate spaces the residences and offices of officials; the less appealing outer peripheries, a system of ditches stretching down to the bay and designed to provide a first line of defence, were occupied by merchants, artisans, labourers and craftsmen.

Moats, a conduit for drinking water and a canal leading from the salt flats near the bay, were among the first infrastructural projects. Ieyasu forced the *daimyo* into providing the funds, materials and labour needed for the massive task of constructing the castle and canals. A single vessel could carry just two of the larger stones, which required as many as 200 men to load. In all, 3,000 ships were used to transport the granite and volcanic materials the sixty miles from quarries on the Izu Peninsula. Once the rocks reached Edo, they were offloaded onto carts drawn by oxen. The larger stones were placed on sledges, wooden palettes drawn by teams of labourers. Seaweed was placed under the sledges to facilitate their movement forward. But for the comic spectacle of hired entertainers, it would have been a Herculean task worthy of heroic depiction. As teams of men from different fiefdoms vied with each other to finish the work in a competitive spirit, they were spurred on by troupes hired to beat drums, blow conches and to mimic the manners of Europeans (southern barbarians as they were called) in lewd dances. In this atmosphere akin to a community festival, the great citadel rose inch by inch.

The castle and its dependent buildings, including the shogun's private residence, a series of secondary fortresses, munitions stores, watchtowers, gardens and teahouses, occupied the centre of the web, with hundreds of warriors, administrators, family members and concubines in residence. Its fortifications were made of stone, grey tiles were baked from clay, the surfaces of its white walls made from lime. Two golden dolphins sat on the roof.

As a symbol of authority it was highly effective, but the sprawling grounds and the fact that it depended almost entirely on the outside for water and food rendered it indefensible. The period of peace crafted by Ieyasu and passed down to his descendants eventually neutralized the building's function as a fort, replacing it with a system of feudal interdependency.

THE MILITARY CITY

The physical arrangement of the city was conceived to embody the hierarchical social order. Ieyasu ruled over the 176 Inside Lords who had shown the prescience to side with him at Sekigahara in 1600, and the 86 Outside Lords who had not. Lords who had fought on Ieyasu's side, together with their families and followers, were allotted spacious residencies close to the castle walls. The Outside Lords were handed plots of land that formed a strategic circle, a first line of defence in the now unlikely event of invasion.

As in all totalitarian states, fear and suspicion dictated policy. Daimyo and their families lived under constant threat of punishment for disloyalty or misconduct. Estates could be requisitioned and families banished to inhospitable provinces or god-forsaken, barely inhabited islands. By preventing horizontal alliances, segregating the population and establishing an extensive network of spies, Ieyasu and his successors made insurrections difficult as no individual group could develop a military or economic base strong enough to challenge the central government.

Dictatorships require loyal retainers, but ultimately, because of the paranoia and insecurity bred by such systems, nobody is beyond suspicion. Lords on both sides of the shogun's loyalty ranking were restricted in the amount of arms they could amass, and the fortifications they could build around their estates. Social contact between the estates was discouraged in an unofficial version of non-fraternization; each estate was encouraged to spy on the next and report any suspicious goings-on. Government inspectors dispatched to keep an eye on the activities of the lords and report back to the castle tightened the surveillance web.

In order to hobble their power and to discourage foment around their still armed retainers and vassals, daimyo were required to leave hostages in Edo as surety for their good conduct. Later, a more unified version of *sankin kotai* (alternate attendance) was introduced. Devised to keep the lords distracted and their coffers depleted, the system required a one-year residence in Edo, another year in the home estate. As these estates were often hundreds of miles from Edo, the bi-annual journey was a colossal undertaking. As a further precaution, barriers were erected at strategic points along the highways into Edo, where a rule of "no women out, no guns in" tightened the hostage system and ensured that the daimyo remained impotent.

With their lacquered palanquins, liveried retainers, horses, spears, banners and decorative halberds, the processions were great spectacles for the townspeople and eagerly awaited events in the high ritual of Edo. A woodblock print by the great Edo artist Ando Hiroshige depicts a daimyo and his retinue crossing the Sumida on their return journey home. Beyond spectacle, they were also reminders to commoners of the authority of their masters.

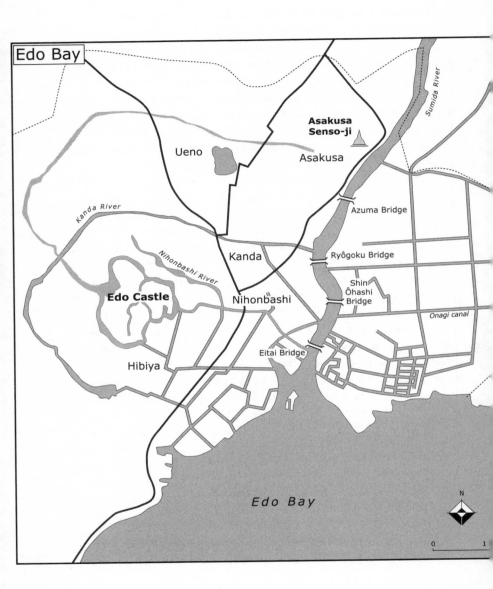

The castle defined the shape of the city. At its feet, Nihonbashi, Kanda and Kyobashi were inhabited by craftsmen, the nuclei of a scheme whereby each trade or craft would occupy an assigned quarter, chandlers in this one, coopers in another. Plasterers were found in Kanda Shirokabecho, for example, scabbard-makers in Minami-Sayacho, indigo dyers in Kanda Konyacho, gunsmiths in Teppocho. Thirty-six approaches to the city gates, called *mitsuke*, were built as security checkpoints. Although the mitsuke have vanished and only a small section of the outer moat exists today, they survive in the names of districts and metro stations like Akasaka-mitsuke, and Yoysuya-mitsuke. The gates were firmly locked at night, a practice that worked for a time before a more natural order asserted itself.

Nihonbashi, connecting the main commercial street of Otemachi with the castle, was an important district from the very beginning. Ieyasu had Nihonbashi Bridge, a 160-foot long wooden construction, built in 1603, making it the starting point for the five great roads that led out of the city. The five trunk roads that converged and bifurcated here were the Tokaido, Nakasendo, Koshu Kaido, Oshu Kaido and Nikko Kaido.

The shogun's perpetual fear of an armed uprising was expressed in the design of the Tokaido road, which was kept narrow enough to discourage the movement of armies, and suitable only for travel by foot or horse. An elaborate system of barriers and checkpoints kept human traffic under strict supervision. Boxes and chests were carefully examined to ensure that no arms, especially firearms, entered Edo. Even a horse required a written permit to enter the city. Like the risks faced by nineteenth-century Europeans travelling in disguise to the holy cities of Lhasa and Mecca, the penalty for trying to smuggle oneself into Edo might easily be death.

All distances were measured from the zero point at Nihonbashi Bridge, a practice that continues today. Travelling to the city with the Dutch trade mission in the 1690s, the scholar Engelbert Kaempfer noted: "Among the bridges, there is one 42 fathom in length, famous all over Japan... It is call *Nihonbas*, that is, the bridge of Japan." The original arched bridge appears much later in the history of the city in Hiroshige's print *Fifty-Three Stages of the Tokaido*. Reflecting its central role in the life of the city, this is print no.1 in the series. The background of the work shows us five towers rising above tiled warehouse roofs. The human elements contain almost the entire social strata of Edo, with a daimyo procession approaching, lance bearer's weapons held aloft, while the riverfront fish-mongers, fearing for their lives, move gingerly back to allow their superiors to pass.

Despite the beauty of the design, the bridge could be a fearful place. Felons were exhibited to the public in fetters at its south end. Adulterers and priests who had committed sexual offences were displayed here before being taken off to the execution grounds. Murderers were placed in a hole with their head and neck exposed. Two saws were placed next to the heads for any passer-by to execute justice should they so wish. Few did. The severed heads were skewered on pikes at the end of the bridge as a warning to would-be criminals. If you had no business with the bridge or the fish market, it was a place to admire from a distance.

By 1608 the moats of Edo castle extended as far as Kudan, a slope where the Yasukuni Shrine now stands. Sixty-six gates, 19 towers and a donjon rising almost 200 feet created an image of fortified majesty endorsed by ritual and protocol. Those who failed to observe even minor rules of etiquette could be subjected to severe punishment. By the time the castle was completed in 1638 it was the largest construction of its kind in the world, though few people living in Edo would have been aware of the fact. Within a mere decade, moreover, the new capital had mushroomed into a major city. Its proportions had already been noted by visitors and favourably compared with other world cities. Visiting Edo in 1611, John Saris, an English sea captain, commander of the *Clove*, the first English merchant ship to visit Japan on a mission to establish a branch of the East India Company, wrote in his journal: "The fourteenth (of September) we arrived in Edo... which made a very glorious appearance unto us; the ridge-tiles and corner-tiles richly gilded, the posts of their doors gilded and varnished." Engaged in a profession that made him acutely aware of fire and water, the captain noted not only the profusion of rivers and canals, but also of stone wellheads hung with buckets that could be used in the event of a conflagration. The main street of the town, he observed, was "as broad as any of our streets in England". This spacious boulevard would have been the prototype for many wide avenues constructed as fire-breaks. Another Englishman, Richard Cocks, visiting Edo in 1616, was better placed to make comparisons. "We went rowndabout the Kyngs castell or fortress," he wrote, "which I do hould to be much more in compass than the city of Coventry."

SOUTHERN BARBARIANS

Japan's first encounters with westerners date from 1543 with the arrival of Spanish, Portuguese, Dutch and English traders, together with numbers of Jesuit and Franciscan missionaries. Although the official reaction to foreigners eventually turned to repugnance followed by animosity, ordinary Japanese were mesmerized by these "southern barbarians" or *nanbanjin*; their clothing, customs, even eating habits all struck them as a mixture of the exotic and grotesque. Many of these Europeans arrived in the company of their Southeast Asian and Indian servants, by way of the East Indies and the Malay Peninsula.

The Portuguese were the first to land, introducing bibles and firearms in a familiar but ultimately unsuccessful strategy, the Church softening up the ground, the military hardening it. Japan's first Christian missionary, the Basque priest Francis Xavier, was powerfully drawn to Japan. "This militant man," as Nicolas Bouvier wrote in *The Japanese Chronicles* (1975), was "attracted by difficult countries, by a slightly melancholic moral rigour that he could sense without formulating... some indefinable quality, born of a tradition of which the West was ignorant." Curious to know more of the priest's doctrine, many Japanese daimyo, aware that Xavier's journey to Japan had begun after the completion of his mission in India, took Catholicism for a new sect of Buddhism.

The tolerant but shrewd Ouchi clan in Yamaguchi, for example, their eyes less on baptism than the Portuguese cargoes from Macao, granted the Jesuit permission to preach in the manner of the bonzes. The uncompromising Xavier took to the streets of the city, denouncing, among other things, infanticide, idolatry and sodomy (the latter a widespread practice at the time among the military and Buddhist clergy). Misunderstandings and offence, both real and imagined, were inevitable. Europeans, ignorant about the Japanese language, found that its vocabulary fell lamentably short of being able to render their message with clarity. Buddhist terminology was used to translate the scriptures; the concept of God came out as the ambiguous *kami,* which could signify any number of gods. The word "sin", faring little better, was termed *tsumi*, meaning the generic "morally wrong". Proselytizing with groups of Jesuits, Xavier did, however, initiate a stream of conversions which by 1600 had reached a staggering and worrisome 300,000—this at a time when the official population of the country stood at a little over twenty million.

The Dutch, more interested in trade than theology, consequently did better after the shogun Hideyoshi turned against a Christian beachhead that appeared to be taking political form. The motives of Europeans were further questioned when Portuguese missionaries, showing a greater enthusiasm for gold than God, began plundering Japan's reserves. In an early purge, the *generalissimo* ordered the crucifixion of 26 Franciscans in 1597. The arrival of the English in 1613 further complicated the situation, introducing unwelcome Catholic-Protestant rivalries. The methods of suppression, though on a smaller scale, were no less severe than those practised by Catholic states like Portugal and Spain on subjects who resisted conversion. Those who refused to recant perished after miserable tortures and ordeals: hung by the feet for days, raped by crowds, boiled alive, thrown into tubs of vipers, or crucified.

SECLUSION

After the suppression in 1637 of a largely Christian revolt in Shimabara on the southern island of Kyushu, Japan entered into a period of seclusion known as *sakoku*, one that would last for almost 250 years. Under this system the building of ocean-going ships was prohibited and sailors who found themselves shipwrecked beyond the territorial waters of Japan returned at their own peril; even those Japanese engaged in trade in such places as Southeast Asia were excluded from returning to their homeland. One troupe of hapless entertainers and their wives, working on the Indonesian island of Java, were never to return home. Under the iron grip of the Tokugawa regime, the influence of foreigners swiftly declined. The motives involved more than mere xenophobia. The Tokugawas were aware of a papal decree dividing the known world into Catholic and Protestant halves. The Philippines had already undergone forced conversion under the Spanish, while the Portuguese held sway over the trading enclave of Macau.

The Dutch, meanwhile, having endeared themselves to a later shogun by supplying a warship to fight against rebelling Christians, were given sole, though still limited, trading rights. Confined to a tiny artificial island in Nagasaki called Dejima, the Dutch and Chinese provided Japan with its only window on the world for the next two centuries. Though a tiny breach in the defences of the country, it allowed for a trickle of scientific and medical knowledge to seep in from Europe. Scientists and scholars like Thunberg, Siebold and Kaempfer were posted to Dejima, and on their return to Europe wrote the first foreign accounts of the country.

As the only westerners tolerated by the new regime, the Dutch were required to demean themselves with displays of cajoling flattery and obeisance in their mandatory visits to the shogun's palace, a practice that continued well into the nineteenth century. The ever-expedient Dutch seem to have felt that the brief humiliation was worth it. Granted an audience in 1822, a Dutch warehouse master by the name of Fischer recorded what was required of a foreigner to make the right impression as he entered the Hall of the Hundred Mats:

> The whole ceremony consists in making the Japanese compliment upon the appointed spot, and remaining for some seconds with the head touching the mats, while the words *Capitan Holanda* are proclaimed aloud. A stillness as of death prevails, broken only by the buzzing sound made by the Japanese to express profound veneration.

The exclusion policy, from which the Dutch and their Chinese rivals were exempted, doubtless hindered the development of the country in many ways, but it also promoted a sense of independence, and a culture less dependent on continental Asia.

PAX TOKUGAWA

The duties of the warrior class in Edo, liegemen in one way or other to the shogun himself, ranged from fairly humble posts guarding the castle gates and blockhouses to senior positions as councillors to leading daimyo. Samurai of any rank could be called to attend or participate in mandatory ceremonies.

The samurai alone had the right to go armed, his two swords, the handles of a long and short weapon protruding from scabbards, differentiating him from the townspeople who were allowed to carry one short and rather blunter sword for self-defence. Farmers had to protect themselves with agricultural tools and implements in the manner of peasants the world over.

With the separation of the warrior and farmer classes, the samurai moved into the *jokamachi*, or "under-castle towns" close to the city fortifications, a pattern that was duplicated throughout the country and formed the standard for urban development at the time. All functions were directed towards Edo castle, the central command organism.

Numbers of samurai, whose masters had been deprived of their positions or who had simply foresworn their allegiance to a lord, roamed the streets of Edo, creating social disorder. Known as *ronin* (wave men), they had no official income or right to fixed residence within the jokamachi. The life of the ronin was a mixed blessing, as they were accorded less respect than fully affiliated samurai in a country where identification was, and to some degree still is, consonant with respectability and recognition. The members of this dispossessed class eked out a living as best they could, hiring themselves as bodyguards to affluent merchants, or as instructors in military science: swordsmanship, equestrian skills and archery. The more intellectually gifted became writers and calligraphy teachers, Confucian scholars or instructors in philosophy and Chinese literature. While employed they could live moderately well. Between posts they were reduced to sleeping in rudimentary shelters or beneath the deep eaves of temple roofs. While their existence may have been precarious, they enjoyed a degree of freedom almost unheard of in a city expressly conceived to inhibit personal choices and freedom of movement.

Swashbuckling and potentially violent gangs of *hatamoto* (bannermen), young samurai who worked directly for the shogunate, were a common feature of life during the early days of Edo. Short of money, they would refuse to settle their bills; when flush, they became violent at an imagined slight when a shopkeeper might offer change for a bill paid. The "White Hilt Gang" was typical of this unstable element on the streets of the city. Their longer than average swords were decorated like their *obi* (sashes) with white fittings. In summer they chose—perversely—to wear long kimonos, in winter short ones, placing lead in the bottom hems and edges of their cloths to make them swing, an effect intended to lend a swagger to their movements.

SWORDS AND INK BRUSHES

The disciplines and moral rectitude of *bushido*, the "way of the warrior", did not preclude blade testing on unwary victims. New swords were routinely tested on bundles of straw, fresh corpses and the dead or still breathing bodies of condemned criminals. With the right to kill any merchant or peasant who failed to show the correct degree of respect, a samurai, selecting some lonely part of the city at night, might easily cut off the head or limb of the first passer-by he met. Needless to say, this privilege, however infrequently put into practice, did not endear the samurai to the townspeople. The retainer of a hereditary post, Yamada Asaemon, otherwise known as Yamada the Beheader, was the most skilful of the Tokugawa executioners and sword-testers.

A massive armed class posed its own problems for the authorities, as rebellions had always arisen from within this group. An edict issued in 1615 requiring samurai to study and master the literary arts with the same vigour they had applied to the martial arts was an attempt, based on the Confucian idea that the pen and sword should be equally matched, to temper the warrior instincts of the samurai. Yamaga Soko, a masterless samurai and instructor in Confucian studies, addressed the delicate question of the peacetime role of the samurai in his work *Shido*, published in 1665: "Within his heart he keeps to the ways of peace, but without he keeps his weapons ready for use..."

Seeking an ideology to legitimize the new order, the authorities created a form of Tokugawa neo-Confucianism that would endorse a strict and confining hierarchical structuring of the classes, one based on laws that could be presented as immutable. The scholar Hayashi Razan, founder of a Confucian academy in Edo, is generally credited with promulgating the philosophy, imported from China, in his capacity as an official Confucian adviser to the shogunate. Razan strove to unify Confucian propriety and its firm rules of conduct with the laws of nature, as this passage from one of his treatises explains:

> Heaven is above and earth is below... we cannot allow disorder in the relations between ruler and subject, between those above and those below. The separation into four classes of samurai, farmers, artisans and merchants, like the five relationships, is part of the principles of heaven and is the Way which was taught by the Sage.

The Sage, of course, was Confucius. Removing the metaphysics required in Chinese tradition, Hayashi created a system of governance offering an ethical basis that would promote the political presuppositions of a new state ideology requiring total obedience to superiors. Confucianism's leaden, didactic literature, however, had a stifling influence on the arts, especially painting. Beholden to the patronage of the Tokugawa court, painters of the great Kano school of artists, for example, sacrificed creativity in their bid to please their masters.

The core hierarchy of the castle and its military personnel, together with a massive concentration of samurai and their retainers, daimyo mansions and a growing number of shrines and temples, required the services of artisans, craftsmen, merchants and labourers, as well as tremendous quantities of consumer goods. Creating the new city that radiated around the castle produced a further workforce of skilled workers: draughtsmen, surveyors, carpenters, plasterers, *tatami* makers, armourers, administrators, scholars and artists. The lively interaction between these practitioners from different classes generated a creative fusion that led to one of the most vibrant cultures in Asia. Such was the influence of the city on Japanese culture that the era came to be known as the Edo period.

Merchants were despised by the ruling elite as their existence was considered to be based solely on the amassing of wealth. As the fortunes of the daimyo were progressively leached by the heavy levies they were forced to pay in maintaining estates both at home and in Edo, merchants and financiers, nominally members of the lower classes, became indispensable to the growth of the city. With an irony increasingly relished by the merchants themselves, their increasing wealth and power led not only to the decline of the old class system, with some *chonin* (townspeople) gaining the upper hand financially, but also to an efflorescence of culture that, to a very real degree, was their creation.

An urban structure was already apparent: the hilly, more prestigious bluffs of the yamanote to the west of the castle, a diluvial terrace with good views across the city, was where the samurai residences could be found, while artisans and merchants were confined to the *shitamachi* or Low City to the east, the marshy, alluvial area most likely to suffer rising tides from the bay and flooding from the river. The expressions High City and Low City first appear in a storybook called the *Eda sangoyu* (Beads of Coral) published in 1690, but the distinction was already well established. The translation of the word *shita* (down) and *machi* (town), the English "downtown", falls short of its acquired meaning. Far more than a mere geographical co-ordinate, shitamachi is a concept and is in many respects regarded as the birthplace of Edo culture, expressed in printmaking, *Kabuki* and the refined mannerisms of the pleasure quarters. On a more mundane level, the people who inhabited the shitamachi were responsible for provisioning the daimyo and samurai families with food, goods and services. Their contribution to the life of Edo, though, belied their low status in the city's social ranking. Their discontent over the long period of the Pax Tokugawa would produce a spirit of defiance.

The citadel and its matrix of subordinate zones and buildings were secure for the time being. The forces that were to eventually subvert the prevailing order were not the rising hordes of fractious warrior clans the Tokugawas so feared, but the relentless tread and grind of culture.

Chapter Three

EDO CULTURE
THE FLOWERING MARGINS
1638-1707

The citadel might have been built to outlast the ages, but no one was under any illusions about the precariousness of life in Edo, a city periodically traumatized by earthquakes, typhoons, tidal waves, floods, epidemics and famine. There was also the ever-present risk of fire among a population living cheek-by-jowl in homes made primarily of wood and paper.

An early test of Edo's ability to withstand disaster and renew itself came on the morning of 18 January 1657, during the rule of the fourth shogun, Ietsuna, when a fire broke out in Maruyama Honmyo-ji, a temple in the present-day district of Hongo. Known as the Meireki Fire, the conflagration followed a drought that had left wells, riverbeds and other water courses depleted and buildings as dry as tinder. Adding to what many townspeople were beginning to think of as divine retribution was a strong wind blowing up clouds of red dust that fanned the flames, driving them over streets and walls. When the doors of a prison at Denma-cho were opened to save its inmates, a rumour spread that criminals were running amok. Responding to the news, the keeper of the town gate at Asakusa hastily ordered the great wooden doors closed. Thousands of townspeople and inmates were roasted alive, jammed against the gate as they tried to flee the flames. When the wind finally abated, a heavy snowfall blanketed the city. People made homeless by the fires perished in the blizzard as they huddled in the cold. The fires and snowstorm are said to have taken some 108,000 lives and obliterated sixty per cent of the city.

Despite its stone and water perimeters the fire had penetrated the castle grounds and fortifications. We can only imagine the sumptuously decorated interiors of the castle, the work of the great court painter Kano Tanyu, that were lost to the fire. The main keep was burnt to the ground. The fire was also strong enough to melt all the gold that was stored in the cellars of the keep. The scene was recorded by the chief stonemason's son:

All around us it grew darker and darker, the people were lighting lanterns to show them the way. About then, the gunpowder stored in the towers began to ignite, and the sound of the explosions rent heaven and earth. With a thunderous roar, the towers crashed burning to the ground.

If the speed of destruction was astonishing, so was the reconstruction. The entire castle, minus the main keep, was rebuilt within two years. A fire-fighting group had already been set up in 1629; now further regulations were introduced to reduce the risk of fire. Thatched roofs were prohibited, streets widened to create firebreaks and fire towers with bells to sound the alarm were erected throughout the city. Despite these measures there were twenty major fires recorded during the Edo period. The shogun's fire brigade was formed some time after the Meireki Fire. Many lords had their own brigades, commoners forming their own volunteer bands. The tattooed bodies and splendid banners of these dashing heroes are celebrated in the colourful *ukiyo-e* woodblock prints of the time. Though fires were an occupational hazard of living in Edo, the townspeople grew philosophical about natural disasters in general. Seeing a redeeming beauty in the fires, they called them *Edo no hana*, the "flowers of Edo".

Unabated, fires continued to be the scourge of Edo life. The cramped downtown districts where merchants and craftsmen lived and worked were especially vulnerable to conflagrations, many the result of arson. The common people, resigned to losing their property and merchandise to fires, came to accept them as part of the price of living in Japan's most dynamic and prosperous city, where even devastating loses could be recouped. Although Edo represented an extremely heterogeneous society, designed to stifle any correspondence or commonality between its segregated classes, the relocation of residents while central parts of the city were being rebuilt had the unplanned effect of blending social classes, with samurai now living, albeit temporarily, at close quarters with craftsmen, resulting in a reciprocal exchange of ideas and skills.

DEFINING THE *EDOKKO*

Living conditions were probably no worse in Edo than any other urban centre in Japan, but as the city grew, its population swelled. The relative isolation of the country spared it many of the diseases common to parts of the world colonized by the western powers, especially the islands and archipelagos of the Pacific, where natives had come into contact with infected European crews. Relatively high standards of cleanliness and personal hygiene, assisted by the introduction of public baths, helped to keep disease in check, but the living conditions of the lower orders were conducive to the rapid spread of epidemics. The preponderance of water, a blessing in normal circumstances, only exacerbated sanitary problems. The Sumida could be counted on to flood twice a year. Filthy fish markets, foul odours and swarms of insects created the perfect setting for frequent outbreaks of cholera.

Among the discomforts of the humid summers were the swarms of mosquitoes that bred in the pools, canals and puddles of the city. Wealthy merchants lived along the more spacious, better ventilated front streets. These solid, fire-resistant homes were usually two storeys high, with attractive tiled roofs. Built of lath and plaster, the walls were finished in a lustrous black paint made from lime, India ink and the ash from incinerated oyster shells, creating an elegantly eerie sheen.

The expansive, free-spending, devil-may-care nature of the townspeople is partly traceable to the conditions in which they lived. With more construction projects, the number of forced relocations and property confiscations grew. Flux and impermanence were permanent features of the city. Common people lived in squalor in warrens of badly ventilated alleys with little sunlight. Many were less than three feet wide, running between single-floored, shingle-roofed row house tenements facing open gutters blocked with raw sewage. Facing the alleys and back streets, housewives made makeshift kitchens where fires could be prepared for cooking. A common toilet could be found in the alley. An Inari fox god enshrined in the depths of the alley provided a degree of spiritual bonding between residents and helped to mitigate their squalor by cohabitation with the divine. As darkness fell, those who could afford to changed into night attire; others slept in their work clothes. Some employees without the means to afford their own accommodation were obliged to sleep on the plank floors of their workplace or spread rush mattresses there. These tiny houses of Edo, locked up and shuttered at night, with their inhabitants laid out beneath transparent mosquito nets made from hemp, cotton or silk, must have been insufferable during the humid summer months.

The people of Edo, though, were a strong, resilient breed. The early Edo period saw the birth of the eponymous *Edokko* or "son of Edo" as he was better known. The received portrait of the Edokko is doubtless exaggerated, but most ukiyo-e depictions and literary accounts concur that he was a reckless type, devoted to gaiety and spectacle. Add to that the forgivable sin of being an inveterate spender, always in search of fineries he could ill afford. Quick to take offence, the male version of the Edokko comes across as a spirited soul whose rough exterior, tinged with vanity, barely conceals the yearnings of a soft-hearted urban dandy.

The type was not universally liked. The writer Koa Jokanbo, in his curiously named *Didactic Clumsy Sermons Continued* (1753), wrote of what he perceived to be the congenital spite, bad manners and upstart views of the Edokko: "The people of Edo wish to be rude; showing respect seems to them a shame. The worst offenders are those of the lowest rank. Some Edo people even make malicious remarks that one mustn't be afraid of samurai and lice."

The first recorded use of the word Edokko appears in a *senryu,* a comic verse published in 1771. By this time, a significant number of Edokko, with roots firmly attached to downtown areas like Kanda, Kyobashi, Ginza and Shiba, had accumulated great wealth in their role as agents and brokers for the government's rice granary in the Asakusa Kuramae district, as dealers in lumber at Kiba, as receiving agents for commodities coming down to the city, or as managers of the thriving riverside fish markets. The downtown areas of Edo were the new market places where trade was conducted, ideas aired, innovation in the arts and the limits of official tolerance tested. Nihonbashi was the home of the newly rising townspeople, the transfer point where patronage of the arts passed from the exclusive domain of the aristocracy to commoners.

Craving all manner of diversion and preferring to spend the little money they had on pleasures and aesthetically pleasing possessions than to save for an uncertain future, ordinary townspeople were brimming with the kind of vitality that is only possible during extended periods of relative peace and economic progress. There was nothing like democracy in the political meaning of the word, but an increasingly strong sense of culture descending to the people. Beneath the heavy machinery of Tokugawa polity could be heard the insistent sound of a restive, demographically ascendant sub-society.

By the end of the seventeenth century, Edo had produced a significant body of merchants whose wealth far exceeded their social status. The wealthier townspeople, who in a very real sense were now Edo's patrons of the arts, refused to give in to the menacing conditions in which even the affluent lived, making instead an aesthetic of it. Requisitioning the Buddhist concept of *ukiyo*, meaning in its pure form "this ephemeral world in which we all suffer," they eliminated the word suffering, reworking the written character to give the more tantalizing reading "floating world". The writer Asai Ryoi offers a useful definition of this attitude to life and art in his 1691 *Tales of the Floating World*:

> ... living for the moment, turning our full attention to the pleasures of the moon, the snow, the cherry blossoms and the maple leaves, singing songs drinking wine and diverting ourselves just in floating, caring not a whit for the pauperism staring us in the face, refusing to be disheartened, like a gourd floating along with the river current: this is what we call ukiyo.

Female beauties, androgynous youths, an atmosphere of pleasure and dalliance set against a consuming passion for culture as a source of gratification: such were the elements of this floating world, avidly supported by the rich, powerful and idly elegant.

BEAUTY AND DESIRE

Using the argument that vice could be supervised and contained, Shoji Jinemon, a brothel-keeper, submitted a petition to the shogun to allow the creation of an authorized pleasure quarter. Five years later he was granted permission. The first Tokugawa shogun seems to have been swayed by the infallible logic, according to a later record of the times, which states:

> Virtuous men have said, both in poetry and classic works, that houses of debauch, for women of pleasure and for streetwalkers, are the worm-eaten spots of cities and towns. But these are necessary evils, and if they are forcibly abolished, men of unrighteous principles will become like ravelled thread.

The legions of unmarried men who moved to Edo from Kyoto, Osaka,

Mie and Shiga prefectures to work and open stores created a male-dominated city. Prostitutes and brothel-owners had already moved their operations into the city from many of the older, more established pleasure quarters of Kyoto, Fushimi, Osaka and Nara, creating a flesh market that was free-wheeling and largely ungoverned. In giving their tacit approval to Jinemon's scheme the authorities hoped to control and regulate the trade, concentrating all prostitutes into a single pleasure quarter, one that would help to close down other establishments, particularly the city's public bathhouses, which featured the services of female bath attendants.

Licensed prostitution had a long, if not particularly august, history in Japan. A pleasure quarter of sorts had existed in Kamakura in the thirteenth century, another in Kyoto during the Muromachi period (1333-1573). The shogun Hideyoshi had authorized a government-licensed quarter in Kyoto, which he modelled on the walled-in pleasure districts of Ming-dynasty China. The site set aside for Edo's new pleasure quarter, a snake-infested bog that bred swarms of mosquitoes in the summer, was unpromising, but Jinemon was an enthusiastic promoter of his project and soon the marsh was filled in, moats dug and sturdy walls erected.

The new quarter that appeared like an apparition above the swamp was named after the rushes and reeds that grew there: Yoshiwara, or Reed Moor. Although the entire complex, with the main streets and houses in place, was not completed until 1626, the Yoshiwara opened for business in the eleventh month of 1617 in an area to the east of Nihonbashi. Early conflagrations were contained and sections of the quarter swiftly rebuilt, but the great fire of 1657, the *Furisode kaji* or Long-Sleeved Fire, was a disaster of such proportions that the entire enterprise was relocated to outlying Nihonsutsumi, an area north of the Asakusa temple. By September of the same year, the new Yoshiwara was open for business.

Situated in the middle of fields, the quarter could only be reached across a raised dyke. Many entered it in litters or on horseback. Because it was built of wood with paper panels and straw mat flooring, fire was a constant peril throughout the history of the Yoshiwara. Fearing that the name might suggest a place of desolation, some artful changes to the Chinese character that spelled out Reed Moor resulted in the more positive "Joyful Moor" or "Field of Good Fortune". (The alteration still left the pronunciation of Yoshiwara intact.)

In what was known as the "Nightless City", as many as 3,000 cour-

Women of the floating world

tesans and prostitutes were supported by teahouse managers, servants, cooks, traders, masseurs, musicians and even clowns. The district was surrounded by strong walls, creeks and drawbridges. The ditch surrounding the Yoshiwara was said to have turned black from all the tooth dye thrown into it. Guards kept watch over the gates to ensure that indentured prostitutes and customers reneging on their payments did not escape, and curfews were strictly observed. Although the pleasure quarters were closely watched, they were to a large extent self-administered special zones, useful to the authorities as safety valves for defusing potential social unrest. Social pedigree counted for little; it was how much cash you brought through the gates of the Yoshiwara that opened doors.

At the entrance to the pleasure quarter were stores and drinking shops. In contrast to those who wished to parade their wealth and hence their ability to buy the services of the costliest courtesans, there were others who valued the way in which the Yoshiwara could conjure up an air of secrecy and discretion when called upon to do so. Among the shops that lined the entrance were those selling *amigasa*, broad-rimmed straw hats for visitors who wished to conceal their identity. Priests, monks and members of the samurai class, though expressly prohibited from doing so, appear to have been good customers.

It was a city where the male population far exceeded that of women and where wives were largely relegated to the roles of matriarchs. Inside the gates of this otherworldly domain men were ruined, and double suicides among thwarted lovers were common, providing promising material for playwrights, painters and writers of illustrated books. It was an illusion of a voluptuous Nirvana. Here, the floating vision of the white-faced courtesan with her multi-layered kimonos, painted toenails and vermillion lips, her wigs ornamented with dazzling tortoise shell hairpins, was enough to ensnare even the most virtuous of men.

Art itself set about the task of portraying a dream-like world that vanished each day with the first light of dawn. The walls and ceilings of teahouses where the most exalted courtesans presided were decorated with paintings by some of the most famous artists of the day. Among sumptuous colours with gold and silver leaf accents, fixtures and fittings were covered in gold-decorated lacquer. For a country that emphasized the virtues of modesty and understatement, the exotic, escapist pleasure palace of the Yoshiwara and its imitators could not have provided a greater, or more subversive, contrast with daily life.

Swords were required to be left at the entrance to the Yoshiwara salons. Besides avoiding the drunken rampages of frustrated violence samurai were occasionally responsible for, it had the unintended effect of levelling class and rank. A. B. Mitford, visiting the quarter in a later age, suggested a further reason for the restriction on swords when he wrote in *Tales of Old Japan* (1871) that "it is known that some of the women inside so loathed their existence that they would put an end to it, could they but get hold of a weapon."

For these women, art and ritual provided a small portal for viewing the outside world. With the first signs of spring, the townspeople began to emerge from their cold winter homes and foul alleys into a city fresh with the reviving scent of blossom. For the women of the pleasure districts, however, there was no such freedom to move around the city, unless, in rare cases, under an escort that would ensure their return. The poet Buson captured the courtesan's sad, vicarious engagement with spring when he wrote:

The plum trees bloom
and pleasure women buy new sashes
in a brothel room.

From the silk divans of the most expensive courtesans to the soiled cribs of the lower order of prostitutes, the quarter offered something for almost every male visitor. In many cases it was the merchants of Edo who could afford the former, the increasingly impecunious samurai who were obliged to use the services of the latter. The authorities were beginning to experience the disquieting realization that money talks.

The highest fees were paid for the services of the *tayu*. Their beauty and skills in music and dance—comparable in many cases to that later phenomenon, the geisha—together with the sheer celebrity of these *grandes dames*, who symbolized for both men and women a magnificently idealized sexuality, explained their pride and price. The *koshi* were next in rank, followed by the less experienced and physically endowed *tsubone* and *hashi*. Lowest in the pecking order were the *sancha* class of semi-professionals, taken from the street or bathhouses.

A great deal of time and money was spent by proprietors on grooming promising courtesans, who were schooled in painting, calligraphy, tea ceremony, poetry, flower arranging and even arts like incense appreciation and sand painting, practices that were normally reserved for the aristocracy. Instruction manuals were studied and training received from senior courtesans and the proprietress of the house. A new client was expected to wait in a reception room normally reserved for guests and servants before being introduced to a courtesan. She would then appear in resplendent attire, seating herself in the best position in the room, in front of the main pillar. A ritual of drinking sake then took place between courtesan and guest, the former reserving the right to reject the latter if he was not to her taste by refusing the proffered cup. Pampered and bred to be arrogant, the upper tier of courtesans nevertheless lived within a rigid system of confinement that made them virtual captives.

FIGMENTS OF PLEASURE

Those who could afford the services of the high-ranking courtesans proceeded to the more regal houses of assignation. The more threadbare visitors to the Yoshiwara made, without the tantalizing preliminaries that characterized the more refined sexual rituals of the tayu, straight for the bordellos where lower ranking women were displayed behind latticed screens. The tayu were known not simply for their beauty and sumptuous dress. They were expected to be accomplished in a number of disciplines, including the tea ceremony, flute and *shamisen* playing, singing, dancing and board games. As witty conversationalists, they were expected to engage in risqué dialogue with customers and also to show mastery of the subtler *double entendre* and innuendo. Tayu were also known for fortune telling and the composition of haiku poems.

The epoch of the tayu witnessed Edo's development as a place *sui generis* with a culture quite distinct from the rest of the country. At its centre was the Yoshiwara, fixated on its own rituals, enforcing strict standards of deportment and a complex protocol, showering itself with festivals and commemorative events. As wealth seeped into the pleasure quarters, attracting the attention of artists and writers, commerce and art transformed the more costly prostitutes into great ladies and the more discriminating brothels into salons. With the patronage of the *chonin*, the Yoshiwara became the seedbed where much of the culture of Edo was nourished and brought to life. Guidebooks were published providing "reviews" of courtesans and explaining the protocol involved in visiting the pleasure quarters. Profiles of the tayu and their particular attributes were published in directories. The guides, called *Yoshiwara saiken*, proved so popular that they were published annually and sold on the streets of Edo.

Men knew that the floating world was essentially an illusion, but this only increased its allure. Assignations with wealthy clients were preceded by the sumptuous procession of a tayu. The sight of these women, idols of the Edo age decked out in lavish robes of damask silk, white makeup, hair held in an extravagant crown of combs and ornamental hairpins, must have been remarkable. The writer Ihara Saikaku described one such procession in 1689:

> The courtesan arranges her clothing so that her red crepe de chine undergarment will flap open to reveal a flash of white ankle, sometimes as high as her calf or thigh. When men witness such a sight, they go insane and spend money they are entrusted with, even if it means literally losing their heads the next day.

Other writers, the popular novelist Shozan among them, became giddy with their own descriptions of the courtesans. Knowing full well that theatricality was a large part of their appeal, he devotes great attention to the costume of one such beauty: "Her dress consists of a long robe of richly embroidered silk brocade. Her head is ornamented by a dazzling glory of hairpins made of the finest tortoise-shell, which glitter around her head like the lambent aureole of a saint."

Expensive, over-ritualized, its formalities flattering the vanities of the client but also testing his patience, tayu culture entered into a period of slow decline at the beginning of the eighteenth century, but not before another incarnation of beauty and desire appeared. In the 1750s the rank of tayu was replaced by that of the equally illustrious *oiran*, a no less intoxicating species of beauty celebrated by writers and artists like Utagawa Toyoharu. The increasingly ostentatious appearance of the oiran eventually led to a decadence that ushered in the geisha.

Oiran wore towering clogs and applied white powder called *oshiroi*, not only to the face, but the nape of the neck, throat, chest, hands and feet. Lips were decorated with rouge made from the juice of the safflower. Oshiroi was derived from a mixture of rice flour, white soil and a liquid extracted from the seeds of the jalap plant. Later on, a facial base powder made from white lead and mercury chloride was used until, in the 1870s, it was found to be toxic. The acme of fashion at one time was to paint the lower lip with iridescent green rouge, a striking effect when seen against blackened teeth. The powder used for blackening teeth was made through a process of oxidization involving a mix of nails and iron filings soaked in sake and tea. Some oiran painted their toenails.

A code of sexualized symbols existed that almost all the inhabitants of Edo would have instinctively understood. Red, symbolizing the transition to womanhood, was considered an erotic colour. A glimpse of bare feet against a line of crimson silk undergarment was considered electrifying. The willow tree, seen growing outside and within the gates of the Yoshiwara, was a symbol of prostitution.

There was a good trade in aphrodisiacs for those who could afford them. Extracts and drinks were made from Chinese and Korean ginseng roots mixed with local herbs that could still be found along the banks of Edo's rivers, tiger balm and pulverized rhinoceros horn. *Fugu*, the Japanese blowfish, purportedly another aphrodisiac, was a favourite among courtesans and wealthy guests, though the poison from the fish, if not properly extracted, could be fatal. The risk seems only to have increased the thrill of sampling the tissue thin slices of fish.

Pleasure boats moored along the Kanda river

The well-off among both sexes assiduously followed the fashions of the Yoshiwara and favoured the stage and off-stage costumes of *Kabuki* actors, wearing vividly coloured satin, crepe silks and damask. To have these fabrics embroidered with metallic threads or hand-painted by an established or rising artist was a hallmark of uncommon prosperity. Syphilitic sores, hidden under gorgeous silks, were often the true mark of the Edo flesh trade, however. Yet it was the rising popularity of the geisha, signalling a change in taste among the Edo populace, that was the harbinger of decline for the courtesans of the Yoshiwara, who would soon become anachronisms.

The Yoshiwara was not the only pleasure quarter in Edo. Others existed at various times at Itabashi, Shinagawa, Senju, Susaki and Shinjuku. And those who could not afford even the most sordid services at the official sites could walk down to Yanagihara (Willow Fields), a section of the Kanda river near Mansei Bridge, where the *yotaka* operated. The name, meaning "night hawks", was given to prostitutes who made a living along the darkened streets and towpaths from a money-strapped clientele of farmers, apprentices and labourers. Customers were led into the rice fields beyond the willows for these short transactions.

Throughout, the Yoshiwara remained the most iconic of Edo's "night-less cities". Its main trade may have been prostitution, but its setting and protocols were sufficiently theatrical to make it one of the central stages for the city's cultural life.

THE GILDED AGE

An extraordinarily efflorescence of Edo arts and commerce took place at the height of the Genroku era (1688-1704). It was a period partially co-inciding with the English Restoration, whose wealth, extravagant gaiety and social mannerisms, confined to a small, highly discriminating but faddish elite, bear some comparison. The culture that bubbled up during this period, however, came increasingly from the Edo masses rather than any cultural elite. The relegation of warfare from daily reality to historical memory, combined with the rapid spread of literacy and learning among all classes, fuelled the growth and exuberance of Genroku culture.

The great literature of the Heian and medieval period, the diaries of noble women, Noh plays, the development of the 17-syllable haiku, the tea ceremony, flower arranging and *bonseki* (the art of creating naturalis-tic scenes using stones on beds of sand placed in a lacquer tray)—all had been focused on the imperial court, religious centres of learning and the military sphere. The women of the great daimyo residences, rarely ven-turing into the streets of Edo, took up similar interests. The monotony of their cultural interests and obligations was occasionally relieved by the ap-pearance of entertainment troupes, puppet shows, performing animals and jugglers, brought from outside.

It was really the commercial districts of the *shitamachi*, however, that became the cultural focus of the new city. Chonin culture and tastes were expressed in forms as diverse as literature, woodblock prints, painting, *rakugo* storytelling, Kabuki, *bunraku* and *joruri* puppet plays, geisha arts, perfume and incense-discrimination parties, sumo wrestling and shamisen music.

For the aspiring Genroku-era writer, there was a surplus of material to draw from. The Edo cast included the newly empowered merchants and their sybaritic, occasionally wayward wives, congenitally unfaithful hus-bands, actors, dilettantes, rakes, courtesans, balladeers and hard-up samurai. These were the ensemble players in a city evolving in wondrous new ways, and it was hardly necessary to create art as there were such vivid characters on every street corner. Even so, the people of Edo seem to have craved a constant fix of entertainment. Thus, the antics and indiscretions of the ordinary life of the lower orders in particular, were freely adapted as subjects for ukiyo-e woodcuts, ballads, storytelling themes, the risqué, often pornographic *ukiyo-zoshi* and the flamboyant new Kabuki theatre.

THE DOG SHOGUN

This belle époque of sorts was presided over by the fifth shogun, Tokugawa Tsunayoshi, a spoilt dilettante with few distinguishing abilities and a crippling dependence on his mother. His 29-year rule was marked by an unusual incidence of natural disasters, including the eruption of Mount Fuji. Though patently neither, he imagined himself an authority on literature and an accomplished Confucian scholar. He was, however, an undisputed authority on Noh drama, but like all things during his eccentric rule he took his interest to extremes. We know, for example, that in one single year, 1697, he performed as main actor no fewer than 71 times in some 23 plays, and a further 150 times in separate Noh dances. Actors who won his approval became affluent; some were even granted samurai status. Performers who displeased him could find themselves living on reduced stipends or in the worst cases banished to the provinces.

One did not have to be an actor to be punished for perceived transgressions. Hanabusa Itcho, a genre painter, was exiled to the isolated island of Miyakejima for a work lampooning a boating excursion taken by Tsunayoshi and his favourite mistress. After the shogunate's attacks on the publishing establishment in 1790, woodblock prints were required to be stamped with an official seal of approval.

The dispensation of favours was often based on the shogun's sexual proclivities, which were said to be largely of the male variety. As with everything else in this age of opulence, Tsunayoshi went to notable extremes. One particular historical record, known as the *Sanno Gaiki*, is explicit on the subject: "The ruler liked sex with males... no matter how humble, if they were handsome, he appointed them as attendants." The document lists 130 such appointees.

Tsunayoshi was unable to produce a male heir to succeed him, and Ryuko, an influential priest and confidant of the shogun's mother, persuaded him that the cause could be traced to his mistreatment of other creatures in a previous existence. As he was born in the Year of the Dog, he would have to take particular care of these namesake animals. Tsunayoshi duly set about authoring his Edict for Loving All Living Things. Dogs were henceforth to be addressed as *O-inu sama* (Honourable Mr. Dog) and accorded burial rites matching their new station. Accounts tell of Edo Castle swarming with countless spoilt and pampered canines. In 1687 orders were issued for the provision of shelters for sick and ageing dogs. Strict penalties were introduced forbidding their mistreatment. Anyone who beat a dog could be subjected to capital punishment. In Edo, in particular, the number of dogs increased dramatically, the streets swarming with often rabid animals that fought and barked at night, depriving townspeople of their sleep. Prisons now had a new type of inmate: people incarcerated on animal rights charges. One man was condemned to death for killing a swallow. This insanity continued until the shogun's death in 1709.

Was an untoward revenge taken out on dogs after the shogun's death? History fails to tell us, but his much put-upon subjects did enjoy a revenge of sorts by naming Tsunayoshi *inu-kubo*, the "Dog Shogun", a title that persists to this day.

Affluence and Patronage

The Genroku age was one of preciousness and extreme dilettantism. One princess newly arrived at the castle from Kyoto and finding the water in Edo too hard for her calligraphy and painting brushes, had water sent to her daily from the imperial capital. If accounts of the day are to be believed, such over-refinements were uncalled for in a city that still remained ecologically wholesome. A Suzuki Harunobu painting from this era, entitled *Picking Herbs on the Banks of the Sumida River*, depicts five women and a boy enjoying a leisurely spring day in an Edo that could still boast natural surroundings.

The townspeople were mindful that ostentation could attract the unwanted attention of the authorities. The trick was to lavish money on luxuries that were unobtrusive. Connoisseurship revolved around the appreciation of finely finished miniature arts: handmade dolls, delicately decorated sword fittings and hair ornaments, subtly carved ivory *netsuke*, tiny boxwood statues, a valuable tea bowl, bonsai dwarf trees and *inro*, exquisitely embossed medicine flasks.

Kimono cloth shops became fashionable at this time, the preserve until then of the privileged classes, who bought fabrics at trade shows or private sales. One of the first shops to appear in 1673 was Echigoya, the forerunner of today's Mitsukoshi Department Store. Echigoya's clientele comprised the new, economically empowered urban masses. The woven and dyed goods, the textiles and accessories sold across the counter in such shops provided work for all manner of artisans, from bleachers, dyers, weavers, brocade and chintz makers to engravers, cotton beaters and needle-workers.

The effects of a commercial revolution that changed Japan's cities beyond recognition can be seen in the woodblock prints of the day, celebrating the life of the merchant quarters. Guidebooks of the time feature shops brimming with customers and goods. Refined pastimes known as *yugei*, the traditional domain of the court, were increasingly adopted by members of the newly wealthy and leisured merchant class. The recreational arts practised by the townspeople of Edo were not confined to aesthetic pursuits only, but might include lessons in gardening, medicine and instruction in board games like *go* and *shogi*.

Those who could not resist the temptation to collect larger, more conspicuous objects such as lacquered chests and gorgeously painted folding screens placed their treasures discreetly in the confines of a *kura*, a fireproof storehouse made from white plastered mud and straw and a heavy tiled roof, bringing single items out for occasional display. The characteristics of the era, a savouring of momentary pleasures unalloyed by intellectual or moral distractions and the cultivation of discriminating tastes, were only defined long after they had vanished.

RED SNOW

An extraordinary event occurred in 1701 that electrified the entire city. Because of its reverberations as both news and as a fitting subject for literature, the story is worth retelling. Assigned to perform ceremonial duties at the shogun's court in Edo, Lord Asano, a daimyo from the western domain of Ako, was provoked into attacking and injuring Lord Kira. Though the reason for the provocation has never been satisfactorily explained, an oversight of etiquette, personal slight or grudge toward Kira—a condescending and spiteful superior by all accounts—have all been mooted. Having violated the strict rule of court banning the drawing of weapons, Asano was commanded to commit immediate *seppuku* (ritual disembowelment). With Asano's death, his vassals automatically became *ronin,* masterless samurai stripped of crest, armour and a banner to serve under. His estates were seized by the authorities, the family castle razed to the ground and his widow driven into taking refuge in a nunnery.

Smarting from humiliation, 47 of the ronin secretly swore to avenge his death. Knowing that they would be under surveillance from the authorities, who posted spies to watch the men's comings and goings, they took a full two years planning their revenge. To allay suspicion, they took up jobs as carpenters, labourers and peddlers, work that would have been inconceivable for a samurai. While quietly hatching a plan of action, Oishi Kuranosuke, Lord Asano's former Elder Councillor, adopted a dissolute lifestyle, drinking and womanizing, a pretence that relaxed Kira's guard.

During the winter of 1703, the ronin broke into Kira's high-walled mansion at midnight. After fierce fighting, in which all the guards and retainers were slaughtered, they searched the grounds for Kira, eventually finding him hiding in a charcoal shed dressed in white satin sleeping robes. After removing Kira's head with the very sword that Lord Asano had used against him at court, they carried the trophy through the snow-blanketed streets of Edo, washed it in a well, which is still there today, and placed it on the grave of their master at Sengaku-ji temple.

While the public in general lauded this violent act of revenge as a heroic deed consistent with the samurai code of absolute loyalty, the shogunate was obliged by its own set of rules to punish the offenders for having assassinated a member of the court. Rather than being decapitated, the fate of the common criminal, the 47 were, after long and spirited debates and deliberations among intellectuals and officials, granted the privilege of an honourable death by seppuku.

The story of the attack by the ronin appeared as a puppet play within weeks of the actual event, an example of the speed with which reality was transmuted into art and entertainment. The story has inspired countless novels, Kabuki plays and films. The best-known theatrical version is the puppet play *Chushinguru* (A Treasury of Loyal Retainers), first performed in 1748. For reasons of censorship, the story was re-situated in the fourteenth century. The poet John Masefield wrote a much inferior English version of the play called *The Faithful.*

Climbing the steps up to the time-weathered graves today, an acrid smell hangs in the air, the tombs banked up beneath clouds of smoke from incense sticks placed there by those who continue to honour the men.

Rudyard Kipling did just this in the spring of 1889, finding that "an animal of the name of V. Gay had seen fit to scratch his entirely uninteresting name" on one of the gold-leafed, lacquered panels of the tomb. "It is the handwriting upon the wall" he added: "Presently there will be neither gold nor lacquer—nothing but the finger marks of foreigners."

THE LITERARY CITY

Simple broadsheets called *yomiuri*, early forerunners of newspapers, began to appear on the streets. These were printed on blocks of engraved wood. Some of these newsletters, also known under the general heading of *kawarabon*, were illustrated. Although subject matter began to edge gingerly in the direction of more sensitive themes towards the end of the Tokugawa period, political commentary at this stage was strictly taboo. Publishers had to content themselves with human-interest reportage: accounts of natural disasters, fires, vendettas, tragedies, double-suicides, stories of strange occurrences and omens, the sighting of supernatural beasts and ghosts.

Providing that hedonism never conflicted with the aims and authority of the shogunate, the chonin were relatively free to indulge a range of tastes, from sexual freedom, literature, fashion, theatre and the arts, to the illustrated books and woodblock prints that, more than anything, captured the spirit of this floating world. *Ukiyo-zoshi* (books of the floating world) portrayed this phenomenon in lurid detail. In contrast to the highly nuanced tea ceremony and Noh play, ukiyo-zoshi titles feature characters whose energy and verve match that of a rising new class in Edo society. The themes in these often insightful documents of the age (adultery, arson, torrid sexual exploits, supernatural tales, fictional adaptations of recent events) were rarely subtle. Neither are the women portrayed as the heroines and victims of these stories the meek, submissive type the Tokugawa government extolled as models of virtue, nor the languid waifs of the later ukiyo-e style.

As literature was expected to be uplifting and even a touch pedagogic, the introductions and closing remarks in ukiyo-zoshi works, however scatological the pages between, were often edifying tracts in the sermonizing manner of the Confucian scholar. The circulation of such books was aided by the stunning growth of publishing in the seventeenth century. Although type printing had been introduced from Korea in the century before, the new spate of commercial publishers favoured wood-block editions of their works, which could be cheaply and easily illustrated. Suwaraya, a bookshop and publishing house located in the downtown Nihonbashi Tori-itchome district, amassed a fortune as its flagship store evolved into a chain. By the beginning of the nineteenth century there were twelve Suwaraya bookshops in Edo. As stores and book lenders for those who could not afford to buy their own books proliferated, so did literacy rates among the townspeople of Edo, creating an avid new reading public.

Books, which had small initial print runs, were extremely expensive. To buy a romance novel would cost the equivalent of one month's food expenses. More serious books, like the novel series of the esteemed writer Takizawa Bakin or scholarly works on Buddhism or Confucianism, cost considerably more. The solution for Edo's increasingly literate residents lay in the rental libraries, which charged less than one-tenth of the purchase price. An 1808 record tells us that there were 656 such libraries in Edo alone. Though there were shops where bibliophiles could find as many as 10,000 titles at any one time, most people rented books from itinerant peddlers who carried titles in backpacks through local neighbourhoods. Books were lent out for five days at a time and were no doubt feverishly read and then passed on to others, the costs split.

Although Kyoto and Osaka initially led the field over Edo, book publishing picked up considerably in the eighteenth century. A useful counterweight to the fires of Edo, which reduced whole districts to the realm of collective, often unreliable memory, were guides to the famous sights of the city. Guidebooks like *An Illustrated Guide to Places in Edo* and *The Naniwa Sparrow* provide invaluable descriptions of the city during the late seventeenth century. Two quite different books, *A Dappled Cloth of Edo* and *Records of Japanese Efflorescence*, were published in 1687 and 1693. These works, documenting the social life of the merchant class as well as examining each residential and commercial block of the city, were extraordinarily precise in their details. *Sharebon* were novels set in the pleasure quarters, which also included practical information.

An interesting system of colour-coding came about. Red-coloured *akahon* appeared in the latter years of the Genroku. Written in cursive script and generously illustrated, these were collections of stories aimed at women and children. They were followed by *kurohon*, black-covered books containing embroidered accounts of historical tales, heroic deeds and lurid ghost and revenge stories. *Aohon* were blue books representing scenes from everyday life. Last to appear were the yellow-covered, *kibyoshibon* books. The authors of these more realistic works, often written in the vernacular and alluding to current gossip and scandals or ostracizing the ideas of Confucian moralists, were more likely to run foul of the censors, though banned books were often simply reissued with new covers bearing different titles.

Real events and scandals, even more provocative than the grimly pornographic works that flourished throughout the Genroku period, appeared in thinly disguised form in plays, stories, ballads, and single-sheet broadsheets similar to the yomiuri. Scandals involving eminent figures, obliquely alluded to but fully understood by the public, appeared in flyers, ballads and the more detailed broadsheets called *jitsuroku* or "true stories". Sexual humour inevitably resurfaced in the enormously popular joke books of the age, which invariably featured cuckolded husbands, lustful wives and the habits of lapsed monks and priests. So great was the demand for anecdotes of this kind that even humble street-corner storytellers like the former dyer Shikano Bunzaemon could make a living compiling their accounts in book form or giving narrative recitations at private parties. The writer Kiseki, though happily exploiting the Genroku *demi-monde* for the contents of his own work, frequently railed against the excessive materialism of the times, the vanity and assertiveness of its women, their immoderate dress and loose morals. Writing in *Characters of Worldly Young Women* about the showy use of costly cosmetics, he observes, "Now young ladies smear it on down to their navels."

GRAPHIC RITES OF SPRING

Makura-e (pillow images) and *shunga* (spring pictures) provided the erotic images deemed necessary for these books to sell in profitable quantities. Shunga are unapologetically explicit images that celebrate the joy of the sexual act. The largely benign intentions of mainstream images (as opposed to sordid or intentionally depraved shunga) are evident in their alternative name, *warai-e* ("laughing pictures"). While not all the erotica maintain the same standard of visual integrity, there is a degree of human warmth in the images produced at this time.

According to John Stevens, an authority on this form of art, the darker aspects of erotic illustration—including sadism, a constant in Japanese erotic art—"became more pronounced in Japanese pornography as the twentieth century progressed, reflecting the brutalization of the human spirit that led to the tragedy of World War II." The fine line between art and pornography is one of those questions that have long vexed the censor. Henry Miller once defined the distinction between the obscene and erotic by saying that you could buy the latter. Shunga were certainly for sale. The fact that their value has risen considerably since they were created, placing them in the category of collectible art, gives pause for thought.

The sense of composition and command of line and form in Edo-period shunga are immensely superior to the crudity of today's mass-marketed pornography. Shunga portrayed not only customers and courtesans, newlyweds or young lovers, but also found an erotic range and depth in the study of the sexual relations between affectionate married couples and the wellspring of vitality that could be drawn upon to keep their graphically portrayed coupling fresh and invigorating. In one print, a couple of indefinable age are fixed by the artist in an erotic pose against the backdrop of an apricot tree, the rough bark of its gnarled branches reanimated by virile blooms.

Shunga artists often employed the services of their wives or even daughters in order to achieve greater anatomical accuracy, which is a feature of their work. Great care was taken when representing the details of clothing, often of a sumptuous, multi-layered kind, and the manner in which it was stripped away or left to hang in voluptuous folds. While such images no doubt served simple auto-erotic needs or shared stimulus for couples, they may also have functioned as manuals for the untested or for experienced viewers intent on expanding their repertoire. Not all of the images, however, particularly the more contorted ones, were to be recommended. One senryu provides a caveat:

> Emulating the postures
> In a shunga book
> They sprained all their joints.

The half-consumed pots of tea, sweets and sake that provide delightful human touches contrast with naked limbs and intent expressions. In other prints fans, leaves of erotic poetry or an overturned bath stool add to the mood of abandonment. An interesting fusion of objects and room décor surfaces in some of the later prints, where the familiar postures of the couple blend with lacquered trays and *fusuma* paper doors, curtains and western clothing.

Suzuki Harunobu was an early master of the suggestive detail. One famous print shows a young man struggling with a woman to retrieve a love letter, their clothes in suggestive disarray. Hanging from a wall behind them, a poem by Chosui reads:

> Stretching across scarlet plum blossoms,
> Bamboo pipes are green.

NEO-CONFUCIAN DOCTRINES

Moderating the irrepressible liberties of Edo was an especially orthodox brand of neo-Confucianism extolled by the Tokugawa regime. Stemming from the twelfth-century Chinese philosopher Chu Hsi, who stressed absolute submission to authority, the ideology held enormous sway with Japan's rulers, who eagerly adapted this system of graduated obedience to suit their needs. In the manner of Japan's other cultural and religious implants, the *Analects* and other writings of Confucius were subjected to an empirical resorting. Confucian doctrines enlisted to serve the Tokugawa state emphasized feudal values designed to support the authority of rulers over the compliant masses. Metaphysics tended to vanish in this rebranded state theology as neo-Confucianism, as it became known, assumed the form of a doctrinaire political philosophy.

The architect of this template for governance was the classical scholar Hayashi Razan, who supervised the founding of the first Confucian academy in Ueno. The institute moved to Soto Kanda in 1691, continuing its work as a finishing school for the sons of the Tokugawas, the elite feudal nobility and military class. A teacher training college was later set up on the same grounds by the Meiji government, relocating to Hongo where it would become the University of Tokyo. Yushima Seido temple's identification with learning continues, evident in the number of students who visit the site, especially in the weeks before entrance examinations, to hang votive tablets of Confucius on racks set up along the covered portico that runs along the main courtyard of the shrine. A pistachio tree, grown from a cutting taken from a tree that stood at Confucius' grave, can be seen at the entrance to the temple grounds. Roosters and "devil dogs" sit on the sweeping tile and copper roofs of the Taisei-den, the Hall of Accomplishment, which enshrines the spirit of Confucius. The temple is situated at the base of a slope that levels out at the banks of the Kanda river. Gazing south from the stone ramparts of Hijiribashi (The Bridge of the Sages), the span that forms an unintentional processional to the temple, the deep green domes of an altogether different deity, the god of the Russian orthodox Nikolai Cathedral, loom over the more occidental domain of Ochanomizu.

Attempts were made to control the freedom of the townspeople through the issuing of countless edicts, regulations and sumptuary laws aimed at reaffirming Hayashi's Confucian social model. The wealthier merchants, their vain wives and spoilt children quickly found ingenious ways to evade these petty laws. Told not to wear silk, they devised kimonos of rough cloth lined with the finest silk available; forbidden to build houses of over two storeys, they added additional levels to existing interiors. Other means were found to circumvent decrees against decorating their rooms with silver leaf or furnishing them with objects covered in gold lacquer. When a decree to prevent commoners from using *kago* (palanquins) was issued in 1681, the general public simply ignored it. The very fact that repeated attempts were made to discourage common people from developing extravagant tastes hints at their ineffectiveness. The townspeople had their own behavioural codes, tastes and aesthetics for governing their lives.

Their preferences, expressed not only in the arts but in clothing, lifestyles and manners of speech, were defined by *iki* (style), *tsu* (connoisseurship) and *asobi* (play). Iki, a sense of stylish flair and bravura, the domain of high-ranking courtesans, actors, young blades and the Edo *flâneur*, has always been difficult to translate because such concepts belong to a sophisticated culture of sensation. Iki was much esteemed for implying sensual promise without revealing too much. The women who worked in the teahouses of Yanagibashi had this special quality, a flair and good taste in dress and comportment that, while flamboyant, eschewed the more florid ostentations of the wealthier Edo townspeople. Only a select number of tsu or *dai tsu* (grand connoisseurs), however, were conversant with the subtleties and code signals of this increasingly intricate world.

THE ART CITY

Painters, former habitués of Kyoto, began to set up schools in Edo under the direction of the master Kano Tanyu. Their work was largely patronized by the aristocracy, however, who appreciated the refined Chinese models used by these artists. While prosperous samurai families, aristocrats and wealthy merchants commissioned expansive paintings to decorate their estates, the townspeople were discovering an inexpensive art form of their own: the ukiyo-e print.

Ukiyo-e images of the floating world appeared in prints, screens, paintings and costume design alongside more accessible paintings that made use of diverse formats: banners, theatre boards and signs, scrolls, lanterns and screens. Almost every available surface of the city could be co-opted for some kind of illustrative purpose.

In the mid-seventeenth century the ancient art of woodblock prints (*hanga*) was revived and invigorated. Woodcuts were printed onto hand-made mulberry-bark paper. Different pressures applied to burnishing, embossing and the use of metal dust on the print surface created texture, depth and lustre. The process of making a full-colour print required the collaboration of the commissioning publisher, who acted as art director and co-ordinator, the artist himself, the woodblock engraver and finally the printer. As public demand for prints grew, so did technical innovation.

Although it is doubtful that Hishikawa Moronobu single-handedly raised the level of the woodblock print to that of art, as is often claimed, it would be difficult to visualize the Genroku period without Moronobu's prints or Saikaku's satirical fiction. Like Saikaku, Moronobu, who probably arrived in Edo after the great fire of 1657, was drawn by the exhilarating complexity and diversity of city life. Grand courtesans and studied images of illustrated albums like *Views of the Yoshiwara* and *Flower Viewing at Ueno* were produced alongside picture-guides to Edo, designs for screens and fans, all manner of erotica and the gritty *Pictures of Japanese Occupations*, a detailed and realistic document, testament to his fascination with the teeming life of the Edo street. Here Moronobu depicts peddlers of bean curd, clam and rice cake, salt-gatherers, washerwomen, fortune-tellers, priests, wrestlers, harlots, apothecaries and fishmongers, all with their trademark quirks and mannerisms. A major chronicler of the newly reconstructed city, Moronobu ensured that ukiyo-e remained the dominant art of Edo.

With a common interest in Edo existence, it was inevitable that Saikaku and Moronobu should collaborate, as they did on a number of books, helping at the same time to stimulate the remarkably close relationship between the ukiyo-zoshi and ukiyo-e. The artists of the floating world, though conscious that their images were embellishments of an already embroidered dream state, claimed that their work, in opposition to the classical painters and their Chinese models, was the truer representative standard of Japanese life, calling themselves *Yamato Eshi*, "real Japanese painters".

The well-established tradition of fusing literature and calligraphy in scroll paintings, a popular derivative of genre ukiyo-e paintings, was something only the aristocracy or wealthy merchants could afford to support. The woodblock print, inexpensive and portable, with its broad range of subjects, was exceedingly popular. More intimate, it functioned as an early form of mass media, offering up-to-date coverage of the floating world and information about the pleasure districts or Kabuki plays. Those who could not afford the folding albums or picture books made from rice paper stitched into double sheets might buy one of the single-sheet prints that were put out as flyers to advertise famous actors and renowned beauties.

Moronobu's earliest ukiyo-e works, known as "primitives", had been monochrome prints. A breakthrough in printing techniques in 1745 allowed initially for two colours (red and green were the usual choices) to be printed directly from woodblocks. Multiple colours and halftones were perfected in the nishiki-e ("brocade picture") prints that followed.

EDO THEATRICS

The most respected and prolific playwright of his day, Chikamatsu Monzaemon lived in Osaka. Much of his work, adapted for use in Kabuki, appeared as dramas for the enormously influential bunraku puppet theatre. There were two bunraku theatres in Edo. A serious theatrical form, puppet dramas enjoyed much respect among adult audiences for their lifelike dramatizations and occasional social and political commentaries. Bunraku and Kabuki competed for popularity in Edo, but after the fire of 1657, which destroyed much of the city, many of the puppet chanters moved back to Osaka and Kyoto. Gradually overshadowing the ballad dramas and hugely expressive puppet theatre, Kabuki was unquestionably the dominant theatrical form of the age.

Fires precipitated a crucial period in the development of Edo. Casting off more traditional influences seen in the culture of the western Kansai region, the rebuilding of theatres saw the emergence of a more unique Edo style and appearance. Kabuki did not always enjoy official approval. The form started as a loose mixture of variety acts performed by troupes of women, who set up their tents and stages on the dry banks of the Kamogawa river in Kyoto. Those involved in these pantomimic performances along the riverbanks were branded *kawara kojiki* (riverbed beggars) and disdained by the authorities. Because the dances were often salacious in nature, and the performers frequently supplemented their incomes with prostitution, female performers were banned by the authorities in 1629 as injurious to public morality, a restriction that, while no longer enforced by law, has been upheld to this day.

The word Kabuki is a compound of three words: *ka* (song), *bu* (dance) and *ki* (acting). Daylong performances of Kabuki attracted audiences from every walk of life, from surreptitious visits by ladies of the shogun's court, who watched from behind screened galleries, to shop clerks and messenger boys. This was the age of such theatrical colossi as Ichikawa Danjuro I, the founder of a long line of Edo Kabuki performers and the exponent of a bold and muscular style known as *aragoto* acting. The coarser, bravura treatment of themes typified by the aragoto style is reflected in its name, which means literally "rough stuff" or "wild thing". Ichikawa created a sensation, making his debut in the role of the martial hero Kimpira wearing stunning red and black makeup alongside actors decked out in flowing demon wigs and silk robes with long trailing hems. Ichikawa's acting career ended abruptly and bloodily in 1704 when he was stabbed to death on stage.

Kabuki's resplendent historical spectacles and real life stories of star-crossed lovers often dramatize the conflict between raw human emotions, sexuality and duty, frequently centring on an ill-starred affair between a young blood of Edo and one of the women of the pleasure quarters. There is a populist, even rebellious side to Kabuki, though, with its brothel-keepers, gravediggers, ferrymen and prostitutes making their own often subversive social commentary. Plays were performed against elaborately constructed backdrops and stage sets. In the late Genroku era, a revolving stage allowed for quick changes of set. Audiences were rarely passive, as the demonstrative Edokko were quick to voice their approval or displeasure with a performance. In this combustible atmosphere theatres were often shaken by fiercely partisan shows of enthusiasm or hostility. At least part of the melodrama—the expansive gestures, larger-than-life costumes and the striking make-up—was due to the dim lighting in the theatres. Young acolytes, stooping beneath actors, held candles attached to bamboo poles to illuminate the thespians' facial expressions.

Lavish costume displays inevitably attracted the attention of the authorities. Though random sumptuary laws were largely ineffective, a Kabuki actor, if he was unlucky enough to be singled out as an example, might have an expensive wardrobe of silks confiscated. The cost of these embroidered costumes, the budget for musicians and scenery and the scandalously high salaries demanded by top actors, meant that theatre owners were often out of pocket.

In an attempt to idolize women and to create the ultimate metaphor for beauty, male actors took on female parts. *Wakashu* (male youths) took on the first roles. The sight of such cloned beauty inflamed enough of the male audience for the *Wakashu Kabuki* to quickly become associated with pederasty. The government soon required all actors to be adult males. Today's *onnagata* (female impersonators) are often older-generation actors, whose skill at portraying the first flush of youth in their subjects is all the more remarkable.

The purpose of the onnagata was to create rather than disguise femininity through highly stylized but transparent techniques, the sexual ambiguity of the performance highly appreciated by audiences. An early onnagata, Yoshizawa Ayame, went so far as to insist that the mannerisms portrayed on stage should extend into real life. Living as women outside the theatre and maintaining the fiction for an adoring public often required keeping a wife or family out of the picture. All this was part of the illusion created by the finest male-female actors. In a short story called *Onnagata*, Mishima Yukio, an accomplished Kabuki critic himself, describes the world of the performer: "The make-believe of his daily life supported the make-believe of his stage performances." This, the main character of the story convinces himself, "marked the true *onnagata*. An *onnagata* is the child born of the illicit union between dream and reality."

Yakusha-e (prints of male actors) were popular. Affairs between actors who frequented the pleasure quarters and exotic courtesans of high rank were the stuff of gossip and the subject of woodblock prints. The ukiyo-painter Katsukama Shunsho started a vogue in producing prints of famous actors, who responded by becoming purveyors of fashion. Expensive cloth, perfumes, toiletries, and even cakes were named after them. When the actor Danjuro (the seventh in line of this hereditary family of thespians) took to wearing a costume with the symbol of a sickle (*kama*) embroidered on it, the design became an overnight sensation that generated much work for the producers of kimonos, dyed fabrics and stylish handkerchiefs. The two syllables added to the Chinese characters for Danjuro's sickle, *wa* and *nu*, formed the word *kamawanu*, which could be read to signify "I don't care," a typical bravura touch that only increased the popularity of the design.

Officially, the status of actors was not much higher than that of outcasts. On stage they were required to wear the simplest of cotton robes; when they ventured out from the theatre quarters they were expected to cover their faces with sedge hats. In practice, the more successful Kabuki actors lived lives of ostentation, surrounded by dozens of servants and doting fans. Theatres competed with each other in the artistry and glamour of their stage sets, costumes, wigs and other accessories. There were sporadic crackdowns, even the banishment of certain actors, followed by a short period of austerity and then the resumption of all the opulence the townspeople of Edo expected from their Kabuki.

There were four theatres in the Low City: the Ichimura-za in Fukiyacho, the Yamamura-za, the Nakamura-za in Sakaemachi and the Morita-za in Kobikicho near Tsukiji. Theatres were occasionally shut down for disorderly behaviour or improprieties, particularly if they involved women of rank. Edo's pleasure quarters, mainly geared to a male clientele, provided rooms where wealthy women could arrange paid assignations with Kabuki actors in much the same way that men bought the sexual favours of courtesans. If *Tosei-otome-shiki*, a book published in 1705, can be trusted, the practice was common knowledge. One rhetorical passage reads, "What do you suppose the theatre to be? It's nothing more than a fror* for male prostitution! It only exists so that women can hire actors for leasure." In 1714 a court lady named Ejima attended a Kabuki per-
~ at the Yamamura-za theatre, where she entertained some actors
with sake. When word got out, the actors were promptly ban-
⌐ ⌐atre destroyed and upstairs foyers where people could meet
⌐rom all other playhouses.

The authorities remained highly suspicious of entertainers and other free spirits. The lower order of wandering entertainers who swarmed into Edo, comprising puppeteers, singers, conjurers, sword swallowers, male and female street walkers, as well as religious quacks, charlatans and bell-ringers collecting alms in exchange for chanting sutras, also concerned those in power. An attitude of open defiance, creeping into Edo literature, was another source of concern for the regime. Testing the limits of authorial tolerance could be a risky undertaking. Baba Bunko, a writer severely critical of the political system, was arrested by the authorities and sentenced to death by crucifixion.

While the Noh stage was the traditional host venue for returning and reincarnated spirits, the wandering souls of warriors, lovers and priests, ghosts and haunted houses caught the popular imagination of early Edo. Lacking the contentious content and boisterous audiences associated with Kabuki performances, Noh rarely attracted the attention of the authorities. Largely patronized by an aristocracy living within the environs of the castle, Noh actors dressed in opulent robes and faces concealed behind masks, performed slow, graceful movements rich in nuance. In contrast to the realistic flourishes and melodramatic plots of Kabuki, Noh presented dramas of the human mind and soul. These were accompanied by restrained dance sequences and the chanting of *utai* music. Stages were small and devoid of all but the simplest background decor: a gnarled pine resplendently green against a gold leaf screen. The Noh repertoire, with its ghosts, spirits, goblins, voices and cries from the nether world, was also peopled by warriors, court nobles, fishermen, monks and peasants—flesh and blood figures spirited across a supernatural stage.

Jidaimono or period plays, on the other hand, were written to excite an audience of merchants and artisans who wanted to be entertained by historical melodramas, warrior tales and stories about the overturning of powerful clans. The writers of a more lurid theatrical form known as *se-wamono* (domestic plays) took their material from real life, changing it into semi-fictional drama portraying scandals, murders and that perennially popular theme, the double suicide of a prostitute and her merchant lover who, financially ruined by the affair, is unable to buy her release from the brothel.

For those unable to afford the theatre or the pleasure quarters, there were entertainment booths set up under the great bridges, along wide firebreaks and crowded crossroads, bazaars, the precincts of temples and shrines and other open spaces. Here they could watch dancers, listen to storytellers, receive a Buddhist exorcism, see strange animals and birds, brought to the country by the Dutch, and people with deformities. Magic lantern shows, impersonators, illusionists and performers of fan tricks were regulars at these venues. The actors who performed in the so-called "beggar's kabuki" did a double turn, painting one side of their face to represent one character, the other in the likeness of a second. Likewise, the two halves of their body were dressed in the clothing of the two respective characters.

Absurd novelties were dreamed up. Performers leapt through baskets bristling with sword blades or rattan hoops blazing with burning candles. Others swallowed rapiers or needles, or gave bizarre musical performances, using an egg or ladle in one instance as a plectrum to play the three-stringed shamisen. Some of the performances were free, though likely to be commercials for snake medicines, wonder powders and other panaceas. Papier-mâché figures called *iki-ningyo* (living dolls), were exhibited in tents. One writer recalled seeing "inhabitants of the island of long arms, the island of long legs, the land of perforated chests, the land of no stomachs, and figures from other exotic lands." Rather more lifelike models of courtesans from the Maruyama pleasure quarter in various stages of disrobing were also exhibited in voyeuristic *tableaux vivants*. Donald Richie describes the scene at Ryogoku Bridge in his book *The Image Factory* (2003):

> Here the onlookers could look at such educational exhibits as a large whale, a brace of dromedaries, an enormous image of the Buddha made of oiled paper over basketry. There were also attractions, which aimed only at entertainment. There was a giant toad made of velvet, there was a cannibal hag from Yotsuya...

APEX OF THE NEW ORDER

With the Tokugawa government struggling to understand the complexities of a new economy rising from beneath, the merchant class emerged as a moneyed elite. As the wealth of the chonin increased and spread to the artisans, labourers and craftsmen who served them, the samurai inexorably lost ground. They still retained their habit of glaring arrogantly at commoners as they strutted and swaggered along the streets of Edo, their swords commanding the respect that comes from fear, but in truth the samurai engaged far less in armed combat at this time than swashbuckling sword films would suggest. The class was gradually becoming impoverished.

Merchants and wholesalers, moneylenders, clerks and brokers who benefited from association with them may have been despised for their money-grubbing, but the samurai increasingly turned to them for employment and favours, merchant families also exerting their influence through intermarriage with members of the warrior class. It was a baffling inversion of the social order, one the authorities never publicly acknowledged.

By this time Edo's prosperity was apparent to even the outsider. Engelbert Kaempfer, a German physician to the Dutch in their trading enclave at Dejima in Nagasaki, visited the Nihonbashi commercial district of the city in 1691, remarking: "On both sides of the streets are multitudes of well-furnished shops of merchants and tradesmen, drapers, silk-merchants, druggists, Idol-sellers, book-sellers, glassblowers, apothecaries and others." Kaempfer noted disturbing shifts in landscape as he entered the outskirts of Edo, passing first the execution grounds at Suzugamori, where heads and bodies in an advanced state of decay were picked over by dogs and crows, then a road along the bay whose slopes were covered with temples and exquisite gardens.

On his second trip to the city he was granted an audience with the shogun Tsunayoshi. His own first-hand observations, included in his history of Japan, published in Dutch, English and French, are of greatest interest. Arriving at the castle moats, he passed over bridges whose pillars were hung with bronze balls, under sloping roofs decorated with golden dolphins. Once inside, the pillars and ceiling beams were made from cedar and camphor, finished in a transparent varnish that brought out pleasing patterns in the grain. The floors were covered in matting edged with gold seam. One detail was of special interest to the European: "I have heard," he wrote "that there is an underground apartment which has a large water tank instead of a ceiling. The Shogun withdraws here when there is thunder because he believes that the force of the lightning will dissipate in the water."

Silver was the currency used in Osaka and Kyoto, gold the standard in Edo, though copper was used all over the country, especially in the retail trade where the bigger wholesalers and shopkeepers had to change this into gold in order to settle their debts. Money changing was the foundation of many family fortunes in Edo. In this intensely materialistic world, Edo merchants, like their Venetian and Florentine counterparts, having brokered more than just trade, had become important patrons of the arts.

A RIVERSIDE HERMITAGE

In sharp contrast with the lavish indulgence in pleasure and the arts spurred on by the courtesan-infatuated townspeople was a modest wattle hut, a hermitage, across the river. This was the new home of the great haiku poet Matsuo Basho. Born to a samurai family in Ueno, in Iga province (Mie prefecture), he showed a great aptitude for literature from a young age. Basho arrived in Edo in 1672 at the age of 28, hoping to pursue his dream of being a poet and teacher.

Basho, with signature staff and sedge hat

In 1680 one of Basho's patrons, the fish merchant and poet Sugiyama Sampu, put a former watchman's hut at the poet's disposal, providing him with food and clothing. This was located on the grounds of Sugiyama's villa in Fukagawa, now firmly situated within the boundaries of Tokyo but then a rural suburb to the east of Edo, from which the city could be observed from a distance. Although far from ready to retire, Basho was following a long tradition in Japan by which a literary man could withdraw from the world, spending his time in a life of quiet contemplation and civilized talks with friends and followers. The poet practised Zen meditation here with a priest named Butcho, who was serving at a nearby temple.

Here he changed his name from Tosei to Basho, in tribute to a banana plantain palm (*basho*) that his disciples planted in the small garden beside his hut. According to his own account, he fondly identified himself with the ragged, easily torn but enduring fronds of the plant, comparing its leaves to "the injured tail of a phoenix". Its flowers, he said, were not bright, "and as the wood is completely useless for building, it never feels the axe. But I love the tree for its very uselessness." The tree, which the poet loved to sit beneath, appears in an early haiku from these Fukagawa days:

Plantain tree in autumn storm
As I listen all night to
Rain in a basin.

One of the least vainglorious artists to have lived in Edo, he appears to have regarded himself as a kind of literary scarecrow. In the days preceding a journey that provided the material for an account entitled *The Record of a Weather-Exposed Skeleton,* Basho wrote: "Following the example of the ancient priest who is said to have travelled thousands of miles caring naught for his provisions and attaining the state of sheer ecstasy under the pure beams of the moon, I left my broken house on the River Sumida in August, among the wails of the autumn wind."

In 1689 he undertook his most famous haiku walk, a five-month undertaking that resulted in his masterpiece, *Narrow Road to a Far Province.* Under the iron rule of the Tokugawas, the roads were finally safe for travellers. After patching his trousers, putting new cord in his hat, and applying moxa treatment to his legs to strengthen them, he set off down the river to Senju, the starting point of the journey, on a day in early spring. Although the riverbanks and the hills of Ueno and Yanaka were covered in cherry blossoms and Mount Fuji lay bathed in the morning light, there was a tinge of anxiety in the departure: "When we disembarked at Senju, my heart grew heavy at the thought of the thousands of miles that lay ahead, and tears welled from my eyes on leaving my friends in this world of illusion."

Although he had a fixed residence, Basho chose to set out on one journey after another. Perhaps he understood that the ordeal of travel would be good for his work. Bidding farewell to his closest friends and disciples at Senju, he strikes a plaintive note in a haiku composed on the spot:

> Departing spring—
> birds cry,
> and in the eyes of fish, tears.

The hermitage and grounds where Basho lived and wrote his best-known journals were preserved until the end of the nineteenth century, when the site appears to have disappeared. After a great tidal wave swept over the area in 1917, a stone frog Basho was said to have liked was discovered, helping to re-establish the location. A second, nearby place of dedication, the Basho House Memorial View Garden, stands on a favourite spot of the poet overlooking the confluence of the Unagigawa and Sumida rivers. A small grove of basho trees complements a statue of the poet kneeling on a *zabuton*, a Japanese cushion, in the flowing, priest-like robes he favoured as he meditates over the scene. The statue is based on a painting by Sugiyama Sanpu. Given the poet's insistence on veracity, the image seated on the plinth is likely to be a reasonably faithful one. Basho's followers might be surprised, though, to see the statue at night, when a time switch swivels the work in a 90-degree arc, illuminating it with a spotlight that allows drivers crossing the nearby Shin-ohashi Bridge and passengers on passing water buses and night cruises to catch a glimpse of the master. The entrance to the nearby Basho Memorial Museum, a research centre with a fine display of the poet's manuscripts and calligraphy, is also marked by a small garden with several examples of the iconic plantain. Another statue, beside the nearby Sendaibori river, shows him in the flat cap and black priestly robes he adopted, holding a wide-brimmed sedge hat and bamboo staff. His face, kindly if slightly weary, gazes into the distance.

THE WIT OF EDO

Haiku had been popular with the townspeople of Edo since the beginning of the seventeenth century. Publishers had brought out manuals explaining rules of composition and providing models for aspiring poets. Humour also flourished in the popular literature, storytelling and drama of the Edo period. Joke books became enormously popular, and there were even joke-exchanging parties held in private homes. Comic writers took as many liberties as they thought permissible. The samurai, Buddhist clergy, Confucian scholars and the more ineffective members of the aristocracy were often the brunt of jokes published in humorous books or told by professional and amateur raconteurs at informal and organized gatherings. The 31-syllable comic poem known as *kyoka* made its appearance into contemporary Edo cultural life at this time.

Comic verse clubs sprung up, places where humorous poetry like *senryu* was read, a genre named after its creator, the poet Karai Senryu, who came to Edo in 1757. The "Toshiwara Group", numbering the publisher Juzaburo Tsutaya and the print artist Utamaro among its members, was one of the best known of the senryu clubs to spring up in Edo. Piercing wit, sensitivity to the foibles and shortcomings of humanity, sharp-tongued commentary on political corruption, insights and epiphanies characterize this immensely popular seventeen-syllable verse.

Although the samurai were often ridiculed in both satirical writings as well as the cruder joke books of the day, some members of this class were involved in comic writings themselves. The samurai scholar, playwright and all-round iconoclast Gennai Hiraga was a leading figure in the world of popular humour. An unsparing satirist, he ridiculed the eccentricities and social foibles of both common people and respected public figures. Literature was beginning to blur class distinctions.

Writers often took their themes from real life. Hardly had an incident occurred than it was being reworked into Kabuki, a puppet play, gazette story or novel. Sensational crimes like murder or arson were especially popular, and if a woman were the main protagonist, writers would waste little time getting to work. One of the best-known stories of this kind, written by Ihara Saikaku, concerns Oshichi, the daughter of a vegetable dealer in the district of Komagome. The tale begins with the chilling line: "A fierce winter wind blew in from the north-east and clouds moved with swift feet through the December sky." The unlucky north-east, gateway for malevolent spirits, would be immediately recognized by the townspeople of Edo as a very ill wind indeed. Taking shelter in a local temple after losing their home in the 1682 fire, Oshichi fell in love with one of its young monks. In the spring of the following year, desperate to be reunited with her lover, she set fire to her own home in the hope that her family would again be forced to return to the temple. Unfortunately, the fire spread to neighbouring houses. Oshichi had barely turned fifteen, but the law was clear on the point of age and culpability: "...should the criminal be fourteen years of age or under: Banishment to a distant island. But when fifteen years of age and over: Burning at the stake." Paraded through the city with other arsonists on the way to the execution grounds at Suzugamori, Oschichi's beauty and fearless demeanour guaranteed her folk heroine status. Her tombstone can be found near Enjo-ji, the scene of the encounter between Oschichi and the banished monk. Actresses chosen to play her part on stage still come to burn incense and offer prayers and fresh flowers at her graveside.

Saikaku, author of the first ukiyo-zoshi, brought a rare maturity to the form with works like *The Man Who Spent His Life in Love* and *Five Women in Love*. Expressing the sentiments of the townspeople rather than the superior classes, Saikaku's work is tinged with a gently reproving cynicism. Commenting on the easy virtues of modern women from the lower orders, he writes, "but this sort of thing, of course, never ever happens among the upper classes." Broadsides against the Tokugawa establishment and conventional tastes were not advisable in such a political climate, but Saikaku discharged plenty of grapeshot. One characteristically cynical remark on the new materialism, of which Saikaku fully approved, is refreshing for its hostility to sentimental clichés about spring blossoms and moon-viewing: "People are not so fond of having plum, cherry, pine, and maple around the house, as gold and silver, rice and hard cash." Nothing, however trivial, unsavoury or ludicrous, is left unexamined. The grasping, capricious, weak-willed men and women he wrote about were real people, recognizable figures from both the mundane and demimondaine world of Edo, who could for the first time see themselves reflected in the mirror of fiction.

BLACK SNOW

Amidst the glittering indulgence and creativity, catastrophes periodically engulfed the city. Earthquakes and fires struck in 1694 and 1703. The year 1704 saw floods that were followed by outbreaks of measles, cholera and plague. On 4 October 1707 strange underground grumblings were heard and intense tremors felt. As the earth around Mount Fuji began trembling and rippling, the snow-covered volcano began to shower ash over Edo. Two days later, the sacred mountain, now enveloped in black smoke, erupted. As fire and lava belched from its cone, the sky above Edo turned bright red. Grey ash and black cinders fell uninterruptedly on the city for the next two weeks, transforming buildings and cityscapes. The city was so dark that people were obliged to carry lanterns during the daytime. Temples and shrines were crowded with people praying for divine intercession.

Inevitably, the shogun's poor administrative skills, corruption and malfeasance were blamed for disasters wreaked by disgruntled gods. As the earth shuddered the city's confidence cracked, and with it grew an uneasy premonition of Edo entering uncertain times.

Period costume worn during a historical parade in Asakusa

Chapter Four

THE RIPENING CITY
1707-1868

If public morale was slipping, so were Edo's moral standards, such as they were. Passers-by on summer evenings, mystified by the loud laughter issuing from the residence of Tanuma Okitsugu, an influential minister to the shogun, were scandalized when they heard the explanation. The Tanuma family, it transpired, had built a sumo hall in their spacious residence, where they amused themselves watching naked women wrestling. Licensed gambling swept through the city at this time, ruining many a wealthy merchant or young Edokko. Temples, organizing fundraising lotteries, were partly to blame for the slide in morality.

Between 1771 and 1787 major fires, crop failures, famines, floods that inundated the lower reaches of Edo and volcanic eruptions endorsed the view that the times were sorely out of joint. Predictably, the city's misfortunes were attributed to the anger of the gods. In this climate of despair Buddhism and Confucianism lost much of their authority. The famine of 1787 was especially harsh, obliging many people to survive on dogs, cats, grass and tree bark. Some citizens of Edo, preferring death to starvation, drowned themselves in the Sumida. Further crop failures and drought, together with exasperation against the government for its mishandling of shortages, led to severe riots.

The Edo period is often portrayed in Japan as a period of peace and stability, but the last 150 years of Tokugawa rule witnessed over 200 urban riots, over a quarter of them during the last ten years of rule by a single family that had held sway for two and a half centuries, deriving its legitimacy not through popular support or royal heredity, but force.

The novelist Bakin left a realistic account of the incidents that followed the riots. The ransacking of the house of a wealthy rice merchant in Kojimachi on the night of 20 June of the famine year sparked the impulse to pillage shops and private homes. Further attacks took place in broad daylight. Once discovered, sacks of rice were split open, strewn across the streets and viciously fought over. Officials who tried to calm the crowds were threatened or beaten up. Hunger and hysteria warped into hallucination. At one point a rumour spread that the devil was leading a particularly savage group of looters. The riots continued for a full month until the arrival of relief boats carrying rice.

When a major fire broke out in 1806, Dutchman Hendrik Deoff, an eyewitness to the conflagration, managed to escape to a field where he could safely observe the scene. "I have never seen anything so terrible in my life," he wrote: "the horror of this sea of flames was increased by the crying and moaning of the women and children as they fled."

Despite the intermittent disasters, the unpredictability of life in Edo and a festering sense of grievance against the authorities, the arts were flourishing. The people of Edo had become besotted with their own culture, the kind of self-infatuation that invariably leads to decadence. By the end of the so-called Bunka-Bunsei period (1803-1830), from the late eighteenth to first quarter of the nineteenth century, Edo had established itself as the undisputed cultural centre of the country.

Exquisite cloths were produced by embroiderers and dyers, finely worked boxwood combs and fragrant wooden pillows, chests, sliding doors, screens, pipes and stencils of intricately patterned fabrics called komon were made by craftsmen. Urban culture flourished through an expanding system of commercial distribution. Design catalogues made by artists like Katsushika Hokusai allowed the public to choose and order prints. To the alarm of the authorities, the merchant class continued to rise above its allotted station in life. The samurai, whose swords and family heirlooms were often to be found deposited in the pawnshop, were losing their authority. In an effort to curb the ostentation, a series of new edicts against luxury were introduced under the shogun Ienari. Prohibitions included the production of ornate combs, the wearing of coral ornaments, restrictions on the giving of elaborate wedding presents, limits on the production of *hagoita* (battledore rackets decorated with images of popular actors) and dolls. Women were prohibited from visiting hairdressers, and mixed bathing at public bathhouses was banned. Efforts to tighten up censorship followed. The Edokko seem to have taken the restrictions in their stride, belittling draconian legislation with humour.

KABUKI ASCENDANT

Kabuki was elevated to an even more exalted level in Edo society than it had already enjoyed, reaching its peak in the nineteenth century. Playwrights could still be punished, though, for presuming to challenge the policies of the government. One actor, Onoe Baiko, was manacled for appearing without a sedge hat covering his face; Nakamura Utaemon found himself in jail after attending a sumo match, while Ichikawa Danjuro VII, making no secret of his flamboyant lifestyle, was exiled.

For those wanting to address reality, to infuse their plays with emotions an audience could understand, it was safer to turn to subjects that were apolitical in content. The Edo-born playwright Kawatake Mokuami, described by scholar Donald Keene as "one of Japan's greatest dramatic geniuses", left behind some 300 plays, blood-chilling dramas revolving around an underworld of thieves, gamblers, extortionists and womanizers. The appeal of plays like this was enhanced by the settings, the thrill of recognition at seeing representations of places like the river banks of Fukugawa, or the statues of the Gods of Good Fortune at Taiso temple near Shinjuku.

Eschewing the all too familiar setting of the Yoshiwara, Mokuami, in his play Kozaru Shichinosuke, tells the story of a dissolute rogue who seduces the maid of a daimyo, forces her into prostitution and proceeds to live off her income. He then murders a priest, only to find out that he was the maid's brother. Overcome with remorse, he asks her to kill him, but when she refuses they enter into a double suicide pact; in Mokuami's darker, more realistic world, however, the couple are arrested and cheated of a more honourable death, the customary climax of traditional Kabuki plays.

This was the heyday of great actors like Kodanji IV, Danjuro VII and Koshiro Matsumoto V, an individual said to be inordinately ugly but able to overcome the audience's revulsion with performances of transcendent artistry. In the refracting mirror of the stage, rogues became saints, the physically deformed became dashing heroes. Costume, makeup, the consummate skills of the best actors and the haunting corners of the half-lit stages all lent themselves to artifice and illusion. An actor playing the role of a beautiful young wife in a classic Kabuki play of this period, *The Ghost of Yotsuya*, a portrait by the author Tsuruya Namboku IV of Edo at its cruellest and most decadent, could reduce an audience sweltering in the summer heat of the enclosed theatres to blood-frozen silence as the poison administered by her husband turned the heroine's youthful face into a hideously aged mask. This is what happened in the summer of 1825 when the play was first produced at the Nakamura Theatre. Enhancing the illusion were the crude forms of illumination that plunged parts of the stage into total darkness and half-shadow. Followed by an eerie green flame, a skilful actor could appear to float as his costume brushed the stage. In its maturity, Kabuki managed the improbable feat of being both melodrama and art.

A combination of a series of theatre fires and the growing permissiveness of actors and audiences led to the transfer of theatres to the Saruwakacho district of Asakusa, then still very much on the outskirts of the city. This did not stop Edo from idolizing its actors, elevating them in the very manner of exaggeration that typified the Kabuki theatre itself to living deities. When death took them, they were accorded the highest honour an actor within the stratified society of Edo could expect to receive. The streets were thronged with mourners paying their respects. A. B. Mitford visited Saruwakacho during its heyday, noting in his Tales of Old Japan how when "two actors called Bando Shuka and Segawa Roko, both famous players of women's part, died at the same time, the people of Yedo mourned to heaven and to earth; and if a million riyos could have brought back their lives, the money would have been forthcoming."

Modest vaudeville houses sprang up at this time, providing a stage for up-and-coming storytellers, magicians and other popular entertainers. The long comic narrative known as *rakugo*, invariably ending with a clever punch-line or witty pun, began to appear at this time. These monologues, which could go on for an hour or more, were enormously popular. Variety halls, known as *yose* or *yoseba*, where professional rakugo storytellers and the hereditary lines of performers they established could perform, opened. Tickets for these alternately serious, edifying and comic monologues were cheap. They had to be, as the audience was made up largely of the residents of the downtown areas whose language and settings were mirrored in the stories.

Master storyteller and former comb-maker Sanshotei Karaku established Edo's first commercially successful rakugo hall. Something very similar to the improvisational style of rakugo was developed into a comic literary prose form by Shikitei Samba, a writer whose roots were in the downtown merchant quarter of Edo. In keeping with the city's commercial spirit and in the time-honoured manner of the amateur wit, Samba's writings often included comical advertisements for shops, including the one he owned himself, a thriving apothecary.

In the same tradition of aspiring men of literature who nonetheless had to make a living was the comic writer Ryutei Rijo, a craftsman who repaired palanquins and created ornamental designs in ivory, bamboo, silver and coral. An accomplished ballad singer, shamisen player and author of the comic novel *Eight Laughing Men*, he exemplified Edo's natural blend of trades, crafts and arts. Samba's irreverent and very funny book, Ikkiyoburo, managed to find its way into print at this time. A series of conversations set in the public bathhouses of Edo, it was one of the last yellow books to be published, as the works of writers like Tanehiko and Bakin began to appear. These were closer in subject and form to real novels. Bakin was the most prolific writer of the day, collaborating at times with the great bohemian genius Hokusai, whose illustrations helped to sell the books. Bakin's house stood at the foot of Kudanshita at a time when the district still had many rural features. Bakin's spring, as it was known, was a nearby watercourse used by the author to prepare his writing brushes.

WOODBLOCK ART

A by-product of the decadence that fed the ripening of Edo was the efflorescence of woodblock art, which reached a degree of perfection at this time. Among the great practitioners of the ukiyo-e print were Kiyonaga, Harunobu, Sharaku and Utamaro. Utamaro's portraits of women in the pleasure quarters, his use of colour, form and style in serialized works like *A Collection of Reigning Beauties* are matchless. A typical Utamaro beauty, languid and willowy, is sensual but attainable. Unlike Harunobu's prints of beautiful, eroticized women in faintly unreal settings, Utamaro's subjects have a plausible sensuality, suggested by intimate, even slovenly touches such as dishevelled clothing, exposed breasts or hair in casual disarray.

The artist spent a good deal of his life in the pleasure quarters, and in one print we see him, clearly in his element, sitting on a verandah at night surrounded by women, raising a cup of sake to one of them as she leans closer. He wears a slightly rakish black kimono, dotted with white spots; two yellow circles are visible on each shoulder, one reading uta, the other maro. Best known for his portraits of courtesans, the artist was interested in women in all their forms, depicting not only the coveted beauties of the pleasure quarters, but peasant women, weavers, dyers and women scouring Edo Bay for shellfish, or cutting mulberry leaves for silkworms.

Utamaro's *The Twelve Hours of the "Green Houses"*, a series of twelve prints depicting in fluid lines a day in the life of a Yoshiwara courtesan, are unsurpassed in their elegance and veracity. The series was published to great acclaim in 1794. A "green house", in its original Chinese connotation, was a nobleman's pavilion, a tall structure where kept women lived. In Utamaro's usage it stands for the more privileged strata within the pleasure quarters of the Yoshiwara. Though not precisely a realist, the artist was able to express psychological moods and nuance through portraits arranged around the twelve-hour zodiacal clock in which the twenty-four hour day is divided into twelve two-hour sections. In the person of Tsutaya Juzaburo, Utamaro had found an imaginative publisher of ukiyo-e and fine quality books by new writers and artists. With Tsutaya's encouragement, Utamaro began working on beautifully illustrated works like the 1786 Edo Sparrow picture book.

Almost nothing is known or verifiable about the life of Sharaku—except for the extraordinary fact that during an intensely creative period amounting to less than ten months in 1794, the artist produced his entire body of known work. The 145 extant prints are almost exclusively portraits of Kabuki actors, an immensely valuable record of the times. The mystery of Sharaku's life and death has never been solved.

Born in Edo in 1760, Ando Hokusai worked tirelessly until the very end of his life, dying at the age of 89, but not before he had published some 30,000 sketches and over 500 books. A man of boundless energy, he took the common people of Edo as his subjects: the peddlers, merchants, shop-girls, litter-bearers, monks, beggars and courtesans. Mount Fuji, standing in the background of many of his prints, forms the central subject of his Thirty-Six Views of Fuji.

Though fully aware of his gifts, he never lapsed into complacency, seeing himself as a student on the path towards an attainable mastery. Sixteen years before his death he wrote:

> I have slowly learned about the pattern of the grass, the trees, the structure of birds and other animals like insects and fish, so that when I am 80, I hope to be better. At 90, I hope to have caught the very essence of

things, so that at 100 I will have reached heavenly mysteries. At 110, every point and line will be living.

Sharp-tongued and cantankerous, Hokusai was by nature a showman whose creative energy drove him to some unusual exhibitions of his skills. These "performances" brought a breath of fresh air to the city. On one occasion, using a barrel and broom as inkpot and brush, he astonished onlookers by painting a colossal portrait of the Indian saint Daruma in the precincts of Gokoku-ji temple. When the shogun Ienari got wind of the event he had Hokusai brought to Asakusa's Denpo-in temple for a demonstration of his powers. The result was an early example of performance art. Turning up dressed in his usual rags, he strode proudly to the centre of the temple's great hall, carrying a box whose contents were concealed from the gaze of the shogun and his retinue of officials. Proceeding to unroll a long sheet of paper, he painted two blue parallel lines representing water along its surface. He then opened the box and out stepped a rooster. Swiftly painting its feet red, he placed the bird on the paper, where it strode up and down, its feet leaving imprints resembling scarlet autumn leaves. Bowing respectfully to Ienari and his astonished retainers, the artist declared, "I have created a landscape for Your Gracious Excellency. It is called *Red Maples along Tatsuta River.*"

If Utamaro provides us with a valuable portrait of the sirens of the pleasure quarters and Hokusai, the little people who made Edo life and culture, Utagawa Hiroshige gives us images of the city itself in over a thousand prints. His best-known work, such as the *Eight Views of Edo and its Suburbs* and the *One Hundred Views of Famous Places in Edo*, are complete series. These valuable documents show us sections of the city founded by Ieyasu and developed by later shoguns. Hiroshige's depictions of Ichigaya Hill, Gotenyama and Nihonbashi are no longer recognizable, but we can still see the outlines and features of Shinobazu Pond, Ueno Hill and Kanei-ji temple, the great Sanmon gate at Shiba and the steep defile of the Kanda canal as it cuts through Ochanomizu. Such works were to exert a powerful influence on later European artists like Van Gogh, Whistler and Cézanne.

The genre best matched to Hiroshige's intensely poetic view of nature was the landscape form. In the early nineteenth century it was still possible to be a landscape artist without even leaving the city. The artist's print of the Suwa Terrace in Nippori depicts people enjoying the cherry blossoms while gazing across rice fields to distant Mount Tsukuba. In Hiroshige's day the shrine was a popular spot for moon viewing and listening to the sound of summer insects like cicadas. In a print showing a large area of rice paddies called Mikawashima Tanbo, north of the Yoshiwara pleasure quarter, the artist shows us migratory flocks of crane alighting in the watery fields. In the desolate south-eastern reaches of Fukagawa, where the Sumida and Naka rivers begin to disgorge into the bay, Hiroshige has a hawk, about to descend on its prey, flying above the scene.

The sacred cone of Mount Fuji looms large in many of these prints, its distant outline often bathed in a crimson and vermillion sunset. Pilgrimages to Mount Fuji were enormously popular during the Edo period. A Fuji cult developed after the hermit Jikigyo Miroku took to meditating on the mountain's summit. Though it was visible from myriad angles within the city, the elderly, infirm and poor were not able to make the pilgrimage. Temple gardens with miniature Mount Fujis provided a novel substitute. Women, prohibited from scaling the real Fuji, were welcome to climb these artificial mounds. By the beginning of the nineteenth century there were Fuji replicas at Fukagawa, Yotsuya, Asakusa, Shitaya, Komagome, Kayabacho and other locations throughout the city. The sites turned into lively, all night social venues, attracting the inevitable vendors of food, religious and non-religious trinkets and fortune-tellers.

In her memoir *My Asakusa*, the actress Sawamura Sadako recalled that on 1 June, the opening day of the climbing season, "devout believers of Asakusa who could not climb Mount Fuji on a pilgrimage used to clothe themselves in white and pray while purifying themselves with cold water."

THE GARDEN CITY

By the first years of the nineteenth century the population of Edo had reached 1.3 million, making it by far the largest city in the world. By the middle of the century, that number had exceeded two million. Despite the burgeoning demographics, the people of Edo still continued to co-exist with nature in a way that is only possible in pre-industrial cities. If we are to believe accounts of the day corroborated in paintings and print, Edo was home to geese, foxes, cuckoos, the Japanese nightingale, swans and the red-crested crane. Boat crews drew water from the Sumida river to brew their tea. Asakusa carp, bass, laver and whitefish were easily taken from its depths. Fireflies could still be seen and cuckoos heard along the Kanda canal; uguisu, Japanese nightingales, were occasionally spotted in Koishikawa, Shitaya and a district that took its name from the bird, Uguisudani—Nightingale Valley.

This was the age of great gardens. Forbidden by the bakufu from spending funds on enlarging their military arsenals, many warriors chose to pursue leisure activities of a cultural nature. Some daimyo, wealthy merchants and later industrialists amused themselves constructing large, ambitiously conceived gardens. Unlike in European cities, these spacious, landscaped grounds were located in the urban centres of Edo. Daimyo residences in the High City were usually built facing ridge roads, providing a sloped area where natural springs could be turned into ponds surrounded by landscaped gardens. The dispensation of space was another reason Edo became known as a garden city. Even relatively low-ranking warrior families could expect to be given narrow but deep plots of land. As the house was likely to be small, their low salaries could be supplemented by growing vegetables on the generous expanse of garden.

Gardening was the exclusive pastime of daimyo and samurai in the early days of Edo, but prosperous merchants began taking an interest in the activity in the nineteenth century. A more modest form of horticulture began to flourish among the townspeople, stimulating nurserymen to diversify their stock and to work within a more public domain. Market gardens in Hakusan, Somei and Sugamo supplied the city with flowers and plants.

Nurserymen were granted permission to hold fairs in temples and shrines. A well-supported plant fair at Yakushi-in temple in Kayabacho, shown in a print from the 1830s by the woodblock artist Hasegawa Settan, includes, besides the standard irises, bamboo and wisteria, a number of imports. The flower fanciers at the fair, a high-ranking samurai, geisha and tonsured monk among the throng of commoners, are seen appreciating such plants as orchids and cactus.

Signalling the arrival of high summer in Tokyo, an early July morning glory fair takes place at Iriya's Kishimoji temple. Horticulturists in the early years of the nineteenth century began developing cultivars around the district of Ueno, a fad that later spread to Fukagawa and Asakusa. The morning glory was originally grown for seeds used in Chinese medicine. An energetic vine whose "glory" is over by noon, the flower has long been associated with the character and spirit of the hard-working, spendthrift Edokko, and their taste for short-lived pleasures.

The cultivation of chrysanthemums by approved growers and their use as a motif was strictly limited to the imperial household until the middle of the nineteenth century, by which time the flowers' popularity made such restrictions unenforceable. Cultivation was a lucrative business, with stallholders attracting customers by fashioning the flowers into statues. Dangozaka (Dumpling Slope) in Sendagi went a step further in 1856 by starting its own chrysanthemum festival. Customers paid a small fee to enter tents where battle scenes and tableaux from plays and romances were on display. The heroes and heroines of these scenes were made from chrysanthemum petals, although their heads were fashioned from papier-mâché. Futabatei Shimei recorded the scene in his 1887 novel *The Drifting Cloud*, one of the first experiments in writing fiction in the spoken vernacular.

> Shaven-headed priests had come and long-haired men, men with half-shaven heads, and men with topknots... Dangozaka was in a state of the wildest confusion. Flower-sellers stood by the usual signboards waving the flags of their respective establishments in the attempt to lure in customers.

Kiku Matsuri (chrysanthemum festivals) are still held at a number of locations throughout Tokyo. The Japanese garden at Shinjuku Gyoen, completed in 1772 after the estate was bequeathed to the loyal Naito clan, provides a matchless setting for chrysanthemum viewing. The current garden, a multicultural masterpiece, is divided into French, English and Japanese sections and also has a large botanical garden full of tropical plants, housed in an old, domed greenhouse. Early November is the best month to appreciate the chrysanthemum. Inside pavilions erected beside the pond and meandering paths at Shinjuku Gyoen, chrysanthemum cascades are planted months in advance.

The temptation to add symbolism to a flower already imbued with all manner of meanings is evident in the inevitable representations of Mount Fuji that appeared at this time. Traditionally, the slopes of the sacred cone are decked out in deep gold and purple petals, the peak, representing snow and autumn shadow, in white and mauve sprays. The poet James Kirkup saw one such display in a Tokyo garden, noting in his 1962 travelogue *These Horned Islands* the "snow-white cloud of traditional formality, shaped like a long French loaf", suspending its "dead-white, airy, colossal blooms just below the cratered peak."

Besides the raising of chrysanthemums, there was a celebrated lotus-viewing spot at Tameike Pond in Akasaka, a peony garden in Honjo and night cherries along the streets of the Yoshiwara pleasure district. At Horikiri Shobu-en, a garden east of the Arakawa river in Katsushika ward, enthusiasts could view the June irises. Irises were first introduced here in the marshes of Horikiri village by a farmer named Kodaka Izaemon in the 1660s. New hybrid varieties were introduced in the early nineteenth century by a descendant of Izaemon, who opened the Kodaka Garden to the public. Among the visitors from Edo was Hiroshige, who included a woodblock print of the garden, Irises at Horikiri, in his *One Hundred Views of Famous Places in Edo* series. The garden was turned over to food production in 1942 during the first lean years of the war, but was re-opened to the public in 1960.

Foreigners who entered the city in the years after the fall of the shogunate were struck by the vast expanses of greenery. Sir Rutherford Alcock, the first British minister to Japan, observed that the city could

> ... boast what no capital in Europe can—the most charming rides, beginning even in its centre, and extending in every direction over wooded hills, through smiling valleys and shaded lanes, fringed with evergreens and magnificent timber.

Judging from nineteenth-century accounts of drinking, boating and versifying parties, gardens were more interactive than the solemn objects of reverence they have become today. Hiroshige portrayed Edo in the years between 1856 and 1858 as a well-watered garden city, an outgrowth of landscaped villages. Thirty-five years later, the British architect and garden designer Josiah Conder was still able to record estates and gardens of staggering beauty and scale in the suburbs of what had become Tokyo. Even as late as 1903, W. B. Mason and Basil Hall Chamberlain, collaborating on a guide to Japan, reported that Tokyo retained a "tranquil and semi-rural aspect owing to the abundance of trees and foliage." Several Edo landscapes exist in Tokyo today, though in much reduced form.

KOISHIKAWA KORAKUEN

Many of the great mansions that once stood within the domain of present-day Koishikawa and the Iidabashi-Suidobashi districts have gone, but others have survived as gardens or areas of pleasure and amusement. Tokyo's oldest garden, the Koishikawa Korakuen, was laid out in 1629. It was constructed under the orders of Tokugawa Yorifusa, founder of the Mito clan, a branch of the Tokugawa family. The work was completed by the head of the second generation of the family, Mitsukuni, a great patron of learning.

Edo-period gardens were greatly influenced by Chinese landscaping styles. Within the garden many famous spots in China and Japan have been recreated in miniature. The name "Korakuen", meaning "a place to take pleasure after", is derived from a Chinese poem by Fan Zhongyan, which reads: "Be the first to take the world's trouble to heart, be the last to enjoy the world's pleasures." Tempering those pleasures, a rice field was created by Mitsukuni in a section of the garden with the intention of teaching his heir's wife the hardships of farming.

A stroll garden with a large central pond, its grounds were designed by Tokudaiji Sahei with the assistance of Zhu Shunsui, a Confucian scholar and refugee from the fall of the Ming dynasty. Mitsukuni took great note of the opinions of Zhu Shunsui, who is said to have designed the Engetsukyo Bridge, an exquisite "full moon" span in the Chinese style. Though largely ornamental, it may very well be the oldest intact bridge in the city. Another Chinese reference can be found in an earthen water-course running through the centre of the garden's small river, a reproduction of a dike that passes through Hangzhou Bay in China. A small hill near the pond represents Mount Lu in China's Jiangxi Province. The slopes of the mound are covered in bamboo grass, while at its base is a pond of sacred lotus. The pulpy, cloud-shaped leaves rise to a height of three feet above the water, their flowers—a symbol of Buddhism—best appreciated in the early morning. The eleventh-century Chinese writer Zhou Tunyi describes its growth, the plant rising like the soul, "without contamination from the mud, reposing modestly above the clear water, hollow inside and straight without."

The Japanese name for the lotus, hasu, is a contraction of hachi-no-su or bee's nest, a reference to the plant's seed chamber. Punctuated by holes, it strongly resembles the cells of the *ashinaga-bachi*, the Japanese paper wasp. Koishikawa Korakuen is today dominated by the curving roof of Tokyo Dome, a baseball stadium, its peace broken by the squeals of passengers from the titanic roller coaster that is the pride of the nearby Korakuen Amusement Park.

To the north of this garden lie the transformed remnants of another estate strongly associated with the Tokugawas. The Koishikawa botanical garden, hidden behind a canopy of trees and the domes of old greenhouses, traces its origins to 1684 when the shogun Tsunayoshi decided to turn the estate into a medicinal herb garden. The original garden can be sensed in the remains of primary broad-leaved evergreen and deciduous forests found on its hilly slopes. Flat stones, used for drying medicinal herbs, are visible in parts of the garden.

Hama Rikyu

In 1654 the younger brother of the shogun Ietsuna had parts of the watery shallows of the bay filled in and built a villa on the reclaimed land. Completed by the eleventh shogun, Ienari, the basic design and scale of the garden remain intact. After the Meiji Restoration the garden was turned into a residence for the imperial family and renamed the Hama Detached Palace. The highlight of the garden is a large tidal pond, with a small tea pavilion at its centre, and islets connected by wooden bridges. The only remaining tidal pond in Tokyo, sluice gates control the ebb and flow of the seawater, which brings in ocean fish such as gobies, black mullet and sea bass. Narrow watercourses were used as duck hunting sites. Enticed into the passages by grain, the fowl were caught in nets. Kamozuka, a mound built to console the spirits of ducks that were killed, can still be seen.

A large black pine was planted in 1704 when the garden was remodelled to celebrate the succession of the sixth shogun, Ienobu. In spite of earthquakes, fires and air raids, the pine has miraculously survived. The eighth shogun, Yoshimune, turned parts of the garden into an experimental farm for the cultivation of new crops and herbs. He is said to have kept an elephant from Vietnam in the grounds. A large garden, with over 600 varieties of peony, it contains areas of crape flowers, cosmos, irises, cherry, spider lilies, wisteria, bamboo and plum.

Close to Hama Rikyu is the diminutive, easily overlooked Kyu Shiba Rikyu, or Shiba Detached Palace, a scrupulously designed and very old Edo-period *kaiyushiki-teien*, or stroll garden, made from reclaimed land near the bay. Floating at the centre of the garden's large pond are five islands. The largest, Horai-jima, a rocky island covered in black pine, takes its name from Taoist mythology, which tells of five islands to the east of China where the immortals lived in perfect harmony. Pines were venerated in China as symbols of immortality, and Taoist teachings encouraged monks to eat cones, resin and pine needles in order to acquire the life force of the tree. To the rear of the garden is a later addition, a hill called Kyua Dai, built for the Emperor Meiji so that he could watch the tides coming in.

KAMEIDO-TENJIN

There were several shrines built to Tenjin, the god of learning, calligraphy and poetry, a typical string of accomplishments demanded by the populace of their hard-working gods. The Kameido-Tenjin shrine was built to the east of the river in 1662. Besides a lake, its main feature was a large wisteria trellis, beneath which visitors would sit sipping from cups of tea or sake. Food stalls and houses of prostitution sprang up nearby, testing among other things the often feeble moral resolve of the priesthood who served at the shrine. Old prints show the Kameido garden as an important feature of the city.

The garden was laid to waste in the bombings of 1945, but a splendid wisteria still attracts swarms of visitors when it blossoms in early May. During the Edo period visitors arrived by boat from Yanagibashi or Asakusa, alighting at the pier in Kameido. Besides the shrine and its wisteria trellis, the other attraction here was a celebrated teahouse, Funabashiya, which served a starch-based confection known as kuzu-mochi. The teahouse, standing beside the entrance to the shrine, opened in 1805 and has been serving the sweet along with green tea ever since.

GARDEN OF THE SIX PRINCIPLES OF POETRY

Construction of Rikugi-en, the Garden of the Six Principles of Poetry, began in the year 1695 under the supervision of Yanagisawa Yoshiyasu, a chamberlain of the shogun Tokugawa Tsunayoshi, a highly regarded litterateur and art connoisseur. Edo gardens were not made overnight.

Designed so that guests could stroll along paths that would reveal fresh perspectives on the miniature hills, teahouses, lake and islands planted with pine, the garden took seven years to complete.

Rikugi-en's name stands for the six principles used in the composition of Oriental poetry, and comes from the *Shi no Rikugi*, an anthology of Han dynasty poems. Although you would have to be a scholar to identify them, the park's pond, flora and stones are said to embody 88 scenes described in the 31-syllable poetry form known as *waka*. The scenery, like many of these stroll gardens, was designed to evoke the spots described at 88 sites mentioned in major Chinese and Japanese literary works, in particular the settings found in two ancient Japanese poetry collections: the *Kokin Wakashu* and the Manyoshu.

Although the garden declined after Yanagisawa's death in 1714, its general contours, pond and rock settings have endured as a reminder of its original form. The Mitsubishi group's founder, Iwasaki Yataro, bought the garden during the Meiji period and had it restored to its original state as a typical Edo landscape garden. In 1934 it was donated to the city and opened to the public.

Blending into the peaceful, wooded grounds of camphor, trident maples, black pines, dogwood and a Japanese red pine dating back to the completion of the garden are over 6,000 deciduous, coniferous and evergreen trees, The pond has become the depository for a host of small creatures—turtles, goldfish, frogs—children's pets no longer wanted by young families living in the cramped, multi-storey apartment blocks around the Rikugi-en. Stealthily re-stocked with aquatic creatures by the neighbourhood, the grounds are also a haven for birds: blue magpies, bush warblers, dabchicks, and migratory species such as the widgeon.

KIYOSUMI-TEIEN

Like many gardens that can be traced back to the Edo period, the Kiyosumi-teien has an interesting history of ownership and change. The garden, located close to the Sumida in Fukagawa ward, was part of a larger estate owned by a wealthy timber merchant named Kinokuniya Bunzaemon.

Timber merchants did particularly well in Fukagawa as buildings in these congested areas burned down regularly. The stroll garden that Kinokuniya built here in 1688 was designed around a large pond. Water

The Kiyosumi-teien garden east of the river

was originally diverted from the Sumida, the pond's level changing with the ebb and flow of the tides in Tokyo Bay. Stone, water and artificial hills were the main features of Edo period stroll gardens. Artificial hills, many in the likeness of Mount Fuji, were designed to be climbed and to provide a panoramic view of the garden below. The garden's central hill, covered in Japanese azaleas, is also known as Mount Azalea.

With the declining fortunes of its owner, the garden fell on hard times. The grounds were taken over in 1878 by Iwasaki Yataro and used as a recreational retreat for Mitsubishi company employees and as a place where business clients and distinguished guests could be entertained. Iwasaki set about restoring the garden, adding some distinctive features. Iwasaki's brother, Yanosuke, an art connoisseur, spent a great deal of time and expense selecting rare and lovely rocks from all over Japan, which were then transported to Tokyo in the company's steamships. A *ryotei*, a traditional Japanese teahouse, was constructed in 1909 to host Lord Kitchener, on his official state visit from England. Overlooking the pond, the ryotei was built in the sukiya style, a domestic architectural form that developed out of the Momoyama period (1573-1615) tea aesthetic.

The Kiyosumi-teien is an all-seasons garden. In spring, forsythia, cherry, Japanese andromeda, quince and azaleas are at their best. Summer sees the blooming of irises, gardenia, hydrangea, crepe myrtle and Japanese catalpa. Drawn by the scent of water in the hot Tokyo summers, serpents slither into the reeds beside the pond, a reminder of the presence of reptiles and animals at one time in this area. During the autumn months, fragrant olive, camellia and red spider come into their own, while winter is the time for plum, wandflower and pheasant's eye.

A LITERARY GARDEN

The laying out of the Mukojima Hyakka-en (Garden of One Hundred Flowers) began in 1804, close to the banks of the Sumida and Arakawa rivers, an area of temples and teahouses that served as a focal point for the cultural and social life of many early nineteenth-century Edo writers and artists. The garden was the creation of Sawara Kiku, a wealthy antique shop owner with an interest in literature. Sawara moved in literary circles and was well acquainted with the painters and poets of the day, numbering among his friends the Confucian scholar Kameda Hosai, the artist Sakai Hoitsu and the writer Ota Nampo.

Sawara set out to design a retreat in the manner of a Chinese literary garden. Friends contributed stones, engraving them with poems that can still be read today. The plum trees, flowers and plants they selected were all closely associated with the pages of Chinese and Japanese classic literature.

Pampas grass, bellflowers, kudzu vine, valerian, irises, cudweed, three pergolas of lilac-blue climbing wisteria, agueweed (a herbaceous perennial), asters and a well known tunnel of flowering, rose-purple coloured bush clover are among the diverse plants in this simple but imaginative garden. Trees include the cherry, deciduous Japanese oak, maple-leafed hibiscus and a very singular maidenhair tree.

Literary pretensions notwithstanding, the garden was created as an ironic comment on, or rebuttal of, the culture of the ruling military class and their fondness for sprawling gardens replete with complex rock settings, clipped hedges and the recreation of famous scenery. A simple pond, grasses and trees growing in the most natural of ways are the extent of this modest garden of little more than two acres.

The garden aroused great interest among the people of Edo and was even honoured by a visit from the shogun Ienari after its opening in 1804. The garden was much visited during the time of the autumn moon, attracting poets who came to write haiku and linked verse. Along with an August "singing insects" festival, the moon-viewing festival is still held every September.

Here, as elsewhere in the city, we are reminded of the paramount importance of gardens, temples and estates, not just as beauty spots, cultural or historical time capsules, but as conservation areas, their borders establishing lines of defence against development.

Shadows over the Bay

By the first half of the nineteenth century, the population of Edo's 1,650 districts was now well in excess of one million. Impressive demographic growth was not matched by development. The degree of isolation into which Edo had hardened can be sensed by comparing the city to the industrialized capitals of the West, and to newly emerging Asian centres of commerce and modernity like Shanghai and Hong Kong. Edo in the 1850s presented an extraordinary contrast. The absence of any wheeled vehicles, metalled roads, trains, carriages or even bicycles must have made it, a city without factories or machines, an unusually quiet place. Flaming torches and candles provided a small amount of light, but most of the streets would almost certainly have been pitch black at night.

Presiding over the decadent early nineteenth-century years of the city, Japan's longest ruling shogun, Ienari, took a dim view of Edo's public morality, though his own life was hardly a model of Confucian rectitude. Censorship, always a fitful affair at best, was more sternly applied under Ienari. Ukiyo-e artists in particular, came in for severe treatment. The great woodblock artist Utamaro, faithful chronicler of the demi-monde, was kept under house arrest, handcuffed and manacled for fifty days to appease Ienari's moral outrage at prints judged indecent and subversive. Other artists, like Utagawa Kuniyoshi, risked a similar fate but persisted in incorporating political satire into their drawings and prints. The main architect of drives to promote public morals, Ienari enjoyed an immodest lifestyle, indulging his pleasures in a flourishing harem of some 600 or more concubines. To further amuse himself, he had a bridge made of sugar—a highly expensive commodity beyond the dreams of ordinary people—built over a pond in his garden.

With the death of Ienari in 1841, further decline set in. Writers, historians and philosophers began to engage in an open debate on the legitimacy of the shogunate, while from outside more foreign ships were appearing along the coast, demanding entry into Japanese ports. Russian vessels were sighted off the northern coast of Hokkaido, while British ships made incursions along the southern shoreline of Kyushu.

In 1837 the Morrison, an American ship returning a group of shipwrecked Japanese sailors it had helped to rescue, was strafed with gunfire when it sailed into Edo Bay. In 1846 another American vessel, the Columbus, arrived in Uraga Bay, demanding the release of shipwrecked American sailors. It was told in no uncertain terms to depart and never return. Three years later the release of the prisoners was obtained after Commander Glynn sailed his ship, the Preble, into the bay, menacing Edo with its guns.

In the face of threats from abroad, attempts were made to reinvigorate the faltering Tokugawa system with a further spate of largely ineffective measures banning improper books, and encouraging authors and storytellers to produce edifying homilies and discourses along neo-Confucian and Shinto lines. Authors were arrested, theatres closed and the pleasure quarters temporarily shut down in a fruitless attempt to turn the Edo lotus eater into an example of moral virtue.

One of the most astonishing confrontations of the century took place on 8 July 1853, when Commodore Matthew Galbraith Perry sailed four heavily armed American ships, two steam frigates and two fighting corvettes, into Edo Bay, discharging a shuddering cannon salute at the Japanese coast that had been off-limits to foreigners for over two hundred years. Perry had sailed on the orders of President Millard Fillmore, who wished to press the Japanese to open diplomatic and commercial relations with the United States. The president had authorized Perry to use any methods he saw fit, adding that "any departure from usage or any error of judgment will be viewed with indulgence." Ignoring Japanese warnings, Perry sailed up the bay to a position where he could, if he so chose, shell the perimeters of the city. Besides a proclamation of intention and a testing of the waters, no Japanese person who saw the ships could fail to notice that the visit was a pointed display of superior western technology and maritime power, a reminder that progress had bypassed Japan.

Perry returned as he promised, on 11 February 1854, this time with a larger squadron of nine ships and 2,000 men. Greeting Perry's "black ships of evil" were a delegation of Japanese armed with swords, antiquated muskets, halberds and assorted medieval weaponry. Uppermost in Perry's mind was less the notion of a mission civilisatrice than the question of trade and the right of American ships to enter Japanese ports.

Armed with another letter from President Fillmore and accompanied by two colossal black bodyguards, Perry was eventually permitted to go ashore. The ritual exchange of gifts that ensued between the uniformed Americans and the Japanese, attired in their finest silks, was telling. Among the gifts given by the Japanese to their American counterparts were a bronze temple bell, a lacquer writing case and a teapot. The Japanese party received samples from a more technologically fixated civilization: a daguerreotype camera, a telegraph machine and, much to the delight of the samurai officials who were able to sit on top of its carriages, a miniature steam train set on a circular track. There were also books, maps, perfumes, and cases of whisky, Madeira wine and champagne.

Adding to the atmosphere of a diplomatic fairground, sumo wrestlers were produced and Perry was invited to punch them in the stomach. Lubricated by the unaccustomed quantities of champagne and whisky drunk in making toasts to each other, one Japanese official, in the pontificating manner common to inebriated Japanese males promoting international friendship, declared, "Nippon and America, all the same heart!"

UPHEAVAL AND MILLENARIAN BELIEFS

Perry's black ships exposed the vulnerability of the Edo bakufu and divided the authorities into two factions: those who wished to open Japan to trade with foreign powers, and those who conspired to replace the weak and discredited regime and place the emperor, and a newly empowered government, at the centre of the state. As if to punish Edo for its intransigence in dealing with the foreign intruders—or so it was interpreted by the townspeople—a violent eruption, known as the Ansei earthquake, shook Edo during the night of 2 October 1855, and again on 11 November 1855. The quakes had been preceded by strange explosions of ground water throughout the city, accompanied by bizarre groans emitting from the earth and flashes in the night-time sky. When the second earthquake struck, its epicentre, around the mouth of the Arakawa river running through the middle of the Low City area of reclaimed land, destroyed over 16,000 homes, leaving some 10,000 people dead. Interminable downpours, flooding and an outbreak of cholera followed the earthquakes. In the absence of a better explanation, the natural disasters, expressions of divine displeasure, were blamed on the appearance of Commodore Perry's black ships.

News of the disasters was spread by printed broadsheets and colour woodblock prints called namazu-e ("catfish pictures"), the name taken from an ancient superstition that earthquakes occurred when a giant, subterranean catfish thrashed its tail. Large numbers of Edo residents took to praying at Kashima shrine, where it was believed a massive rock formation plunging deep into the earth possessed the power to subdue the fractious fish. Yonaoshi, or "reform the world" beliefs, sprang up like millenarian cults among the more optimistic Edo residents who imagined that these were signs portending the birth of a new world. The period from Perry's arrival in 1853 and a second mission the following year, and the final overthrow of the shogunate in 1868, was characterized by assassinations, intrigues, coups and countercoups, culminating in civil war. A revival of emperor-worship fuelled by ultra-violence and xenophobia was embodied in the rallying cry: "Revere the emperor, expel the barbarians."

Even some of the newcomers had their doubts about this strangest of encounters between the US and Japan, a country that had sealed its border during the Jacobean period and only opened them in the reign of Victoria. Townsend Harris, the first American consul-general, wrote gravely in his journal on 4 September 1856: "Grim reflections—ominous of change—if for the real good of Japan?" The same thoughts are echoed in the diary of Henrikus Conradus Joannes Heusken, Harris' Dutch interpreter, whose entry reads, "I fear, oh my God, that this scene of happiness is coming to an end and that the Occidental people will bring here their fatal vices."

Sporadic resistance to the inevitable continued. On the snowy morning of 24 March 1860, Ii Naosuke, Lord of Hikone, chief counsellor to the shogun, was assassinated outside the palace gates by a group opposed to all agreements with the "western barbarians". The assassination, which left Ii's body and those of his guards lying bloodied in the snow, only succeeded in weakening the Tokugawa ancien régime.

These were dangerous times for foreigners living in Edo and the foreign settlement at nearby Yokohama. The British legation had already been attacked in 1861, and a British merchant, Charles Richardson, cut down by samurai after refusing to bow to a procession of ex-daimyo. Another British casualty, the delegation's residence, was blown up in 1863. An American businessman, Francis Hall, wrote in 1859 that he would "start out for a walk by putting a revolver in one pocket and a copy of Tennyson in the other."

Though an age of unease, of portents and consultations with the supernatural, there was still time enough for novelties, new sights and experiences. In 1863 an enterprising Portuguese businessman exhibited an Indian elephant in the Ryogoku district, causing much excitement. The creature was depicted in countless prints, with text describing its size, history and eating habits. The satirical journalist Kanagaki Robun, writing the commentary for a diptych print by Yoshitoyo, was so impressed as to lapse into the rhetoric of the fairground tout:

> It understands what people say and it can guess their feelings and it puts out fires and drives out harmful pestilences. It gets rid of poisonous things. For those who see it, the seven misfortunes will decrease and the seven fortunes will grow.

As opposition to the status quo was reaching critical mass, a strange delirium overtook the eastern seaboard towns and villages of the country in the autumn of 1867. Stepping into the chaos were briefly lived millenarian cults, delirious mobs parading Shinto images through the streets of Edo and shouting quasi-religious slogans. When they were not looting the houses of the rich or indulging in bouts of eating and drunkenness, hundreds of thousands of exultant people, both men and women, stripped off their ordinary clothes, making their faces up in outlandish visages. Dancing half-naked in the streets and dragging customers from restaurants and shops to join in the debauchery, crowds beat gongs, chimes, whistles and drums to the defiant singsong refrain of *Ee ja nai, ka, ee ja nai, ka!* ("Anything we do is OK. Why not? What the hell!"), proving the point by wearing outrageous costumes, cross-dressing and openly having sex in alleyways. While the lewdness and abandon were signs of crowds venting frustration at the insecurity of the times, their songs and slogans ridiculing the policies of the shogunate and the mismanagement of the economy helped to hasten the end of the old order.

Violence blended with more superstition. People's worst premonitions seemed confirmed with the sudden death from a rare disease at the age of 37 of the Emperor Komei in 1866, and in the same year the passing away of the shogun Iemochi. More unnatural events took place in the frenzied autumn of the following year when talismans and amulets inscribed with the name of Ise shrine, the most sacred religious site in Japan, rained down on Edo and other towns along the eastern seaboard, a good omen according to those who interpreted such things.

The inevitable occurred in the February of 1868 with the departure into retirement at Kannei-ji temple in Ueno of the last shogun, Yoshinobu. Rebels against the new order took up arms, staking out positions on the hills above Shitaya, the location of present-day Ueno Park and Kanei-ji, one of the Tokugawa shogunate's mortuary tombs. Some three hundred soldiers were killed in the short but fierce battle that ensued, and as many as a thousand houses destroyed by shells that fell short of their targets before the rebels finally surrendered. On the day the battle was fought, torrential rains caused Shinobazu Pond to flood. Many of the soldiers had to fight in knee-deep water as cannon rounds directed respectively from the second floor of a teahouse and from a cave shrine dedicated to the Inari fox god, roared overhead.

Shortly after the event, Hozumi Eiki wrote a haiku called *On Fleeing the Battlefield at Ueno*. Its evocation of horror is more powerful when you understand the age-old association between the nightingale and the coughing up of blood:

Rain washes away
The blood: Just at that moment
A nightingale sings.

The battle was an act of gallantry with little hope of succeeding, a model of the kind of noble failure much beloved of the Japanese and, in the dramatization of history so characteristic of this storytelling city, an example of events instantly requisitioned as literary and theatrical narrative.

Chapter Five

MEIJI IMPERIUM

1868-1912

The emperor, Son of Heaven, remained in a hermetic seclusion in his palace in Kyoto. But even there, behind high walls of clay and tile and the nine gateways that led to the imperial presence, life was stirring. The first two Englishmen to be granted an audience with the mythical emperor, Sir Harry Parkes and A. B. Mitford, encountered a fifteen-year-old adolescent dressed in a robe of white brocade, with trousers of vermillion silk trailing several yards behind him. His teeth, the astonished guests noted, were lacquered black, the upper lip gilded, the lower painted crimson; sooty arcs had been painted high on his forehead above shaven eyebrows, and his cheeks were rouged. Mitford captures the occasion:

> We were standing in the presence of a sovereign whose ancestors for centuries had been to their people demi-gods... The sanctity of their seclusion had been inviolate, they had held no intercourse with a world of which they knew nothing. Now, suddenly, the veil of the temple had been rent, and the Boy-God had descended from the clouds to take his place among the children of men... and had held communion with *The Beasts from Without.*

Under the new, as yet uncertain order, those members of the samurai class who had remained loyal to both shogun and emperor were ruined overnight, forced in many cases to sell off their family heirlooms, even used clothes. *Daimyo* compelled to maintain large estates in Edo now packed up their possessions and left for the provinces, taking their families and retainers with them. Hundreds of acres of choice land fell vacant. These well appointed plots formed the core of the modern, westernized city that would soon grow. Many of the estates were used by foreign legations.

The departure en masse of an entire social class, about to be rendered anachronistic by reform, triggered civil disorder as *ronin* and thieves, the two practically synonymous at this historical juncture, set about occupying these mansions, using them as strongholds from which to rape, plunder and murder in the manner of marauders. Trade slumped as merchants closed down their shops, traders sealed their warehouses and thousands of townspeople fled the city, leaving Edo vulnerable.

Land prices fell and so did the population, from two million to 600,000. Grass grew in the streets outside the abandoned residences of the daimyo. The future business quarter of Marunouchi, Nihonbashi and the administrative district of Kasumigaseki languished as their great mansions were deserted and empty streets invaded with weeds. Pedestrians venturing into the area, even during daylight hours, risked attack by armed robbers. The novelist Nagai Kafu, born in 1879 and a child at the time, captured the sense of insecurity in an autobiographical story called *The Fox*.

> The talk was uniformly cruel and gory, of conspirators, of assassinations, of armed robbers. The air was saturated with doubt and suspicion. At a house the status of whose owner called for a moderately imposing gate, or a mercantile house with impressive godowns, a murderous blade could at any time come flashing through the floor mats, the culprit having stolen under the verandah and lain in wait for sounds of sleep.

Order was restored with the arrival of the boy emperor who, with a retinue of one thousand soldiers, entered the city on 26 November 1868. The streets on that day were completely silent as the emperor made his slow procession towards the castle. Things livened up the following month when a national holiday was declared and 2,563 barrels of royal sake were distributed throughout the city.

RESTORATION AND RENEWAL

The policies initiated after the arrival of the young emperor were defined by the word *ishin*, usually translated as "restoration". More accurately, the term stood for renewal, a revitalization involving the collective energy of the entire populace. Emperors to this day are invariably called on to provide commemorative verses when the occasion calls for it, a court tradition members of the royal family seem to genuinely enjoy. The Meiji emperor's verse in honour of the new age was nothing if not prophetic:

It is time for men
Who were born in the land of warriors;
It is time for them
To make themselves known.

In a charter oath that called upon the people to renounce much of the past in an effort to become as powerful as the West, the young emperor told them that "knowledge shall be sought throughout the world," a pledge that was firmly honoured. *Fukoku Kyohei*, denoting "Rich Country, Strong Army", a fresh slogan for an age characterized by rallying cries, captured the aspirations of the times.

Edo had acquired its new name Tokyo, meaning "Eastern Capital", on 13 September 1868. For several years the two names co-existed. As the feudal bastion transformed itself into a modern city, even the perception of time changed, or at least the method of fixing it, with Japan adopting the western calendar on 1 January 1873. The perceptions of foreigners also underwent changes. The travel writer Isabella L. Bird, visiting the city in 1878, summed up the distinction between the names when she wrote, "It would seem an incongruity to travel to Yedo by railway, but quite proper when the destination is Tokiyo."

While most people embraced the new order, the sense of unease at the encounter with the outsiders was expressed by a radical political movement whose slogan, *Sonno joi*, can be translated as "revere the emperor, expel the barbarian." The imminent dissolution of the feudal samurai class and its replacement by a conscript army, along with the arrival of the "barbarians" themselves, engendered yet another instance of xenophobia in the form of the League of the Divine Wind. Members of the league held that self-purification and sincere living would cause the Japanese gods to send a *kamikaze* (divine wind) to expunge foreign influences. In the meantime, its followers took more practical steps by carrying self-purifying salt on their persons in the event that they met someone in western dress. Money of foreign design or provenance was handled only with the aid of chopsticks.

The more western-allergic ex-samurai sought further protection by covering their topknots with metal fans when they rode under the newly installed telegraph wires. Rumours had already spread among common folk in the countryside that the wires were somehow connected with black magic rites practised by Christians. In the end samurai managed to keep their titles and modest stipends, but in all other respects they were turned into superannuated warriors.

THE NEW AGE

The promulgation of the Meiji constitution took place on 11 February 1889. Materially it made little difference, but psychologically a great shift took place. Members of the merchant class, in particular, may have made themselves affluent, but their prestige and self-esteem had been relatively low. Now they were liberated from the shame of a rank that left them wealthy but despised. Playwright Hasegawa Shigure, a native of Nihonbashi, described the sense of release experienced by her father with the declaration of the Meiji constitution as "the end of the old humiliation, the expunging of the stigma they had carried for so many years as Edo townspeople." Outcast groups like the *eta* were emancipated from their wretched status. The stigma ran far too deep, though, to be so easily waved away with the mere signing of a document.

In this new age, overtures were made to the foreign powers and audience quickly sought with the emperor. The *Japan Times Overland Mail* commented on this extraordinary turn of events in the 13 January 1869 issue:

> ... an Imperial demi-god, unapproachable, sacred from the eyes even of his own nobles: in December asking admission within the circle of civilized sovereigns, attempting the part of a constitutional monarch and preparing to receive the representatives of a score of foreign nations and foreign services, every individual of which the law, but a few short years ago, enjoined each true Japanese to slay, should he dare to pollute the soil of Nippon with unholy tread.

The emperor found himself in a role he was born for. His position in this new order was clear. A divine ruler, embodying the revival of traditional moral values, he was also expected to symbolize the progressive doctrines of Meiji, to steer the nation in the manner of a benign philosopher-king to the forefront of the civilized world. Any lingering reservations were assuaged with yet another rousing slogan typical of early Meiji's ambitions and optimism. "Japanese Spirit and Western Culture" implied a fruitful convergence of refined abstraction and materialism.

By the early 1870s the majority of Japanese, caught up in the head-long rush to acquire western knowledge and technology, had abandoned their desire to cling to or recreate the past. Though with some difficulty, the new government set about trying to transform the manners and cultural habits of Tokyo, prohibiting public displays of nakedness that might upset the sensibilities of westerners, forbidding lighting bonfires on the streets, washing dirty dishes in the river and urinating in the gutters in front of shops. Confusing the similar Japanese ideograms for urinal and post box, one incident saw a visiting group of farmers mistake a post box for a public urinal. Like the Tokugawa elders before them, the Meiji authorities were uncomfortable with unregulated pleasure. Writers were repeatedly inveighed to be more high-minded, to eschew low-life themes for more pious and patriotic subjects.

Certain practices and punishments associated with a feudal, pre-modern Japan were gradually abolished. Among the more draconian penalties scrapped under the new Meiji enlightenment were burning at the stake, crucifixion, torture to extract confession and the tattooing of criminals. It also banned the public display of heads, but not before one or two foreign photographers had recorded the grisly scenes.

A Foreign Settlement

Some of these early foreign residents could be found living in Tsukiji, where a daimyo estate had existed until recently. The name Tsukiji, signifying reclaimed land, was a reference to the mud flats that once stood between branches of the Sumida river. Tsukiji's long association with fish began with the founding of the city and when catches were landed and auctioned on a nearby beach. Sparsely populated, its festering mud flats and brackish wells made it one of the least desirable areas of the city. If that were not enough, its areas of vacant ground were used as a noisome dump for refuse. The only space at the government's disposal to offer to foreigners as a port settlement, the area was duly cleared, its legions of scavenging crows and kites dispatched, and orderly streets and graceful houses built over the tips. Marvelling at the changes, one Japanese writer watched the new settlement rise "month by month, until the new buildings resembled the teeth of a comb in closeness and orderliness. There was no longer any stinking refuse or hollow places filled with stagnant water at Tsukiji."

Yet the new settlement, failing to attract the number of merchants it had expected, was doomed from the start. For one thing, the shallow harbour precluded the thriving maritime trade the Japanese had anticipated. There was also a psychological barrier; Tsukiji's river-facing, gated settlement cooped within canals reminded foreigners of Deshima in Nagasaki, the man-made island built to house and confine the Dutch traders during the xenophobic Edo era. Many subsequently moved out, drawn by the cooler slopes and better facilities of nearby Yokohama. The death knoll of the settlement came in 1872 with the great fire that devastated large parts of the city, including much of Tsukiji.

The area had provided early foreign residents with glimpses of a life yet to change. Junks with large saffron and white sails passed along the canal here on the incoming tides, loading up on timber, while ferryboats transported people from bank to bank. Ernest Satow, a British diplomat who wrote extensively about these early years of contact between Japan and the West, recalled his impressions of Tsukiji:

> Curious duck-shaped boats of pure unpainted wood, carrying a large four-square sail formed of narrow strips of canvas loosely tacked together, crowded the surface of the sparkling waters. Now and then we passed near enough to note the sunburnt, copper-coloured skins of the fishermen, naked, with the exception of a white cloth around the loins, and sometimes a blue rag tied across the nose, so that you could just see his eyes and chin.

CITY TRANSFORMATIONS

Westernization was initially slow to sink in, but the stage props—the red-brick buildings, horse-drawn trolleys and top hats—appeared quickly enough. Western-inspired fads, fashions and conveniences grew rapidly after a number of national exhibitions displaying modern machinery, gadgets and devices were held in Ueno Park. The times and the exhibits were new but Edo had had its own share of exhibitions. One memorable event, organized by Hiraga Gennai in 1757 and held in the grounds of the Confucian Yushima Seido temple in the Soto-Kanda district, displayed rare species of birds, shellfish and plants. Edo had always been good at combining commerce, worship and the arts.

A Hiroshige print depicts townspeople flying kites on the slopes of

Kasumigaseki during the New Year's holiday. Kite flying had long been popular among Edo's lower orders. Flying their kites above the heads of the warrior class is said to have given them a momentary sense of imagined superiority. An ideogram is written boldly on the kite at the top of the print, the first Chinese character of the publisher's name responsible for the print series, an astute way to advertise the company.

What was new in these Meiji-era events was the intent that exhibitions should be insistently modern and firmly urban. A circular sent out to exhibitors before the event warned darkly that no fish, exotic birds, rare plants or older works of art were to be presented. The First National Industrial Exhibition held on Ueno Hill in 1877 focused largely on manufacturing, metallurgy, machinery, agriculture and gardening, though one exhibitor managed, in the spirit of the Edo period fairground, to sneak in a ten-foot-high treasure ship made of sugar.

If early visitors to Tokyo were surprised by the size and sprawl of the city, they were also struck by how quiet it was. The atmosphere of a provincial town was probably due to the lack of machinery, the absence of horse-drawn traffic clattering over cobblestones. Carts were drawn by men. In the very first years of Meiji there were still no wheeled vehicles in Tokyo. Carriages drawn by oxen could occasionally be seen, but these were restricted to members of the imperial court in Kyoto. The townspeople generally travelled on foot, even along the great highways like the Tokaido. Those who could afford to, rode horses or were carried in simple palanquins called *kago*, hung from a single pole balanced between the shoulders of bearers.

A new Japanese invention called the *jinrikishaw* was well suited to Tokyo's narrow streets and lanes. In another concession to western sensibilities, rickshaw runners were required to cover themselves in more than the traditional loincloth normal at the time. Many of the rear parts of rickshaws were decorated with images clearly influenced by art emerging from the pleasure quarters. The owners of these new conveyances were required to remove the more suggestive decorations. The sudden appearance of the rickshaw spelt the end of palanquins, which disappeared virtually overnight.

FASHIONS AND FADS

The cultural schizophrenia of the times, with its willingness to jettison traditions and customs that might offend foreigners or make them form a low opinion of Japan as a backward society, resulted in some odd revisionism. The novelist Mishima Yukio, that arch-critic of Meiji capitulation, looked back on the era, likening it to "an anxious housewife preparing to receive guests, hiding away in closets common articles of daily use and laying aside comfortable everyday clothes, hoping to impress the guests with the immaculate, idealized life of her household, without so much as a speck of dust in view."

The modification of social practices in the early Meiji years, partly inspired by fear among the Japanese that they would be mocked by foreigners, resulted in curious measures. Ancient phallic stones were covered up or consigned to the storerooms of temples, a prohibition on the long-established practice of mixed bathing was soon enforced, traditional buildings not deemed to be western enough were threatened with demolition; even the performance of Noh dramas was brought into question. Public spaces around the approaches to Tokyo's main bridges—a semi-free public domain where a lively mix of food vendors, tricksters, mountebanks and prostitutes gathered, erotic shows and ribald melodramas were performed in reed-screen playhouses, and satirical verses criticizing government policies stuck to the bridge stanchions—came under official control.

When the new Shimbashi railway station was unveiled by the emperor on 12 September 1872, those invited to attend the opening ceremony, with its bunting, flags, cannonades and other unfamiliar western-style trappings, were warned not to turn up in traditional working clothes, *hanten* jackets or country-style *momohiki* pants, or to display any form of nakedness. In an age excessively concerned with outward appearances, it was another example of the easy translation of Victorian propriety into Meiji prudery.

A fad for eating meat was endorsed by Fukuzawa Yukichi, one of the leading intellectuals of Meiji, who advocated that its consumption would improve the nation's physique. The emperor himself soon declared that he would henceforth eat meat. Although there had been hunters' markets in Edo, where permitted meats such as boar, poultry and deer were sold, often under the euphemistic labels of "medicine" or "mountain whale", a combination of Buddhist strictures against the eating of animal flesh and its prohibitive cost obliged most people to depend on fish for their animal protein. Far more than just a fad, eating meat represented the breaking of a Buddhist taboo on the consumption of animal flesh. With the state bent

Walking the new westernized streets of Marunouchi

on elevating Shinto, with its emperor-centred worship, one wonders if this was not a deliberate violation.

Meat may have become a permanent fixture on the Japanese table, but a lingering distaste for the slaughter and handling of animal flesh, and its association with Edo's outcasts, persisted. Butchers making deliveries to Keio University, where the students seem to have been inordinately fond of beef, would hear the striking of flints, a traditional cleansing ritual, as they passed through the gates into the main campus.

No sooner had the emperor become an avowed carnivore than the empress gave up the practice of teeth blackening, quickly followed by the ladies of the court. Sports and leisure activities grew, with clubs and societies for such western pursuits as boxing and billiards; horse racing took place at Kudan and Ueno. Steam paddleboats plied the Sumida, where metal bridges replaced wooden ones. A French restaurant opened in Ueno; men grew luxuriant moustaches and hung gold watch chains from their waistcoat pockets. The Edo-born satirist Kanagaki Robun captured the mood of the times in a withering parody on the aping of western customs, called *Eating Beef Stew Cross-Legged*. He may have had a popular beef stew dish of the day called *kaika nabe* (civilization hot pot) in mind.

The emperor had led the way into the new age by having his topknot cut in 1872, and wearing western clothing for official appearances. The government had ordered the cutting of topknots the year before, equating the practice with feudalism. The lyric from a popular song at the time corroborated the view: "If you tap a shaven and topknotted head you will hear the sound of retrogression... but if you tap a close-cropped head of hair you will hear the sound of civilization and enlightenment."

If the samurai were required to cut off their topknots, women, inspired perhaps by the example of the empress, underwent a more voluntary makeover into the new age. Returning home one day, playwright Hasegawa Shigure was astonished to find her mother performing "the usual maternal functions without the smallest change," but with an entirely different face. Accustomed to seeing a woman with shaved eyebrows and to smelling the acrid scent from the iron oxide solution that women still used at home to blacken their teeth:

> The mother I now saw before me had the stubbly beginnings of eyebrows, and her teeth were a startling, gleaming white. It was the more

disturbing because something else was new. The new face was all smiles, as the old one had not been.

While all of these western developments were doubtless exciting to behold, some of the charms of Edo, its easier relationship to time and space, were being forfeited in the rush for modernity. Fukuzawa Yukichi, in a book called *Western Clothing, Food and Homes*, spoke of the necessity to "familiarize oneself with the reading of time; all people carry a watch in the West to know the time without relying on temple bells as in our country." One can only imagine in a city devoid of trains, horse-drawn tramcars and bellowing rickshaw pullers, the pleasant sensation at hearing those felicitous bells.

MEMOIRS OF A CITY

Private journals and memoirs play an invaluable role in our ability to reconstruct the past of a city that was changing daily. Hasegawa Shigure, born in 1879 into a merchant family living in Nihonbashi Odenmacho, spent much of her childhood among the dark and narrow back streets and black plaster-walled storehouses of a district whose surroundings had changed little since the Edo period. Hasegawa's childhood years are described in detail in her *Old Tales of Nihonbashi*. Her home was located near the site of the city's main prison at Kodenmacho. By Hasegawa's time the area had become open ground for acrobats and freak shows—one of her family's sidelines was renting monkeys to itinerant street performers—but the prison remains a sinister presence in her work.

Another invaluable account of the mid-Meiji period in downtown Tokyo appears in the memoirs of Tanizaki Junichiro, under the title *Childhood Years*. Born in 1886, Tanizaki grew up in Nihonbashi, an area close to Hasegawa's home, before moving across the Nihonbashi river to Ningyocho. Despite its proximity, Ningyocho, the centre of the grain trade, was quite a different place to Nihonbashi, the merchant heart of the city. Tanizaki lived a few doors down from the western-style rice exchange building, which is still there in a back street of the district. The area was also something of an all-purpose leisure quarter, with shops, restaurants, entertainment halls, theatres and geisha establishments concentrated into an area a little west of Suitengu shrine, where a monthly market always attracted a large crowd. Like Hasegawa, Tanizaki was weaned on stories from the Kabuki repertoire as well as the amateur theatricals seen each month at a local temple.

Though there was much to admire about the strides made during the early years of Meiji, there was something immature, even a touch pathetic in Japan's need for approval, its fear of ridicule, the unconsidered excesses that seemed to endorse the denigration of its own native culture. Classic painters like Hashimoto Gaho and Kano Hogai witnessed their works being sold on the street for a pittance. In a frenzy of cultural vandalism, ancient Buddhist buildings were desecrated and works of Buddhist art burned for fuel. The destruction and theft of hundreds of thousands of priceless statues, paintings, temple bells and other ritual objects began when the Meiji government, in an effort to elevate Shintoism, ordered the separation of Buddhism from state Shinto, ending centuries of religious syncretism. The worst of the violence against Buddhism was over by 1871, but not before Shinto zealots had destroyed much of its tangible heritage.

Even the great Zojo-ji temple in Shiba, one of Edo's great religious complexes, was not immune to new developments. Zojo-ji was chosen by the Tokugawa clan as their ancestral temple. Ieyasu chose the location as part of a scheme to protect Edo from evil spirits. This south-eastern purification gate into the city lay close to the bay and the Tokaido Road, so it also served as a post station for travellers and pilgrims. The splendours of the grounds in its Edo prime were manifest. A wooden slope and lotus pond stood behind the temple's hundred or more buildings, dormitories and refectories, where a shrine dedicated to the lute-playing goddess Benten could be found. Contemporary accounts describe the temple's woodwork, a riot of beams, joinery, transoms and trellises covered in the ornate pine, crane, peony and Chinese lion motifs and reliefs much beloved of the Tokugawas. The mausoleums of the shoguns stood behind black-lacquered gates amidst stately rows of bronze lanterns. Because the site contained the mausoleums of the now deposed shoguns, the authorities moved swiftly to deprive it of much of its former power and wealth. The new leaders of the Meiji government showed their contempt for the outgoing Tokugawa by confiscating the temple, turning the grounds into a park and removing six of the mummified shogun to the rear of the Main Hall. Nothing was actually destroyed, but slow neglect served the same end.

One did not have to be a member of the aristocracy to suffer the indignities of relocation, as space, including temple lands, was appropriated by the authorities in the name of development. In Nagai Kafu's 1909 novella, *The River Sumida*, an anxious family faces the prospect of losing its traditional grave-site: "As a matter of fact," the daughter says, "they're widening the streets, and the cemetery in Komagome is to be cleared away. And so we'll have to move Father to Yanaka or Somei or somewhere."

THE HYBRID CITY

Tokyo began to look like a different city, a veritable hybrid. This was most noticeable in individual buildings rather than entirely re-conceived zones. Single designs, however bizarre they might have looked to outsiders, stood as beacons of modernity. The Tsukiji Hoterukan, a hotel built for westerners and one of Meiji's early meeting places between the two worlds, was a prime example of this new, syncretic architecture. The building had a short life, but was enthusiastically recorded by photographers, painters and print-makers. In these works we see a Japanese garden, castle turret and wind-bells vying for attention with European-style furnishings, sash windows, and a verandah faintly reminiscent of the British Raj. If it was an occidental building, it was of a type never encountered in the West itself. Buildings like this represented a desire to move into the future, combined with a reluctance to entirely jettison the past. Jinnai Hidenobu, a scholar of urban morphology, has written:

> Many architectural masterpieces of this time reflected the plurality of demands growing out of a mixture of old and new values, in which an admiration for western structures signalling a new epoch coexisted with an unwillingness to discard trust in castle architecture as a symbol of stable social status.

After a major fire in 1872 destroyed Ginza and Tsukiji, the authorities became convinced that wooden buildings should be replaced with fireproof materials like brick. An understanding of the ferocity of the fires that periodically laid waste to parts of the city can be had from the account of a conflagration at a similar time in the district of Asakusa, recorded by James Hingston in his two-volume travelogue, *The Australian Abroad*. Taking a rickshaw to the Yoshiwara, Hingston suddenly found himself in streets blocked with dead bodies, full of the cries of firemen and stretcher-bearers:

The earth was strewn everywhere with smoking and smouldering wood ashes, reddened now and again into a glow as the wind came their way. The fireproof stores or go-downs stood in bold black relief over the frightful scene, and looked like giant monsters standing sentry in the fiery, infernal regions. The smoke was unbearable to the eyes, making them smart and water in a way that stopped all progress through the streets of this fire quarter. Away on every hand it looked like a wilderness of flame and smoke...

Regardless of the horrors, the ever-pragmatic residents of Tokyo saw these disasters as a much-needed opportunity for urban renewal. The reconstruction of Ginza, acquiring at the same time the name Rengagai or "Bricktown", was overseen by an English engineer named Thomas J. Waters. The inspiration for the buildings, paved streets and pavements was London's Regent Street. The architectural era is often referred to as the "English period." There were almost a thousand brick buildings in the area when the project was finished, not a single one of which survives today.

The spectacle of so many western-style buildings concentrated in one street and several back streets attracted enormous interest. More visitors arrived in 1874, when the country's first gas lamps appeared along the Ginza. Three years on, the Kabuki theatres were gas lit, dispelling their shadows and perhaps a little atmosphere as well. Introduced a good sixty years later than in European cities, Japan's experience with gas lighting was a short one.

Few people wished to live or work in Ginza's brick structures. Unlike wooden buildings, which encouraged a circulation of air during the unbearably humid summer months, the brick buildings trapped the air. Neglected corners of interiors soon turned into fine incubators for mildew and nests of centipedes. Vacated by more reputable tenants, the buildings fell on hard times as street and circus performers, acrobats, jugglers and itinerant entertainers with their dancing bears and monkeys moved in. The façades, overlooking an avenue lined with cherry, maple and willow trees, remained impressive, a leafy, cosmopolitan boulevard much as it was intended to look.

Despite its shortcomings, the new Ginza was a showcase for Japanese modernity. Foreigners were less easily persuaded. In her long forgotten book, *Jinrikishaw Days in Japan*, Eliza Ruhamah Scidmore, an American who lived in Japan for three years during the formative 1880s, wrote:

> This is not the Yeddo of one's dreams, nor is it an Occidental city. Its stucco walls, wooden columns, glaring shop windows, and general air of tawdry imitation fairly depress one. In so large a city there are many corners, however, which the march of improvement has not reached, odd, unexpected, and Japanese enough to atone for the rest.

One hears the same kind of remark today from expatriate residents of Tokyo. Over the following decades the original coordination suffered as hybrids were added that further offended the classically trained sensibilities of some foreign visitors. The guidebook writer Philip Terry, describing the area in 1920, dismissed it: "size without majesty, individuality divorced from all dignity and simplicity, and convenience rather than fitness or sobriety are the salient characteristics of this structural hodge-podge." Yet despite its shortcomings, the rebuilding established the Ginza as a centre of commerce and urbane leisure.

THE ROKUMEIKAN: WESTERN TASTES

The mix of neoclassical, colonial and northern European, adapted to the Tokyo climate, was most visible in the ministry offices of the Marunouchi area, whose confining walls, gates and bridges were systematically dismantled during the early years of Meiji. These buildings have long gone, but an idea of this style can be seen in the Koishikawa Botanical Garden, where the former hall of the Tokyo Medicinal School still stands.

Another pseudo-western building that ended up looking more exotic than anything in the West was Mitsui House, Japan's first bank. The structure was designed by Shimizu Kisuke II, a master carpenter who had worked as a building contractor in the foreign settlement of Yokohama. The stone-faced, timber-framed building, with verandah, open galleries, tiled roof and a central bell tower reminiscent of traditional castle architecture, was one of the first examples of a western-style building by a Japanese architect; it only survives in photographs and prints. Woodcut prints were often visual hyperbole, but in the work of artists like Utagawa Kuniteru II there is a remarkable similarity between print and photos. With such an extraordinary building, there was apparently no necessity for exaggeration.

Where others embraced the process, Nagai Kafu had mixed feelings. There is a touch of rebuke in his 1931 novel, *During the Rains*, when, casting an eye over the type of city that rose from the impulses of the Meiji era, he wrote, "... when a city aped the West to the degree that Tokyo did, the spectacle provoked in the observer is an astonishment, along with a certain sense of pathos." Soseki Natsume, the foremost novelist of his time, shared Kafu's reservations about the speed with which Japan was assimilating western civilization, warning that the country was plunging headlong into a nervous breakdown not unlike the one always simmering beneath the surface of his own unstable personality.

Other designs of the period were moderately successful, in spite of incongruent settings. In the 1880s the wealthy entrepreneur Shibusawa Eiichi commissioned a leading architect to build him a grand, European-style villa at the confluence of two waterways in Nihonbashi. Tanizaki Junichiro remembered it from his childhood, recalling its graceful galleries and pillars: "The barges and lighters that moved up and down the stream past the 'palace' were strangely in harmony with it, like gondolas moving on a Venetian canal." Other villas followed, many of them swept away or damaged beyond repair in the great 1910 flood.

The English architect Josiah Conder arrived in Japan in 1877. Conder not only worked as an architect, but also taught at the influential College of Technology, an institute destined to become Tokyo University. His statue stands today in the grounds of the main university campus at Hongo. Tokyo's premier showcase for "civilization and enlightenment", an example of daring social *élan*, was Conder's Rokumeikan, or Deer Cry Pavilion. The two-storey brick building was a mix of high Victorian, Italianate and airy Moorish galleries, topped with a French *belle-époque* roof. Guest suites boasted alabaster bathtubs. The pavilion, with its ballroom, promenade halls, music and reading rooms, was a venue where Japan and the highest western representatives could mingle over ice-cream sorbets, Havana cigars and games of billiards and whisk. The spacious dining room was presided over by a French chef who served such unfamiliar dishes as red snapper casserole, Hungarian-style leg of lamb, roast quail and that redoubtable Victorian favourite, plum pudding. American cocktails and German beer were served in the bars. The music was provided by a German band playing mazurkas, waltzes and polkas, and a French orchestra performing operettas. It was a finishing school for Tokyo high society and the setting for balls, charity bazaars, tea dances and banquets. Yet the French author of *Madame Chrysanthemum*, Pierre Loti, found the Europeanized mimicry distasteful, dryly observing: "They danced quite properly, my Japanese in Parisian gowns. But one senses that it is something drilled into them that they perform like automatons, without any personal initiative."

Serious intentions, however, underpinned the costumed events at the Rokumeikan. The government hoped that this display of easily assimilated cultural practices would earn it enough respect to be treated seriously by the western powers, that it would persuade them to forfeit privileges maintained through the Unequal Treaties. The agreement permitted among other things, a system of extraterritoriality, by which foreigners accused of crimes committed on Japanese soil, were exempt from trial in a Japanese court. A masquerade ball held in 1887 was lampooned as an example of the degree to which high-ranking Japanese officials could go in order to curry the favour of westerners and to prove that they were familiar with the social graces. Times had clearly changed, and what might once have been lauded as enlightened behaviour was now sneered at. In a comment on the humiliating efforts of the government and Prime Minister Ito, the public dubbed them "the dancing cabinet". When it became apparent that the western diplomats who attended these functions were happy to feast and dance, but unwilling to revise the treaties, the glittering evenings at the Rokumeikan came to an end. Converted into the Peers' Club in 1899, then into a bank and insurance company office, the building was eventually demolished in 1940. Photographs and a model of the Rokumeikan can be viewed at the Edo-Tokyo Museum in Ryogoku, east of the Sumida. Also to the east of the river, in Hirai, a district of Edogawa ward, a fragment of the original building can be found in a most unlikely location. One of the Italian-style bronze chandeliers from the ballroom has mysteriously found its way into the Buddhist prayer hall at Tomyo-ji temple where, fully reinstalled, it no longer casts light over a glittering crowd of socialites, but a modest congregation of Buddhist worshippers.

MITSUBISHI MEADOW AND LONDON BLOCK

Given the number of western engineers and architects in Tokyo, it is not surprising that many of the city's public edifices bore a remarkable likeness to Victorian buildings. The Mitsubishi Group, a huge financial and industrial conglomerate, had already bought up large plots of land for property development in the Marunouchi area. The "Mitsubishi Wasteland", as it was known, hardly lived up to the pastoral associations conjured up by its name. According to those who knew or assiduously avoided the area, the land, though only a stone's throw away from the inner moat of the palace, was a forlorn and lonely place. The poet Takahama Kyoshi spoke of it as an "abode of foxes and badgers", of weed-covered hillocks where aristocratic gardens had once stood: "Marunouchi was a place of darkness and silence, of loneliness and danger."

As the model for the area was the financial district of London, it came to be known as "London Block". Conder completed the first brick buildings here in 1894. The four-storey, redbrick structures with white stone quoins faced onto streets lined with a very modern civic mix of trees and electric poles. The pride of Meiji-period Tokyo, the area stood for progress, but as an exercise in transplanted town planning may have been less successful. Paul Waley observes that the buildings:

> ... have that late-Victorian London air of Marylebone High Street or parts of Kensington, but without the architectural conviction and spontaneity that grows out of native soil. Photographs of the London Block in its early days reveal a pronounced sense of unease. The buildings need carriages and trolleys and the bustle of late-Victorian and Edwardian London. Instead, all they have to look out on is a few rickshaws and the occasional disoriented passer-by.

The piles of these ostensibly stable western buildings were sunk into earth that, at Edo's beginning, were mudflats. The narrator of Kawabata Yasunari's novel *Thousand Cranes* (1949) describes the area in the post-war years before Mitsubishi demolished the last of the London Block's redbrick structures:

> As the train approached Tokyo Central Station, he looked down upon a tree-lined avenue. It ran east and west, almost at right angles to the railroad. The western sun poured into it, and the street glittered like a sheet of metal. The trees, with the sun behind them, were darkened almost to black. The shadows were cool, the branches wide, the leaves thick. Solid Occidental buildings lined the street.

Conceived during the Meiji era, Tokyo Station was completed in 1914

There were strangely few people. The street was quiet and empty all the way to the Palace moat. The dazzlingly bright streetcars too were quiet. Looking down from the crowded train, he felt that the avenue alone floated in this strange time of evening, that it had been dropped here from some foreign country.

With the completion of Tokyo station in 1914 the area managed at last to shrug off any lingering associations with its original name, Mitsubishigahara, the Mitsubishi Wasteland. The terminus was now firmly established as the new "doorway to Tokyo", a role formerly enjoyed by the Ginza. With the station in place, many imposing buildings like the Marine Insurance Building and the Marunouchi Building, the nation's largest office complex, were erected. Imposing brick structures went up in the nearby Kasumigaseki district, housing ministries, the Metropolitan Police Department and the Supreme Court.

Begun in the last days of the Meiji period, Tokyo Station, designed by Tatsuno Kingo, a former student of Josiah Conder, was ready just two years into the new Taisho era. The building marks the beginning of modern Japanese architecture. Faced with locally made bricks, the main structure was built from steel imported from Britain and the United States. Tastefully rendered in the Queen Anne style consonant with Beaux Arts tastes, the building, modelled on Amsterdam Centraal station in the Netherlands, survived the 1923 earthquake but lost its two upper storeys and cupolas in the Second World War.

Despite the impermanence of many of the buildings Conder designed during his long years in Tokyo, his pioneering of the grand style in public architecture left a lasting legacy. The Tsunamachi Mitsui Club, a 1913 Conder building, remains in much the same state as when it was inaugurated. Its similarity to some of the features of the Rokumeikan provides us with an insight into the way the upper classes socialized during the Meiji period. Several of Conder's students went on to design distinguished buildings of their own, among them the first Imperial Hotel, the Imperial Theatre, Akasaka Palace and the neoclassical Bank of Japan.

THE CLOUD SURPASSING PAVILION: AN ASAKUSA WONDER

Height had always been synonymous with power and mystique. Sacred mountains were worshipped, the tallest shrine trees revered; towering castle keeps were intended to impress, pagodas to suggest the celestial reaches. By the 1880s the old limits on height had begun to be exceeded. One of the most remarkable was the twelve-storey Ryounkaku (Cloud Surpassing Pavilion), destined to become the symbol of Asakusa at this time and to be much reproduced in postcards. Constructed in 1890 under the supervision of a British engineer called W. K. Barton, the 216-foot redbrick, octagonal tower was the tallest building in Tokyo. Lit up at night by electric arc lights, the building may have been a little like the Great World in Shanghai. Despite its pretensions to modernity, it even resembled a Chinese structure of the Tang or Song periods.

Yet where the six floors of the rather more risqué Chinese version offered singsong girls, peep shows, fan-tan tables and earwax extractors, the floors of the Ryounkaku were mostly packed with imported goods, restaurants and an observation deck near the top replete with telescopes; the ninth floor was reserved for art exhibitions. Japan's first elevator ran up to the eighth floor, while its illuminated windows, 176 all told, made it highly visible at night. Even during the daytime, the tower could be seen from as far away as Mukojima, east of the Sumida, and Atago Hill towards the bay. The alleys to the north of the building, packed with brothels, were less visible from a distance. If the Rokumeikan, commissioned by government fiat, represented the western tastes and aspirations of the Meiji elite, the Ryounkaku was an early symbol of mass culture and entertainment.

TOKYO SLUMS

As grand western-style buildings were being built and the first trade fairs took place, Tokyo was discovering the concept of poverty, something that had always existed but had never been classified as a social ill. The area of Shitaya Mannencho was counted among Tokyo's *sandai hinminkutsu* or "three great ghettoes". (The other two were Shiba Shinamicho and Yotsuya Samegabashi.)   The areas were essentially the scheme of Edo-period government officials keen to relocate undesirables, convicts and beggars into strictly confined zones. Beside social outcasts, the row house here was also inhabited by labourers, itinerant street merchants and performers. Airless places with no view of the sky, single rooms measuring from four-and-a-half to six tatami mats might accommodate a typical family. Compounding space deprivation were the shared toilets and the brackish communal wells residents were obliged to use. Residents who could survive these privations might be faced with cholera epidemics caused by rats, with pestilential insects and transmissible diseases like tuberculosis.

Writing in September 1892 from the fetid room he shared with nine others in a hostel in Shitaya Mannencho, one of the worst of the Meiji slums, the youthful journalist Matsubara Iwagoro could say in all truth that "I saw there stranger natural objects, more mysterious products, and more astonishing artefacts than in any museum or in any kind of fair or factory." On his own initiative, Matsubara, in the employ of the *Kokumin* newspaper, had taken the unprecedented step of researching his accounts of the poor by living and working among them, sharing a room in a lodging house and working on a subsistence wage as a porter. While clearly honing his journalistic skills and instincts, Matsubara appears to have been entirely sincere in his desire to get to the bottom of his story by experiencing the deplorable conditions of the Meiji poor. As George Orwell would do much later, Matsubara's newspaper reports were compiled and appeared in book form under the title *In Darkest Tokyo*. Another pioneering work, *Japan's Underclass* by Yokoyama Gennosuke, appeared a few years later. In these very contemporary examples of reportage we learn exactly who the poor are, hearing the stories and sharing subsistence meals with the rag pickers, tinkers, rickshaw pullers, ditch diggers, peddlers, umbrella repairers, jugglers, sutra preachers and quacks who inhabited the three slums and the hovels of Asakusa and Honjo.

The impact of these two books, human documents of a kind never seen before in Japan, was felt even among literary circles, influencing the work of writers like Higuchi Ichiyo and Kunikida Doppo. Tokuda Shusei, one of the most accomplished novelists of the Meiji and Taisho periods, was one of those writers who chose to find his material and characters from the experiences of an urban working class. Closely in touch with his own society, he drew many of the subjects of his naturalistic novels from the life of ordinary people in the Morikawa district of the city's Hongo ward where he lived. The life of a maid working in the house next door became the main character of his 1908 novel *The New Household*; the early years of his marriage, the material for two works, *Mould* and *Footprints*; the life and trials of a former prostitute, a friend of his wife, the substance for the 1913 novel *Festering*.

Novelist Higuchi Ichiyo was a Meiji-era figure who knew the underside of Tokyo better than most of her literary contemporaries. Published in 1895, Higuchi's masterpiece, *Growing Up*, concerns the plight of a young girl living with her elder sister in one of the licensed quarters of Tokyo who is doomed to lose her childhood freedoms the moment her sexual awakening is sensed by the brothel owners. Its portrait of the plight of young women trapped in circumstances that pass for tradition is one of the most poignant social novels of the day. At one time Higuchi, who died from consumption at the age of 24, lived in a narrow house on the street leading to the Yoshiwara, a result of a series of financial disasters suffered by her family:

> Nowhere a decent house, only rows of low tenements, ten and twenty to the row, their roof lines sagging, their front shutters carelessly left half open. One hears no rumours of rich men in these parts.

Higuchi was able to observe at close quarters how the "Yoshiwara moat, dark like the smiles of the black-toothed beauties, reflects the lights and the sport in the three-storey houses near enough to touch." From such surroundings she was able to observe the comings and goings of the district, the sale of young girls at the entrance, the removal of dead bodies late at night. Before the girls entered the pleasure quarter they would pass by

The young novelist, Higuchi Ichiyo

a willow tree, taking one last look back at the life they were about to forsake. The tree has been moved several times in its long life, but the "Look Back Willow", as it is poignantly called, is still alive, a straggly but enduring specimen standing on a busy street corner in front of a garage.

Higuchi's fiction, reflecting the wit and cynicism of Saikaku, a writer she much admired, is refreshingly unsentimental. Unlike Kafu's women, reminders of a lost age, Higuchi's flesh and blood prostitutes are symbols of failure and penury. We see the Nightless City, its denizens and those who live nearby for what they are: a priest who compromises his position for wealth and status, a grasping grandmother in the money-lending business, a confectioner who cheats his customers by diluting his products, parents who, watching their children blossom into adolescence, can observe, "there are times when daughters are more valuable than sons." Her descriptions, sympathetic but heavy with irony, never attempt to gild the sordidness of the quarter:

> It's one thing to see a woman of a certain age who favours gaudy patterns, or a sash cut immoderately wide. It's quite another to see these barefaced girls of fifteen or sixteen, all decked out in flashy clothes and blowing bladder cherries, which everybody knows are used as contraceptives. But that's what kind of neighbourhood it is.

The plight of prostitutes was never alluded to in the work of Edo artists like Kitao Shigemasa and Katsukawa Shunsho, though the explicit eroticism of the shunga drawings reveals the real purpose of the quarter. Accounts by foreigners resonate with the later writings of Higuchi. A. B. Mitford, for example, writes of visiting the Yoshiwara just after nightfall, when the women

> ... take their places, side by side, in a kind of long narrow cage, the wooden bars of which open to the public thoroughfare. Here they sit for hours, gorgeous in dresses of silk and gold and silver embroidery, speechless and motionless as wax figures, until they shall have attracted the attention of some of the passers-by, who begin to throng the place.

Kafu, writing some two decades after Higuchi and Mitford, is more wistful as he bemoans the changes assailing the district:

Prostitutes on display at the Yoshiwara

In the autumn of 1908, when I came back from several years abroad, I felt like an old devotee for whom the rules had been turned upsidedown. There were beer halls on the old central street of Yoshiwara, and the harmony of "the two rows of lanterns, that first sign of autumn" had already been destroyed. The rows of ladies waiting in the houses had disappeared. The Five Streets were dark, the rickshaws along the embankment were conspicuously fewer in number.

EMINENT FOREIGNERS

As the great Meiji experiment moved forward, foreigners working at the delegations were now joined by specialists co-opted by a government eager to catch up and perhaps even overtake the West. Two German doctors were invited to oversee a school of medicine in Shitaya, Italians came to teach the arts and music, two French jurists were recruited to work on the drafting of new legal codes. The American professor of zoology, Edward Sylvester Morse, discoverer of the Omori shell mound in southern Tokyo, was another foreign specialist who, along with the American scholar, James C. Hepburn, set about compiling the first Japanese-English dictionary. Engineers, lecturers and architects followed.

With the Japanese acquiring so much expertise from the West, some foreign settlements like Kobe went into a slow decline. Lafcadio Hearn, the most influential western writer in Meiji Japan, described the naiveté and disillusionment of some outsiders with little grasp of the capacity of the Japanese:

> Within two decades from the founding of the settlements, those foreigners who once imagined it a mere question of time when the whole country would belong to them, began to understand how greatly they had underestimated the race. The Japanese had been learning wonderfully well—"nearly as well as the Chinese." They were supplanting the small foreign shopkeepers; and various establishments had been compelled to close because of Japanese competition.

For Hearn, arriving in the city in December 1895 to take up the prestigious chair of English Language and Literature at Tokyo Imperial University, the prospect of living in the new capital was irksome in the extreme. He defined Tokyo as the "most horrible place in Japan", and in his view it was not even Japan but an invented city of "dirty shoes,—absurd fashions,—wickedly expensive living,—airs,—vanities,—gossip." Settling into an undistinguished-looking house in the suburb of Ushigome, Hearn noted that the road outside the house his family rented was being dug up to make room for water pipes, requiring him to step around a series of ditches before reaching his door, another sign of the restless development gripping the city. He found some consolation at the rear of the house, where a field and hill, covered in cypress, pine, bush clover, bamboo and sorrel, provided shelter for rabbits, foxes, owls and pheasants. Behind dense layers of vegetation, an ancient temple known as Kobudera (the "gnarled temple") and its equally ancient abbot were much more to Hearn's liking. This is where the writer, among grounds overgrown with weeds and scattered with Buddhist statuary, was able to retrieve some of the atmosphere he savoured at former habitats in the Japanese provinces.

The first foreign tourists began to appear at this time. Tokyo now formed part of a New Grand Tour of the Far East, one that might include a spell in Shanghai and Hong Kong. Others, like Hearn, were more serious, intent on accomplishing something in Japan. Yorkshire-born

Isabella L. Bird, author of the travel classic *Unbeaten Tracks in Japan*, arrived in Tokyo in 1878. A devout Victorian Christian with unflinching moral views, she was by the standards of her day an open-minded writer driven by a strong spirit of inquiry. Dependent on the good graces of her hosts and interpreter when she ventured into remote parts of the country never visited by foreigners, she was an adaptable traveller, prepared to make do with simple, unfamiliar food and to respect local customs. She delighted her hosts when she removed her muddy boots at the entrance to houses and inns, something few foreigners seem to have done at the time. (Even a much later visitor, George Bernard Shaw, obdurately refused to remove his shoes when stepping onto the delicate straw tatami mats used as interior flooring.)

Bird took a rickshaw in the company of Basil Hall Chamberlain to the Senso-ji temple in Asakusa, where she found "much that is highly grotesque at first sight. Men squat on the floor selling amulets, rosaries, printed prayers, incense sticks, and other wares. Ex votos of all kinds hang on the wall and on the great round pillars. Many of these are rude Japanese pictures." Encountering the temple's main altar, she found a concentration of...

shrines and gods, gigantic candlesticks, colossal lotuses of gilded silver, offerings, lamps, lacquer, litany books, gongs, drums, bells, and all the mysterious symbols of a faith which is a system of morals and metaphysics to the educated and initiated, and an idolatrous superstition to the masses.

The essence of these scenes has not changed a great deal since then, though the following description of the worldly pleasures co-existing easily with the sanctity of the inner temple most certainly has:

Behind the temple are archery galleries in numbers, where girls, hardly so modest-looking as usual, smile and smirk, and bring straw-coloured tea in dainty cups, and tasteless sweetmeats on lacquer trays, and smoke their tiny pipes, and offer you bows of slender bamboo strips, two feet long, with rests for the arrows, and tiny cherry-wood arrows, bone-tipped, and feathered red, blue, and white, and smilingly, but quite unobtrusively, ask you to try your skill or luck at a target hanging in front of a square drum, flanked by red cushions. A click, a boom, or a hardly audible "thud," indicate the result. Nearly all the archers were grown-up men, and many of them spend hours at a time in this childish sport.

Whether or not Bird understood or was informed of the real purpose of the booths and their "sport" is not clear.

John Russell Young, accompanying the former US President and First Lady, General and Mrs. Grant, on their tour of Japan in 1879, compared Tokyo at this time to a series of villages, an analogy much favoured by writers ever since. Using the spelling still then common among foreigners when writing about the new capital, he observed:

> It is hard to realize that Tokio is a city—one of the greatest cities of the world. It looks like a series of villages, with bits of green and open spaces, and enclosed grounds breaking up the continuity of the town.

The Grants were well received. On a visit to the Shintomiza, a theatre in the Ginza, the audience were treated to an inventive display of international goodwill in the form of a dance finale in which a troupe of geisha from the Yanagibashi pleasure quarter appeared in red and white stripped kimonos beneath which star-spangled singlets could be seen. Their fans, an indispensable item in geisha dances, were decorated with Japanese and American flags.

The ebullient Clara Whitney, daughter of American missionaries and educators who had moved to Tokyo in 1875, was in the audience and recorded the performance in her diary:

> Each girl was dressed in a robe made of the dear old Stars and Stripes, while upon their heads shone a circlet of silver stars. It made the prettiest costume imaginable. The stripes constituted the over-robe itself while one sleeve slipped off from one shoulder revealed a sleeve of stars below, their girdles were dark blue, sandals, red and white, and presently they took out fans having on one side the American and upon the other the national flag.

The Grants seem to have thrown themselves into the life of the city, joining the throng lined up along the Sumida for the annual summer opening of the river. The always-enthusiastic Edward Morse was there too, noting what he saw: "It was a startling sight when we got near the place to see that the fireworks were being discharged from a large boat by a dozen naked men, firing off Roman candles and set pieces of a complex nature. It was a sight never to be forgotten: the men's bodies glistening in the light with the showers of sparks dropping like rain upon them..."

Victorian writers and travellers continued to be curious about a country that had hardly been visited since the reign of James I. Rudyard Kipling was in Tokyo in 1889. In a description not unlike some of the images in woodblock prints made at the time, he marvelled at Tokyo after dark, where "half the town was out for a walk, and all the people's clothes were indigo, and so were the shadows, and most of the paper lanterns were drops of blood red." The 24-year-old Kipling, an unknown journalist, was mightily impressed by what he saw, filling his letters with descriptions that have the freshness and spontaneity of eyewitness accounts. Tokyo was a city that...

> ... roared with life through all its quarters. Double lines of trams ran down the main streets for mile on mile, rows of omnibuses stood at the principal railway stations... All the trams were full, all the private and public omnibuses were full, and the streets were full of "rickshaws". From the seashore to the shady green park, from the park to the dim distance, the land pullulated with people.

Though only a handful of the best have survived, the Meiji period saw the first wave of books on Japan and orientalism. It seems that almost every literate traveller felt compelled to publish impressions of the country. "Not to have written a book about Japan," Basil Hall Chamberlain remarked in 1890, "is fast becoming a title of distinction."

BOSTON BRAHMINS
Once the perfumed phial was open some of its essence vanished. Chamberlain was right when he wrote, "For Old Japan was like an oyster—to open it was to kill it." Old Japan had struck a chord with an unlikely group of American scholars, art collectors, aesthetes and aristocrats from New England who, repelled by American ostentation, detected in the high culture of Japan—in Buddhist ritual, Shinto purity, the austerity

of Zen, the code of the samurai and the cultivation of an aesthetic way—values akin to those of their Puritan ancestors.

Among the Bostonians drawn to Tokyo was Edward Morse, he of the famous shell mounds, now firmly established as professor of zoology at the Tokyo Imperial University. Ironically, at a time when many people in Japan were eager to bury the past and to allow westerners to cart off valuable works of art to Europe and America, Morse was about to introduce the study of archaeology, the preservation of heritage.

Sensing the evanescence of Old Japan, and the disinclination of the Japanese themselves to preserve it, Morse was instrumental in urging institutions such as the Peabody Academy of Salem and the Museum of Fine Art in Boston to establish major Japanese collections. There were private collectors, too, like Isabella Stewart Gardner and the wealthy Bostonian physician, William Bigelow, who purchased literally thousands of Japanese artworks. Morse's colleague, fellow Bostonian Ernest Fenollosa, was considered at the time to be the premier authority on Japanese art. By the early 1880s, Fenollosa, now converted to Buddhism and campaigning vigorously among government circles for the preservation of Japanese art in the face of the mania for all things western, had made the acquaintance of a remarkable Japanese by the name of Okakura Kakuzo.

One incident testifies to the linguistic dexterity and quick wit of this extraordinary man, who was fluent in English. Accosted on a New York street by a fellow who imagined he could score a quick laugh at the expense of Okakura and his group, all dressed in traditional Japanese attire, the man asked, "What sort of 'nese' are you people? Are you Chinese, or Japanese, or Javanese?" Okakura answered immediately, "We are Japanese gentlemen. But what sort of 'key' are you? Are you a Yankee, or a donkey, or a monkey?" In his poem *Gerontion*, T. S. Eliot has the tall figure of Okakura, dressed in formal kimono at a private museum in Boston, "bowing among the Titians."

Okakura's position, that Japan was an integral part of Asia and that "the ideals of Asia are one," was the very opposite of Fukuzawa Yukichi's contention that Japan "should leave Asia and enter the West." Author of *The Ideals of the East*, Okakura was appalled at the blind thrust towards western culture at the expense of the Japanese arts, observing in his highly influential *The Book of Tea*, "Civilization and Enlightenment did not bring a real civilization to Japan, but it rather brought materialism which should be removed."

Okakura's art instincts, like those of his English equivalent John Ruskin, were unimpeachable. Okakura and Fenollosa's crowning achievement was their involvement in setting up the 1889 government-backed Tokyo Art School in Yanaka, with its focus on the study and practice of Far Eastern art. Modern painters like Hishida Shunso and Yokoyama Taikan, exponents of a newer Nihonga style of painting, were products of the school, along with practitioners of bronze casting, traditional metalworking and ceramics.

The rapture at living in an oriental capital, exemplified in the works of millionaire-turned-writer Percival Lowell, was by no means shared by all Bostonians of culture and good taste. The Harvard historian Henry Adams complained of Tokyo's sweltering summer heat and offensive fields of night soil: "Tokyo is beastly," he groaned, "nothing but a huge collection of villages, scattered over miles after miles of flat country; without a building fit to live in, or a sewer to relieve the stench of several hundred thousand open privies."

Human waste was proving a profitable commodity with suburban farms on the fringes of the city using it as compost for growing fresh vegetables. Waste from samurai households commanded a higher price than that from commoners, as it was reasoned they enjoyed a better diet. Wealthy farmers and village heads generally monopolized the right to collect premium night soil from the residences of the daimyo. Those who suffered most from the noxious smell were those living along the banks of the Sumida and Ara rivers, where the night soil was transported in boats that made no efforts to conceal their load.

DISTINGUISHED JAPANESE

Besides the "Boston Brahmins", there were a number of eminent Japanese like Okakura residing in Tokyo. One of the most distinguished figures of the age, a strong advocate of westernization, was the author and educator Fukuzawa Yukichi, founder of a Tokyo academy that later became Keio University. An independent thinker and fierce critic, he facilitated an experiment in free thought and open political debate, strongly influenced by British utilitarianism and the primacy of modern education, which was short-lived but highly influential. Fukuzawa's face appears on today's ¥10,000 note, Japan's highest denomination.

Fukuzawa started out as a student of Dutch but quickly switched to English, gaining a reputation as a translator, a skill which qualified him as an attendant to the head of the first embassy to the United States in 1860. Two years later he joined an official delegation to Europe and an overseas trip to America again in 1867. His first book, *Conditions in the West*, established him as a serious authority on western matters. In a rebuttal of the Confucian view of a social order used to legitimize Tokugawa authoritarianism, he wrote in his popular *An Encouragement of Learning*:

> It is said that heaven does not create one man above or below another man. This means that when men are born from heaven they are all equal. There is no innate distinction between high and low.

Keio University, the institute Fukuzawa established, was, along with Waseda University and Tokyo Imperial University, the nerve centre of westernization, and it was in such a liberal milieu that such talk of social levelling and the championing of the rights of women could be conducted. The catchphrase that best sums up the early aspirations of the Meiji era, *Bunmei Kaika* ("Civilization and Enlightenment"), coined by Fukuzawa in one of his other books, was nothing if not cultural.

A leading figure in Meiji letters, Mori Ogai was a graduate of the medical school of Tokyo Imperial University and an early exponent of the so-called "I-novel". Close to the confessional diary form, it soon became the preferred medium of expression among writers of the Japanese romantic and naturalist movements. These authors were faced with the subordination of the individual to the greater interests of the state demanded by the Meiji constitution, whose promulgation seemed to dash the hopes of many artists and intellectuals that a people's rights movement might provide a vehicle for creative dissent. Mori departed from the naturalist view, however, preferring like Natsume Soseki to elevate the role of reason and intelligence in an effort to create order through literature and science amidst the chaotic collisions of the old and new that characterized the Meiji period.

The importance of place in Tokyo novels of the time can transform narrative accounts into something akin to a city itinerary. In Mori's *The Wild Geese*, we read that:

Okada had regular routes for his daily walks. He would go down the lonely slope called Muenzaka and travel north along Shinobazu Pond. Then he would stroll up the hill in Ueno Park. Next he went down to Hirokoji and, turning into Naka-cho—narrow, crowded, full of activity—he would go through the compound of Yushima Shrine... going through the Red Gate, he would proceed along Hongo-dori until he came to a shop where people were standing and watching the antics of some men pounding millet. Then he would continue his walk by turning into the compound of Kanda Shrine.

It is still possible to plot a literary route through this part of the city. Finding the shop where the two men pounded millet might be difficult, but the original Red Gate is still there, along with Kanda shrine, better known as Kanda Myojin. Muenzaka, however, has undergone some changes since Mori wrote the following:

> Even in the days I am writing about, the Iwasaki mansion was located, as it is today, on the southern side of Muenzaka, though it had not yet been fenced in with its present high wall of soil. At the time dirty stonewalls had been put up, and ferns and horsetails grew among the moss-covered stones. Even now I don't know whether the land above the fence is flat or hilly, for I've never been inside the mansion.

The high walls described by Mori remain, screening off the mansion from passersby, though the grounds and house are now open to the public. Another monument to Meiji syncretism, the mansion was built for Iwasaki Hisaya, son of the founder of the industrial giant Mitsubishi. The 1896 estate, a short walk from the lotus pond in Ueno Park, was, like so many of the grand buildings of the time, the work of Josiah Conder. The coffered wood ceilings, fluted columns framing the entrance porch, parquet flooring, stone fireplaces and Japan's first western toilet evoke a world of privilege. The overriding style is Jacobean, but traces of myriad western design forms can be found, including a second-floor colonnade recalling the Ionic style used in Pennsylvania country residences, while interior decorative motifs are Islamic in provenance. Set apart from the main house, a dark wooden building, part Gothic, part Swiss country cottage, houses a billiard room. Conder employed fluted columns to frame the entrance porch,

The 1896 Iwasaki Mansion in Muenzaka

along with a colonial style verandah and gold-embossed wallpaper. Gas-powered steam radiators placed throughout the house were an early form of central heating. These were refinements beyond the imagination of the common Tokyo dweller. Typifying the trans-cultural habits of the day, members of the family would change between Japanese and western footwear and clothing as they passed from one section of the house to another. A gloriously befuddled ensemble of styles, the mansion is a fine example of *fin-de-siècle* Tokyo eclecticism.

New Civilization

The ex-samurai turned oligarchs were quick to introduce far-reaching economic reforms, but these were not matched by meaningful political initiatives. The new Meiji constitution created a Diet consisting of the House of Peers and a House of Representatives. Granting the vote to only a small number of wealthy landowners, it remained resolutely authoritarian and patriarchal, a blend of traditional Japanese and German governance representing at best a limited interpretation of democracy.

The works of reform-minded writers and thinkers like Adam Smith, John Stuart Mill, Herbert Spencer, Guizot and Rousseau were now available in translation and much read by advocates of more radical change. Inspired by these possibilities, new groups like the Freedom Party and People's Rights Movement emerged, none with more than a limited hope of success.

An early casualty (some would say beneficiary) of the cultural purges meant to abolish or sanitize the past in order to curry favour with the West was Kabuki. The theatres returned from banishment in the east to the centre of the city. The Shintomi-za was rebuilt and the Kabuki-za located in its present position in Higashi Ginza. New, more respectable plays were written for what was originally a plebeian art form associated with the pleasure quarters, and powerful older works diluted. To some degree, elevating Kabuki to a national art form had the effect of neutering it. The great Kabuki exponent, Ichikawa Danjiru IX, was instrumental in this transformation of robust, earthy performances into more institutionalized dramas. At the opening of a theatre in 1872, dressed in white tie and tails rather than the racy kimonos normally associated with him, he summed up the new order when he declared, "The theatre of recent years has drunk up filth and smelled of the coarse and the mean," going on to assert: "I am deeply grieved by this fact, and in consultation with my colleagues I have resolved to clean away the decay."

The emperor's attendance at a Kabuki performance in 1887, following a similar visit to see a sumo tournament, was an official endorsement that would have been inconceivable a mere two decades before and sealed the fate of Kabuki as a respectable performing art. The new Kabuki-za theatre that opened in 1889 was notable for its western, faintly Renaissance-style exterior. An alternative existed at the Miyatoza in Asakusa. Regarded by aficionados as the last holdout of Edo-period Kabuki, the theatre was still in business during the Taisho period, though by then it was competing with music halls and motion picture palaces.

Despite the purges Kabuki actors remained enormously popular in both their roles and as arbiters of style and taste, and the theatres were just as well attended as ever. The requisitioning of Kabuki and its transference from the low to higher city helped to create new audiences among the elite and nascent middle classes. Tickets for the Kabuki were still beyond the means of many ordinary citizens. The *yose* variety halls were the best alternative to the new, "improved" Kabuki performances. These were local affairs, obviating a trip from the eastern low-lying areas of the city, which even in the late years of Meiji were not as well served with public transport as the central districts. The playwright Osanai Kaoru commented on this feature of Tokyo life:

> There were no electric trolleys and no buses and taxis... horse trolleys ran along the main streets of the Low City. It was a very rare occasion indeed when the Tokyo person set out for Ginza or Asakusa after dark. He would for the most part range no farther than the night stalls in the neighbourhood or perhaps a temple or shrine fair. Yose was his one real diversion.

Besides fairs and flower exhibitions, the larger temples and shrines like the Asakusa Kannon offered diversions as well as the prospect of merit gaining through religious observations. More akin to a complementary world than a parallel universe, there was no apparent conflict between devotion and entertainment, the world of non-attachment and the performing arts. Piety had its place among the figures kneeling among clouds of incense before a dimly lit altar at the rear of the main hall, but once outside, life came bubbling up to the very steps of the temple. Basil Hall Chamberlain and W.B. Mason, authors of an 1891 guide to Tokyo, strongly recommended a visit to the temple:

> ... for it is the great holiday resort of the middle and lower classes, and nothing is more striking than the juxtaposition of piety and pleasure, of gorgeous altars and grotesque ex-votos, of pretty costumes and dingly idols, the clatter of clogs, cocks and hens and pigeons strutting about among the worshippers. The temple authorities welcomed the crowds of pleasure seekers and their donations and didn't question too closely what went on inside some of the tents erected right inside the precincts of Senso-ji.

Whether W. E. Griffis, an early tourist, understood that the archery galleries were a subterfuge for prostitution is not clear in his description of the grounds of Asakusa as "the quaintest and liveliest place in Tokyo", where the visual feast included "performing monkeys, cheap photographers, street artists, jugglers, wrestlers, life-sized figures in clay, vendors of toys and lollipops." Yet a later passage seems to suggest that he might have had more than an inkling of what went on:

> At the north end are ranged the archery galleries, also presided over by pretty black-eyed Dianas, in paint, powder, and shining coiffure. They bring you tea, smile, talk nonsense, and giggle; smoke their long pipes with tiny bowls full of mild, fine-cut tobacco; puff out the long white whiffs from their flat-bridged noses; wipe the brass mouth-piece, and offer it to you; and then ask you leading and very personal questions without blushing...

Alongside the clay figures noted by Griffis were highly realistic papier-mâché dolls. The old hag of Adachi Moor, a notorious character known to entice travellers into her hut before robbing and murdering them, was a particularly frightening figure for children. The print artist Tsukioka Yoshitoshi, whose early work depicts scenes of appalling violence and horror, produced a triptych on the subject, showing a pregnant woman, bound, gagged and hanging by her feet as the celebrated hag sharpens her knife beneath her swollen abdomen. Big-nosed westerners were less harrowing as subjects for dolls. Curiosities more than monstrosities, they were invariably depicted with red hair and blue eyes. The ever-sympathetic Clara Whitney visited the displays in 1875, noting with amused appreciation: "A lady and gentlemen with flame-red hair and azure eyes were standing arm in arm":

> ... a red-haired beauty rode a velocipede, one walked with a crutch, and another swept while a gardener very lifelike sat by a flower bed smoking an English pipe, and a little boy had a string of balloons. It was all very well done. Wonderfully lifelike—even the redheaded individuals, who were ugly to be sure, looked like some I have seen before.

Tokuda Shusei, in his novel *Rough Living*, gives us a similar mix of the sacred and earthbound when describing the visit of his main character to Nishi-Arai Daishi, a temple in one of the poorer districts east of the river:

On leaving the main hall, Oshima roamed around the expansive temple compound, halting to observe some sort of sea mammal on exhibit and a rural, itinerant juggler... she loitered for a while in a rough, barren playground where cherry trees had recently been planted. Then she went around back to the cemetery. She witnessed an old peasant receiving the incantation of sacred waters from a priest, and she paused in front of rows of statues of Saint Kukai, a candle burning in front of each figure. In a nearby grove, a crowd had formed to see a scrawny monkey in a sailor's suit walking a tightrope.

It was just as well these earthier plebeian forms of entertainment were surviving, as culture was increasingly being appropriated by the new establishment. In the days of Edo the Kabuki theatre and the pleasure quarters had done more than set the styles. In a very real way they were the inspiration and setting, the incubators of culture. The latter continued their basic function as houses of prostitution during the Meiji period, but lost much of their lustre as *demi-monde* institutions where artists, writers, musicians and wealthy patrons could indulge in, but also transcend, carnal pleasures in the fruitful symbiosis of higher aims.

Osanai Kaoru, recalling perhaps the glory days of the Yoshiwara, lamented the decline of the courtesan into "a tasteless chalk drawing" and the degeneration of the Yoshiwara clientele into a shabby crowd in "workmen's jackets and flat-top haircuts and rubber boots". There was a barely concealed sneer in this rebuke of the masses for their unschooled tastes, but also a sense that, not only had the colour and refined taste been leached out of the place, but also the human drama. Recalling that Yoshiwara had often acted as a stage for Edo-period plays, Osanai offers more regrets tinged with bitterness:

No playwright would be silly enough to put the Yoshiwara of our day to such use. A chance encounter under the lights of the beer hall at the main gate would most likely involve a person with a north-country accent and a home-made cap, and his uncle, in the city with a petition to the Ministry of Commerce and Agriculture. The customer sweetening his coffee with sugar cubes in a western-style salon, given a farewell pat on his new muslin undershirt, would most likely be a numbers man in a visor cap, or a wandering singer of Osaka balladry who does the outskirts of town. No one could think of the Yoshiwara as in the slightest degree a romantic setting.

For entertainment of a more refined kind, people who could afford it now went to the geisha houses. The great fire of 1911 dealt another blow to the Yoshiwara, although it was hastily rebuilt in the hybrid style of the day: a Japanese frontage here, a European tower or miniature wing of a château there. There were several Yoshiwara rivals, well-established pleasure quarters that could offer some of the older graces. One of these was at Nezu, near the campus of the new Imperial University at Hongo. A little too close to the students for the authorities, who wanted to protect the best and brightest from temptations and distractions, the Nezu quarter was duly moved to Susaki in Fukagawa, an area of reclaimed land near the mouth of the Sumida. The dispersal of pleasure quarters reflected the dismembering of the mercantile culture that had marked the Meiji period.

THE WILLOW WORLD

The great pleasure districts of the late Edo and Meiji periods were Yanagibashi and Shimbashi. The etymology of the name Yanagibashi is much disputed. It may have derived from the willows (*yanagi*) that lined its embankment and the approach road from Asakusa Bridge, which still retains its trees in homage to the past, or it is possibly a phonetic warp from Yanokibashi, "Armoury Bridge", a reference to an arrow depot used by the shogun's troops located in the same area. Just as plausible is the theory that the name was taken from Yanagiwara, meaning "Willowfield", the area on the banks of the Kanda river at its confluence with the Sumida.

Yanagibashi seems to have begun as an entertainment district by developing an association with the much larger licensed quarter of the Yoshiwara. *Chokibune*, narrow sculls powered by single oarsmen from their moorings along the Kandagawa, were used to ferry customers up to the brothels and teahouses located in the marshy fields and paddies north of Asakusa. The Kandagawa boathouses were also the departure points for customers going to the great shrine to Tenjin out at Kameido to the east. Lanterns lit the doorways of Yanagawa restaurants until the early post-war period. One or two riverside restaurants still remain, but now it is mostly apartment owners who enjoy the river views.

Mendicant musicians and balladeers would be paddled up to the gardens of the Yanagibashi geisha houses and restaurants, where they serenaded visitors in the manner of Venetian gondoliers. The gardens, with their cherry trees, wisteria trellises and azaleas, were extensions of the river bottom mud, adding a natural touch to the contrivances of the pleasure quarter.

In its heyday, Yanagibashi's geisha were highly regarded. The area received a fair number of literary tributes, the equivalent then of free advertising or critical endorsement. "The great metropolis of Edo," Ryutei Tanehiko wrote in his *Geisha Tora no Maki*, "is honeycombed with canals and waterways, and wherever they flow, the water laps and washes the city's many geisha. In Yanagibashi, the geisha bloom in rivalry like primroses in the grass." A later writer, Tanizaki Junichiro, wrote in his *Childhood Years* memoir that he "never once came across anyone who communicated even a trace of the stylish femininity so characteristic of the Yanagibashi geisha."

Edokko, still clinging to the nostalgia of a period they made their own, seem to have preferred Yanagibashi and its stylish women, skilled in the shamisen, dance and the arts of conversation, to its brasher rival Shimbashi, much patronized in the early Meiji period by reformist politicians hailing from the somewhat *déclassé* prefectures of Yamaguchi and Kagoshima. The air of elegance which its clientele of Edokko aficionados of pleasure, patrons of the arts and wealthy philanderers, once imparted to the district, was considerably diluted by this new breed of bureaucrats and entrepreneurs ushered in by Meiji. Though Yanagibashi remained one of the most respected geisha quarters during this period, it had already lost some of the special élan that set it apart.

Because of its position at the confluence of two rivers, Yanagibashi was the preferred venue for the grand annual "opening of the river" marked by a huge fireworks display at the end of July. Its restaurants, commanding exorbitant prices for the privilege of viewing the show in the company of geisha and an elite clientele, were reserved months, sometimes years, in advance. Although one of the great observances of the Edo period, fire concerns and the increasingly malodorous waters of the Sumida caused the event to be terminated. The displays were revived in 1978 but the venue was relocated further up river, dealing a crippling blow to Yanagibashi. Retaining walls placed here during the high-growth 1960s were perhaps a necessary evil given the frequent flooding and subsequent loss of life and property, but such precariousness was part of life in the floating world.

Although the old wooden teahouses synonymous with the district have almost vanished, Yanagibashi geisha are still in demand as entertainers for riverboat parties. It is still possible to see stylishly robed women lifting their kimonos as they gingerly make their way across the gangplank and descend onto the deck of a pleasure boat strung with paper lanterns.

Geisha in Rivalry

Shimbashi, Yanagibashi's great rival, had a similar system, with boats functioning as houses of assignation, a subject much beloved by *ukiyo-e* artists. A woodblock triptych by Torii Kiyonaga, entitled *A Moored Pleasure Boat beneath the Bridge*, showing gorgeously clad geisha seated under roof awnings, is typical of the genre.

After the great fire of 1872 that destroyed much of the city, including Ginza, Shimbashi geisha were the first of their breed to move into the new redbrick buildings replacing the old black plaster walls that formerly characterized the district. The Victorian furnishings, floral wallpaper and the chintz and velvet may have borne a superficial resemblance to the guest parlours and drawing rooms of high-society London and New York, but the lack of proper ventilation, with air trapped in rooms already stuffy with the fumes from oil lamps, must have been more ordeal than elegance in the humid summer months.

As the Shimbashi area grew, so did its entertainments. The Kabuki Theatre was within its orbit, so too the later Shimbashi Embujo theatre. As the Shimbashi geisha's star rose, a simmering rivalry sprang up with the geisha houses of Yanagibashi. By the 1910s the two districts were the city's premier geisha quarters. In Kafu's novel, *Geisha in Rivalry*, the writer portrays the insincere, coldly calculating women of Shimbashi, but also gives us a sense of the strictly tiered world of the Tokyo geisha. During a theatre performance

> ... geisha in groups of four or five at a time came incessantly to pay court at the boxes of the powerful teahouse mistresses of the Shimbashi district. Not only geisha, but also actors, other entertainers, and professional flatterers who happened to pass by bowed ceremoniously before

them, and a ceaseless traffic of ingratiating gifts of fruit and sushi rice sandwiches and the like flowed toward their boxes.

Kafu's disapproval of the scheming geisha in his novel did not detract from the pleasure he took in the company of such women, nor his belief that in the *karyukai* (the flower and willow world) the flavour of Edo culture was preserved. If the geisha were the earthly equivalents of Benten, the lute-playing goddess of art and beauty, they were also, as Kafu showed, made of flesh and blood. In his illustrated series *The Twenty-four Hours at Shinbashi and Yanagibashi*, the print artist Yoshitoshi Tsukioka took a similar interest in the foibles and weaknesses of geisha, and the impact of western culture on Meiji Tokyo. Images of photographers, gas-lighters, rickshaw-pullers, and references to newspapers, all novelties at the time, make their appearance in this set of prints.

By Yoshitoshi's time, the strictures governing the lives of geisha and courtesans in the Shimbashi and Yanagibashi districts, as well as the Yoshiwara, had been considerably relaxed since the Edo period. Geisha were able, should they so desire, to spend the night with a guest. The new freedoms led to predicaments, which the new, vigilant media only exacerbated. The narrative cartouche accompanying one of the prints of a pregnant, clearly worried geisha reads:

I hear the newspaper hawker's voice.
There seems to be no way
To delete the bad mouthing
Of these despicable jealous editors.

THE PERFORMERS

At the same time as Kabuki was being gentrified by having its links severed with the now languishing pleasure quarters, a small revival of the musical narrative form of chanting known as *gidayu* was taking place in Tokyo. In 1877 the new Meiji government lifted its 1629 ban on women performing in public. By the early 1880s several young female narrators had begun appearing in the theatres and music halls of the city. The most famous of these performers was Takemoto Ayanosuke, a woman of striking beauty and musical talent. Enormously popular with Tokyo audiences, she was well known enough to receive a mention in Mori Ogai's novel, *Wild Geese*.

In the great print artist Kunichika Toyohara's portrait of her, this hardworking Meiji beauty appears in a radiant purple, floral-patterned kimono. Beside her is a cup of water and cloth for wiping the sweat from her face during performances.

Western theatre was being introduced to the urban elite of Tokyo and other Japanese cities. The radical activist Kawakami Oyojiro and his wife, an ex-geisha by the name of Sadayakko, were early pioneers in the popularization of western-style drama. The fact that Kawakami could get away with riding a bicycle onto the stage in the role of Hamlet, without a suggestion of dissonance, was simple: both character and machine were modern and unfamiliar to Meiji audiences. The couple took their company on extended tours of Europe and the United States, presenting colourful costume dramas and digests of Kabuki. What they offered were exotic but abridged versions of Kabuki to hugely appreciative audiences, and they received favourable reviews wherever they went.

The creators of popular entertainment turned to the city and its burgeoning population for their dramas, seeking out human interest stories, scandals or, even better, outrageous crimes for their narratives. There was nothing like a good murder, particularly if the victim was a woman associated with the pleasure quarters, to arouse the interest of the public, playwrights and the more sensational novelists of the day. A crime with all the right elements to appeal to the public and lend itself to literary adaptation occurred in the autumn of 1897, when a man named Matsudaira Noriyoshi murdered his common-law wife, named Kono, a serving woman in a geisha district who had amassed some money. After strangling her, he mutilated her face in an effort at delaying her identification, then wrapped the naked body in straw mats and rolled it down the steep embankment of the Kanda river at Ochanomizu. The murderer was soon arrested, the incident giving the newspapers an unexpected boost in circulation. The story was quickly written up as a play, making a well-received debut on—of all places—the Kagura stage of the Meitoku Inari shrine. Perhaps it was not such an unusual setting for the day as it might sound now. Tanizaki recalled seeing "card-sized pictures of Kono's mutilated face among the usual pictures of actors and geisha" in the shops and stalls at the Suitengu shrine fair in Ningyocho.

EDO NOSTALGIA, MEIJI REALITIES

Nature and art were no longer the city's sole agents of transformation. Factories began to spring up like noxious mushrooms. Despite the cement works, commercial shipyards and factories disfiguring the east bank of the Sumida, Kafu could satisfy some of his cravings for old Edo in Fukagawa, the flood-prone flatlands where Basho's retreat once stood. Three important Edo writers much admired by Kafu were associated with the district: Kyoden Santo, an incisive commentator on the customs of the pleasure quarters; Tsuruya Namboku IV, one of Edo's foremost playwrights; and Takizawa Bakin, a writer of highly popular moral romances. Given its literary credentials and partial physical survival in the alleys, teahouses and brothels compressed into an area known as Monzen-Nakacho ("Central Quarter in Front of the Gate"), it was not surprising that Kafu, in his 1909 *Song of Fukagawa*, could write: "My longing to take refuge in Fukagawa was irresistible." Yet like so many of the districts that Kafu patronized and wrote about, exterminating forces were never far away. Besides the terrible death toll they produced, the great floods of 1910 and 1917 washed away a great deal of the area's history.

The transformation of a feudal city into a modern one came at a very high cost. Configured around a natural landscape of hills, valleys, ponds and rivers, the city's trees and woods were now cut down, undulating areas flattened, watercourses filled in, place names changed. With the abolition of the aristocracy, residential estates were converted into public buildings and embassies, or passed into the hands of the remaining nobility and military elite. The disappearance of panoramic vistas, greenery and fine scenery did not completely erase the collective memory, thanks in large part to the visual records found in woodblock prints and the descriptions of districts preserved in the repository of the city's literature. By the end of the Meiji period many streets had been widened to make way for trolleys or to act as firebreaks. Others disappeared altogether. Canals, rivers and other watercourses were much reduced. Districts like the Ginza, Mitsubishi Meadow and Nihonbashi were soon unrecognizable.

Only the means was new for a city long accustomed to renewal; instead of fire, earthquakes and typhoons, planned change was now the order of the day. Many welcomed the changes, happy to exchange the dank, ill-lit and crowded *uradana* or back alleys for the opportunity to move onto street fronts. Open drains ran down the middle of these earthen grids. When it rained the boards over the drains often came off, sending up raw sewage.

It is a convention of sorts for people returning to a place after an absence of some years to lament change in the form of elegies to the past. Those like Kafu who could afford to, lived elsewhere, but sharing his strong nostalgic bent, they were quick to condemn any form of modernization. In the government's view, alleyways and the row houses that stood along them represented a serious health and fire hazard and would have to be torn down. In Kafu's view, these micro-districts were valuable beyond measure:

> Its downright homely sentiments and downright homely way of life come together in every object in the alley—latticed sliding doors, wooden ditch covers, clothes-drying decks on the roof, wooden gates, fence-top spikes. One must admit that the backstreets constitute a world of artistic harmony born amid confusion.

Novelist Tayama Katai shared Kafu's alarm at the changes, writing: "Bridges were rebuilt, there were evictions after fires, narrow streets were widened. Day by day Edo was destroyed." The transformations, however unwelcome, provided rich themes for writers with nostalgic tendencies. As Meiji superseded Edo, and even that era began to show the first signs of ageing, Tayama could cast a regretful eye over its imminent demise. "In the confusion something still remained of very early Meiji," he wrote about the Nihonbashi district, "I grow nostalgic for it, that air of the degenerate."

Hasegawa Shigure, too young for the carefully crafted nostalgia of older writers such as Kafu, compared the dark back streets of the old merchant quarter with Kanda to the north, where she sometimes stayed with an aunt. Here she got a glimpse of the new world emerging on her doorstep:

> She took me to see the Nikolai Cathedral, then under construction. It was when I stayed with her that I first heard the sound of violin and piano and orchestra. In our part of the Low City such sounds and such instruments were quite unknown. So it was that I first caught the scent of the West.

The Josiah Conder-designed Nikolai Cathedral in Ochanomizu

For Kafu, many of the new buildings that people were starting to live in were dreary in the extreme, especially the incongruous non-Japanese structures springing up in the downtown areas to the east of the river. He railed against the unexamined imitation of the West and the new hybrid culture it was producing in his *Diary of a Recent Returnee*, *Sneers*, and a short story published in 1909 called *A Song of Fukagawa*. In the tale a young man recently returned from the West takes a trolley car east. When a power failure strands him in Fukagawa, once home to a thriving Edo pleasure district, he ventures into a drab and claustrophobic city where:

> ... Western-style buildings standing unevenly on the opposite corner, some tall, some short, looked utterly impoverished, like shacks without depth or weight. Perhaps this was because they were all nooks and windows, devoid of ornamentation. The power lines crisscrossing overhead formed a frenzied obstruction to the transparent winter sky. Utility poles, made out of timbers so raw they might have been felled just yesterday, jutted out along the street, threatening to block the view com-

pletely. Slapped indiscriminately onto the poles were signs painted in awful colours, flaunting an utter ignorance of design.

Kafu's changing viewpoint, shared by many of his generation, is commented upon by the critic Kato Shuichi; writing about the Meiji period, he observes that "the alienation of the artist drove him either into a nostalgic yearning for the culture of the Edo period, or into an infatuation with the West."

By the early 1890s this infatuation was already showing signs of disillusionment, a reaction to over-hasty westernization expressing itself in a fresh interest in traditional values and culture. Reflecting increasing disenchantment with the aims of materialistic progress, a new term, *bunmeibyo* (civilization disease) was coined. This coincided with the first, troubling signs of a resurgent nationalism. Accused of a slight against the imperial shrine in Ise, the minister of education was assassinated in 1889; the following year, the foreign minister, criticized for dragging his feet over negotiations for treaty revision, was seriously injured in a bomb attack.

THE NIHONGA SCHOOL

A dual process of assimilation and subordination of western influences was taking place in painting. Cultural preferences were evident in the way artists affiliated themselves with either the western styles of painting (*yoga*), or Japanese (*nihonga*). The western school of artists worked mostly in oils and watercolours, the Japanese fraternity in traditional mineral pigments. Although its main aim was to reassert a Japanese identity through the recovery of its cultural past, there were modernist elements in nihonga. To that end, traditional genres and subjects would be reinstated in the newer context of a more occidentalized Taisho Japan. A great many nihonga artists devoted themselves to *bijinga*, representations of female beauty.

The newer canons of feminine beauty were explored in the nihonga paintings of artists like Yamakawa Shuho and Kobayakawa Kiyoshi, who were intrigued by the creative possibilities offered by mingling progressive western styles with more orthodox Japanese ones. Though marginalized for being women artists, several female nihonga painters like Kajiwara Hisako and Uemura Shoen appeared at this time. Within the nihonga school, Okakura Kakuzo, an advocator of the classical heritage and Buddhism, emphasized the need for individual self-expression and innovation in art, a view shared by other late Meiji and Taisho artists like the novelist Soseki Natsume and sculptor Takamura Kotaro.

Renewed interest in Japanese art and architecture among scholars and collectors abroad was evident in the second half of the nineteenth century. The Impressionists were among the first to be influenced by the art of the ukiyo-e. Japanese prints had already started circulating in Paris as early as 1856. Artists like Degas, Monet and Manet either owned or were inspired by exhibitions of prints by the likes of Hiroshige. Van Gogh's 1887 painting, "The Courtesan", rendered in the striking colours of Provence, is actually a reproduction of a figure by the artist Eisen Kesai. Shops selling Japanese furnishings and *objets d'art* were opening in Paris and London. Books like Edward Sylvester Morse's *Japanese Homes and Their Surroundings* had a later impact on the tastes of the Art Nouveau movement.

Woodblock prints also underwent a transformation in the early nineteenth century as tastes changed. Prussian blue, similar in tone to the colours of indigenous indigo fabrics, became popular. Imported synthetic aniline dyes associated with western modernity began to usurp traditional organic pigments that had animated prints with such restrained verve. Chemical pigments were introduced to prints in the 1860s. Enthusiastically applied, they give the prints of this era a gaudy, exaggerated or fanciful appearance, but are invaluable documents of the period, their over-animated fusion of steam engines, penny-farthings and electric lamps with blue skies and cherry blossoms embodying the exuberance and optimism of the times.

The great Meiji print artist Kobayashi Kiyochika preferred a more realistic, nuanced approach, turning to delicately graded nocturnes, even when he was depicting trains. A master of pathos, Kobayashi's print of a little shrine standing in the fields outside the Yoshiwara is prescient. Looking at the print, we sense that as the new city expands, the shrine and the courtesans who patronize it, depicted at twilight with exquisite melancholy, are doomed.

So, to some extent, was the woodblock print as it was overtaken by newer western techniques of copperplate printing and lithography. Some woodblock artists, sensitized to the new influences, responded with prints depicting the encounter between Japan and the West. Kiyochika's prints of locomotives and Yoshitoshi's images of brick buildings, rickshaws and gas lighting brought the modern world into the floating world.

With the widespread adoption of not only western political systems and technology but also social values, institutions like the Yoshiwara and art forms like the erotic shunga became an embarrassment. Western Victorian sensibilities were appalled by the Yoshiwara, but there were others who took a lively interest in the place, recognizing its vigour.

Many writers and artists of the day lived in the contiguous districts of Yanaka, Nezu and Sendagi, within walking distance of Tokyo University and the Tokyo School of Fine Arts. Along with Tenshin, Natsumi Soseki had a house in Yanaka, where he wrote two of his most popular novels, *I Am a Cat* and *Botchan*. Mori Ogai had lived in the same house some years before, moving to a more permanent residence in nearby Sendagi. Kafu visited the house, noting the kind of austere good taste one would expect from a disciplined master of Ogai's rank: "Save for the hanging and vase in the alcove, the room was quite bare... In the middle of it was a desk, again bare, actually more like a table, a single board with four legs and no drawers, and no ornamentation."

NATURE AND NOSTALGIA

Despite creeping industrialization, human interaction with nature and seasonal change survived within the sinews of the city. The muddy back alleys that froze in winter, resonating with the sound of *geta* (wooden clogs), became steamy passages of fermenting heat in the summer. In eulogizing beauty and mood, writers preferred to associate the season with floral aromas and women faintly damp with perspiration than with the pungent smells of decay. At the high point of summer, notorious then as now for its stifling humidity, a mid-year celebration called *chugen* took place during which temples placed their priceless treasures in the sunshine, airing them in an effort to protect them against insects and mould. This was often the only chance for ordinary people to view exquisite works of art often kept in the dark recesses of the temple.

Writers could find inspiration in the lotuses at Tameike Pond, under the cherry blossoms at Asukayama, along the embankments of Mukojima and in countless other places. In Kawaguchi Matsutaro's novel *Mistress Oriku: Stories from a Tokyo Teahouse*, the main character recalls: "You know, you could drop a line in the river from the garden of my place and catch a sea bass. The tide brought them all the way up here. In summer you could jump in from the jetty—people didn't swim so much as just cool off in it. That shows you how clean the Sumida river was back then."

Teahouses along the river served as venues for the powerful and wealthy, hosting statesmen, business elites and the new industrialists. Restaurants and teahouses also played a central role in the cultural life of the city, developing carefully nurtured affinities with the world of Kabuki actors, bunraku puppet masters, *koto* performers, the better-off gidayu chanters and the idly elegant.

In Kawaguchi's novel, a series of linked stories based on the real life proprietress of the teahouse, her reputation for mature beauty and generosity earns her many admirers among the young, gifted but inexperienced men of the entertainment world who petition her to manage their sexual initiation, a practice apparently quite common at the time. A true daughter of Edo, Oriku embodies the values of a former age. Devoted to her business and customers, kind-hearted and discreet, she exemplifies the true qualities of Edo that the author implies had become increasingly rare by the Meiji era.

By the late years of Meiji an exquisite culture of taste, embodied in the teahouses and cherry trees that lined the embankments of Mukojima, a place of tranquillity and spiritual refreshment, was still possible despite the new smokestacks and spillage from coal barges. Egrets stood in the shallow water of rice paddies abutting the nearby Mimeguri shrine, red-footed gulls floated on the waters between the ferry crossings. The devout continued to make pilgrimages here to the shrines of the Seven Gods of Good Fortune, and poets gathered for meetings at the Hyakka-en Garden, but the effects of encroaching industrialization were obvious. The haiku poet Kikakudo Kiichi, who had managed to live in near blissful seclusion like an Edo-period aesthete in a nook of land near the shrine, soon found his one-floor home swallowed up by a factory.

In Kawaguchi's tale, a grim future devoid of the beauty and finer aesthetics associated with Mukojima is not foretold in the tea leaves, but in the appearance of a shoe factory whose owner buys up land next to the teahouse. Nearby jetties are soon requisitioned for industrial cargos, and a new bathhouse and inn beside Chomei-ji temple sticks up a dazzlingly vulgar sign. "It's what happens when people abuse the invention of electric lighting," Oriku muses as she passes the advertisement: "They say something invented means something destroyed, and it's true. I dare say electric lighting will destroy the beauty of Mukojima." Dependent for their livelihood on the views of the river and of embankments synonymous with the works of poets and woodblock artists of a previous age, Oriku rightly surmises the situation: "Once the scenery's gone, we're through."

The artists and literati who were drawn to the area were gradually displaced by wealthy businessmen and politicians who built villas along the river. "After the flood of early August 1910," Kafu wrote, "almost everyone departed... In the changing times since, as the outskirts of the city have moved on, the cherry trees along the river embankment have died one by one." The ever-vigilant Kafu noted the changes with a moist eye and dry pen in his 1909 short story *The Peony Garden*. Kafu's Sumida is a lightning rod for the changes being carried out in the name of progress. The story begins promisingly, with a gentleman of the old school and his geisha companion hiring a boat to view the peonies at Honjo, east of the river. Here is Kafu's trance writing at its best in the narrator's spellbound description of the scene:

> The rich green of the Kanda Canal in the rising tide shone like a freshly polished sheet of glass, catching the sun as it sank into the grove of the Kanda Shrine. At the mouth of the canal where barges and little boats were collecting, the waters of the Sumida spread before us, the more radiant for the depth of the scene. Along the measured lines of the stone embankments, straggly willows waved in the breeze, quiet and languorous beyond description.

As they pass beneath Ryogoku Bridge, "the sky descended to cap the mouth of the river, the smoke from the factories spiralled upward." Arriving at the garden they find that "even the blossoms that had not lost all of their petals were faded badly, their hearts black and gaping... Are these the Honjo peonies? Are these all?" the narrator's companion asks disconsolately. The district of Honjo where the garden stood for so long is now, in keeping with the plaintive tone struck by the story, an area of small sheet metal factories and used car dumps.

The writer Ryunosuke Akutagawa spent much of his childhood in the watery lowlands of Honjo. Recalling in an essay how his father had seen the apparition of a fox spirit in the form of a young warrior, driving it away with his sword, the writer conveys a strong sense of the loneliness of the area before industrialization.

> Corpses made the strongest impression on me in stories I heard of old Honjo, corpses of those who had fallen by the wayside, or hanged themselves, or otherwise disposed of themselves. A corpse would be discovered and put in a cask, and the cask wrapped in straw matting, and set out upon the moors with a white lantern to watch over it... And how is it now? A mass of utility poles and shacks, all jammed in together.

Edo and Meiji-period literature, as this passage attests, paid a great deal of attention to locale, something that is less important to today's writers. Yet lovers of language and literature will even now find themselves intrigued by the urban geography of Tokyo, where so many streets have hidden meanings and allusions implanted in their names. Because it is not possible to experience the city in its entirety, it must be explored street by street, district by district in an episodic manner, which may be the reason it provided such a promising structure for fiction. Little remains today of the physical fabric of late Meiji Tokyo, but in the profoundly nostalgic descriptive novels of writers like Kafu and Tayama Katai, we can not only follow the social trends of the age, but sample its tastes and moods.

Asakusa, that playground for the townspeople of Edo, was just across the river from Mukojima. The entertainment quarter developed a stronger, albeit sleazy, identity during the Meiji period. The indulgent climate of Asakusa found people suddenly possessed of new, liberating passions. Mori Ogai has the main character of his novel *Vita Sexualis* describe walking through the area around the Senso-ji temple:

> Passing behind old men and women on bended knees, their bodies bent like lobsters as they muttered their incomprehensible prayers... We came out on a narrow street lined with archery shops. I was amazed to find in each of these shops a woman whose face was covered with white paint... Their eyebrows had been sketched on as high as possible, sometimes even up to the borders of their hair. Their eyes were strained open as wide as possible. Even when they talked or laughed, they tried not to

move that part of the face above the nose. I wondered why the faces of these women looked as if they had been prearranged. Though I didn't understand what I was witnessing at that time, I later learned that these faces were for sale. These were the faces of prostitutes.

Mori's novel first appeared in serialized form in his literary magazine *Subaru* (The Pleiades) on 1 July 1909. The authorities, conscious of the fact that Ogai held the exalted rank of surgeon general, hesitated until the end of the month before banning the story on the grounds that it might have a harmful effect on public morals. Commenting on the decision, writer and critic Sato Haruo wrote: "Because the author treated the problem of sexual desire, the authorities considered this a novel of sexual desire."

By now something else, more troubling than censorship, was happening in Japan. In 1895 the country had won its war with China, its subsequent annexation of Formosa a warning of incipient colonial ambitions. Even Lafcadio Hearn, who preferred the Old Japan, wrote of a "nation regenerated through war... The real birthday of New Japan—began with the conquest of China." A patriotic fervour swept through the entire nation with these victories, whetting its thirst for more territorial expansion. Between 1904 and 1905 Japan successfully waged a war against the Russian Tsarist empire. Japan's surprise attack on the Russian fleet at Port Arthur and its campaign to drive out the Russians from Korea was a costly and protracted undertaking, but resulted in a humiliating defeat for Russia. The defeat of a massive European nation by a small Asian country established Japan as a world power to be reckoned with. In 1910 it annexed Korea.

From the Japanese perspective, however, the conditions that concluded the Russo-Japanese War of 1904-05 were unsatisfactory. In the view of the protesters who gathered in Hibiya Park on 5 September 1905 the government had failed in pressing its advantage, giving in to poor terms dictated by the western powers when they signed the Portsmouth Treaty of that year. The police were powerless to control the crowds, who vented their frustrated nationalism with attacks on government offices, police boxes, newspapers, the American legation and Christian churches, ten of which were destroyed. It was all part of the disturbing cross-cultural currents stirring in Tokyo in the last decade of Meiji.

AN IMPERIAL SHROUD

While attending graduation day at Tokyo Imperial University on 12 July 1912, the emperor complained of tiredness and shortness of breath. He had been suffering from kidney failure and diabetes for years, refusing treatment for both. His first thorough examination revealed that he was suffering from uremic poisoning, a fatal condition in those days. As the emperor's body was considered divine, his doctors were not permitted to administer injections.

With the news of the emperor's declining health, crowds gathered in silent vigil in the palace plaza. Passing tramcars were slowed down and blankets, rough cloth and sacking placed over their rails to muffle the noise. A scheduled display of fireworks along the Sumida was cancelled, street festivals scaled down and great quantities of sesame seed burnt at temples throughout the city, where it was believed that the smoke exorcised evil spirits.

A little after midnight on 30 July special newspaper extras announced the death of the Meiji emperor. The same papers declared a five-day ban on music and dance. All performances at theatres and music halls were forbidden. The imperial funeral took place on 13 September. The country may have modernized itself during the years of Meiji, but when it came to ritual obsequies, tradition held sway. According to Shinto rites that went back over a thousand years, the funeral ceremony took place at night, preceded by a cortege drawn by five white oxen, escorted by bowmen and banner-bearers, and attendants bearing fans, staffs and halberds. Utility poles and windows along the route were draped in black and white to resemble ceremonial lanterns; two feet of sand was strewn on the roads to muffle the sound of the passing wheels. The main character of Oswald Wynd's 1977 novel *The Ginger Tree* observes the scene:

> The marchers on foot looked dressed for the Noh drama, in medieval robes with the flowing lines which said China, not Japan, all in white except for some of the head-dresses. Banners had black characters on white, fastened top and bottom to white painted bamboo poles. Elaborate though all this was it was also almost without pomp, the opposite of a state funeral circus in the West, as though here the object underlying pageantry was silence.

Following shortly upon the announcement of the death of the emperor, the nation had another momentous event to fathom: the *junshi* of General Nogi and his wife. Meant to express fealty, junshi was the act of suicide committed by a samurai upon the death of his master. The practice had not been much heard of since the seventeenth century, when it had been effectively outlawed. Taking up brush and ink as the practice required, the general wrote his farewell poem and then prepared the instruments of death. After helping his wife to sever her carotid artery, he then performed the most demanding form of ritual suicide, requiring a horizontal and then vertical slash to the stomach and abdomen. General Nogi appears to have accomplished the complete ritual without fainting, as his naval uniform was neatly re-buttoned when the body was found.

The death pact revealed a strong division of views among the public, some excoriating the general for belittling all the achievements of the previous decades, others seeing heroism and loyalty, a reminder of lost values. The suicides overshadowed the emperor's funeral itself. Many newspaper readers struggled to comprehend what had taken place. Soseki Natsume expressed bewilderment when he wrote, "I had almost forgotten that there was such a thing as junshi." Another writer of significance, the novelist Shiga Naoya, thought that Nogi was simply *baka na yatsu*—"an idiot". For the majority of Japanese, the suicides tarnished the hard-earned modernity of the era, even if they would be re-honoured in the 1930s by a government more interested in martial traditions than modernity.

The general's house is still there within the grounds of Nogi shrine, eerily preserved, the deathly atmosphere of its rooms much the same as it was in 1912. In a later age, under even more different circumstances, another general, Douglas MacArthur, planted a magnolia tree in the shrine garden in Nogi's memory, on the spot where the couple's bloodied clothes were buried. The house stands on Nogizaka (Nogi's Slope), a rare instance of a road being named in honour of a person. Now a very central district of Tokyo, it appears to have been semi-rural during the general's time—if his complaints about foxes attacking his poultry are anything to go by.

Soseki Natsumi, arguably the greatest writer of the Meiji era, majored in English literature at Tokyo Imperial University before going on to studies in London. Soseki's central theme was the isolation and loneliness of the Japanese intellectual. Born and bred in Edo, Soseki established a pattern replicated by many writers who, initially besotted with all things foreign and contemporary, became increasingly disillusioned with outside influences, ending up more than ever traditionalist.

Soseki had stepped into Lafcadio Hearn's shoes at Tokyo Imperial University, a difficult act to follow by all accounts, though he appears to have made a good job of it. Hearn had entered a faculty peopled by gifted but fractious students known to disrupt lectures if they were not to their taste. "His lectures," one student later recalled, "were revelations to us, at once poignant and lucid." This view is corroborated by one of Hearn's colleagues, who chanced upon his teaching one day. Opening the door and entering, he found the first two or three rows of students in tears: "I do not know what it was all about. It is a rare event for a Japanese to be in tears; even a coolie is ashamed of it, and with men of higher rank it is much more striking than it would be in England. Hearn had been reading some very simple English poem; and there was the effect."

Soseki was never affiliated with any literary school or movement. In one of his finest works, the 1914 *Kokoro*, he examines the friendship between a younger and older man, the former embracing the new age, the latter witnessing the junking of much of his own culture in the rush to acquire western learning, technology and tastes. After writing a confessional letter to his young friend, the older man, referred to in the novel as *Sensei* or "Master", commits suicide. The year is 1912, one marked by the death of the Meiji emperor. Sensei notes in his letter that "I was overcome with the feeling that I and the others, who had been brought up in that era, were now left behind to live as anachronisms."

Like General Nogi, Sensei, reading a newspaper account of the suicide on the day of the emperor's funeral, senses the passing of an irretrievable era. He resolves to commit suicide himself, an act lending itself to two interpretations: self-execution as high symbolism, or the copycat annihilation of an overwrought neurotic. In either instance, it signalled the death of a difficult age.

Chapter Six

TAISHO STYLE

1912-1926

As Nagai Kafu saw it, the Great Meiji Flood, the 1910 inundation that submerged almost the entire part of the lowland city to the east, and the dreadful Yoshiwara fire the following year signalled the end of a period in the life of the city. More accurately it was the death of the emperor himself, a year later, that brought about the great social shifts.

There are certain historical periods that resonate with a style that is inimitable, but easily reconstructed in fictional settings. They last for only a few intense years. The Restoration period in England, coinciding with the florid tastes and theatricality of Japan's Genroku age, was one such period, the Belle Époque another. The Taisho era (1912-26) was another special time. During this period the authorities temporarily relaxed their hold on civil conduct, a reaction perhaps to the physically and morally corrupted state of its central symbol, the emperor.

The oppressive climate of late Meiji soon lifted as the firm manner of the former emperor passed into the limp hands of his son Yoshihito, the new Taisho emperor. Although monarchs were supposed to fill only symbolic roles as heads of state and Shinto divinities, their character and deportment might define the age. In recent years historical revisionists in Japan have tried to polish the image of the Taisho emperor, but the fact remains that he was virtually incapable of fulfilling even the simplest of ceremonial duties. Dogged by poor health, weakness of character and a reputation for drinking, womanizing and eccentric behaviour, he was said to be fond of dressing up in western-style military uniforms in the manner of Kaiser Wilhelm II and throwing extravagant parties at the ostentatious Akasaka Detached Palace. An inferior successor to his father, his conspicuous defects made a mockery of the idea that a Japanese emperor was a manifest deity. Attending a Diet session, the poor fellow is said to have rolled up an important document and used it as a telescope to observe the proceedings. Quietly removed from the public's gaze, he was henceforth rarely seen in public. Nothing pertaining to the emperor's condition appeared in the press, but rumours of his eccentricity and debauchery must have circulated freely. The public instinctively took advantage of an emperor sidelined by a publicly unacknowledged mental infirmity.

Overlooked until recently, this important and highly distinctive period in the arts carried political and social resonances. Fertile social unrest was fuelled by the relaxation of government surveillance and censorship, a closer questioning of social inequalities and the traditional position of women, the introduction of worker's unions, the encouragement of big business and the long overdue development of parliamentary procedure. The writer Nitobe Inazo took up the banner of modernity when he urged a more cosmopolitan outlook, encouraging his readers to become "world citizens".

The struggle for a modern cultural identity was one of the main themes of the era. The 1914 Taisho Exposition, though primarily aimed at promoting industry, helped to establish the independence of the new age. Its booths, including a gas-heated bathtub, the country's first escalator and tableaux from Japan's colonized territories of Taiwan and Korea, were staffed by Tokyo geisha. It was a major success. Even the new emperor, still able to make public appearances at this point, attended the event. Before leaving he bought a bag of jellybeans. Several pavilions at the exposition in Ueno reflected an interest in prevailing European architectural tastes and trends, such as the Viennese Secession movement and Art Nouveau. A second exposition, held in 1922, attracted seven and a half million visitors. The themes this time were modern living, the exhibits ranging from cable cars, escalators, a refrigerator and new styles of western architecture, including a reconstructed apartment house, examined with intense interest.

MAGAZINES AND MOVEMENTS

The transference between Euro-American and Japanese cultures proved immensely stimulating for both the wealthy elite and the majority. Education and the growth of the press were helping to drive urbanization and mass culture. The appetite of the newly educated classes for printed matter stimulated journalism. Within just two years the literary magazine *Bungei-Shinju* achieved a circulation in the hundreds of thousands. All tastes were catered for, not just the highbrow, with huge initial sales of

Cover of the radical
art magazine, *Mavo*

magazines like the popular *King*, paperback pocket books, and *enpon* (one-yen books).

The pioneering magazine *Hosun*, first published in 1907, focused on small format prints and *manga*, devoting considerable space to the changing appearance of Tokyo. In 1910 the sculptor and free-style poet Takamura Kotaro published an essay in the literary magazine *Subaru* entitled "A Green Sun". Its advocacy of total individualism and freedom in the arts, a complete break with the past, created quite a stir. It struck a deep chord with a group of young writers and artists who went on to publish a magazine called *White Birch*, arguably the most concept-forming publication of the period. The magazine featured the work of new writers like Shiga Naoya. Their work, though naive in its idealism and hopeful humanism, stood for the worship of the individual, an enormously appealing message for the young.

Satirical magazines had already appeared during the late years of Meiji. The best known, *Tokyo Puck*, lampooned the new fashions. The Tokyo of the 1920s saw the birth of another audacious magazine, *Mavo*. Inspired by Futurism and Dadaism, it attempted to turn conventional magazine methods on their head, sometimes quite literally, with whole pages of text or linocut prints appearing upside-down. Feminist literary magazines like *Myojo* (Morning Star), a publication devoted to poetry, and popular magazines aimed at women, such as *Nyonin Geijutsu* (Women's Arts) and *Fujin Koron* (Women's Forum), began to appear during these years.

Some of the most popular and emblematic images of the time were created by Takehisa Yumeji, a gifted painter and illustrator whose portraits of the "new woman" appealed to the masses. In 1914 Takehisa opened Minatoya, a Tokyo shop and café where he sold kimonos and illustrated stationery of his own design; the shop acted as a salon where artists of all stripes, particularly women, could gather.

BLUE-STOCKING

Another women's magazine, the enormously influential *Seito* (Blue-Stocking), had been brought out by the group Seitosha (the Blue-Stocking Society) in 1911. Edited by Hiratsuka Raicho, the magazine, originally published as a literary journal promoting creative writing, altered course and took up the cause of women's rights. It promoted the idea, still shocking to many outside the relatively progressive urban centres, of a "new type of woman", independent of the "good wife, wise mother" ideal promulgated during the Meiji era. The first issue of the magazine carried Hiratsuka's famous proclamation:

> In the beginning Woman was the Sun. She was a genuine being. Now Woman is the Moon. She lives through others and glitters through the mastery of others. She has a pallor like that of the ill. Now we must restore our hidden Sun.

This was stirring rhetoric, but in many instances, of course, the New Woman was humoured yet expected at the same time to fulfil her traditional filial duties. In cities like Tokyo, however, education (the first women's university was established in 1918) and a fledgling feminist movement facilitated the efforts of some women to work outside the home.

In addition to their roles during the Meiji period as teachers, nurses and midwives, women began to take up posts, albeit minor ones, as clerks in government departments, typists, telephone operators and department store salesgirls. The working woman of the 1920s might be employed as an office worker, bank teller, "elevator girl", or even in the recently unthinkable position as chauffeur, bus conductress or journalist.

The press took much delight in excoriating this new breed, but some women of advanced ideas responded by going into print themselves. Hiratsuka, who favoured cohabitation over marriage, was different in that she put theory into practice. Her writing was enough to turn the faces of the Meiji-born male an apoplectic blue, as these published samplings of her views on marriage illustrate:

> I have such antipathy toward the institution of marriage I cannot even bear the names husband and wife.

> Not to marry is all the more natural since marriage prescribes unfavourable claims and duties to the woman.

In her autobiography, she wrote that "my aversion to authority has lasted to this day, and will probably stay with me until the end of my life." Her organization was also known as the Hongo Group as the offices of her publication were located in the Hongo area, a popular district for writers and artists.

Spurred on by women like Hiratsuka, the True New Women's Society was formed in nearby Hakusan in 1913. There were other women whose mere existence exacerbated anxieties over gender issues and modernity. In her *Modern Girls, Shining Stars, the Skies of Tokyo*, Phyllis Birnbaum profiles five outstanding Japanese women, all connected in some way with the arts. Each of these women came of age during a period in Japan when the concept of women's rights was first being aired. Matsui Sumako, Japan's first western-style actress, caused great excitement with her electrifying performances of self-possessed, individualistic women. Living a private life much the same as the characters she played on stage, this talented actress, much to the delight of the media, caused one scandal after another. It is more difficult writing about the complex life of Takamura Chieko, a painter who ended her days in a Tokyo sanatorium and is best known in

Japan as the subject of a collection of love poems entitled *Chieko's Sky*, written by her husband, the sculptor and poet Takamura Kotaro. Birnbaum re-examines the couple's relationship and questions whether Kotaro really helped to liberate his wife, or destroyed her talent with the demands of his own ego. Yanagiwara Byakuren, a minor aristocrat forced by her family into marriage with the wealthy owner of a coalmine, is known in Japan for throwing both her husband and the country into a storm with the publication of a letter in the *Asahi Shimbun* newspaper informing him of her intention to file for divorce. The fact that Yanagiwara also happened to be a gifted poet and stunning beauty assured her a place among this rich group of highly individual Japanese women. Uno Chiyo, another of Birnbaum's subjects, passed away in 1996. Celebrated for her passionate private life and semi-autobiographical novels and stories, she seems to have lived exactly the sort of life that best suited her, blithely ignoring most of the advice of friends and family.

ART AND EXPERIMENT

Many of these new ideas and the climate of intellectual freedom they helped to create came from abroad. Strindberg, Proust, Eliot and Rilke were enthusiastically read in translation. In an early example of the Japanese love of compounds, students from the better institutions, thirsty for new ideas, talked passionately of "DeKanSho", standing for Descartes, Kant and Schopenhauer. Russian novels and German philosophy were discussed in the "milk bars" of Ginza where earnest young people came to be known—as yet without too much of a censorial tone—as Marx boys and Marx girls. One could become acquainted with the works of Goethe, Carlyle, Baudelaire or even Lao-tze by reading their books in translation, by attending the People's English Academy and the Athenée Français or by attending lectures at the Liberty English Academy in Kanda. The Bengali poet and philosopher Rabindranath Tagore visited Tokyo in 1916, casting a spell over all who met him. The future Nobel laureate formed views still worth pondering:

> The Japanese do not waste their energy in useless screaming and quarrelling, and because there is no waste of energy, it is not found wanting when required. This calmness and fortitude of body and mind is part of their national self-realization.

The Literary Society was formed in 1909, training actors for performances of modern plays. *Hamlet* was performed in 1910 and Ibsen's far more contentious *A Doll's House* a year later. Audiences paid keen attention to the contents of plays by the likes of Maeterlinck and Hauptmann staged at Tokyo's New Theatre.

The actress Matsui Sumako was synonymous with the experimentation and daring of the new age. A survivor of two unhappy marriages, Matsui's portrayal of Nora in the Japanese version of *A Doll's House* embodied the new woman. Passionately discussed in magazines and the popular press, her role as Nora as well as her refusal to comply with the notion of marriage and male authority as sacrosanct constituted a troubling challenge to Meiji patriarchy. Matsui rose to fame as one of the founding members of the Geijutsu-za (Art Theatre), which was largely responsible for bringing western plays to Tokyo and the provinces. In her personal life she provided a parallel script to her acting. Barely surviving the opprobrium of the early years of Taisho, a woman like Matsui could not have existed in early Meiji. Her performance in *Salome* had been compared with that of the slightly older actress and early exponent of western theatre, Sadayakko. After Sadayakko and Matsui actresses became a permanent fixture in the modern Japanese theatre. Her final affair, with her theatre director, the playwright Hogetsu Shimamura, a married man who had abandoned his family to move in with the actress, ended when he unexpectedly died from influenza. Intense to the end, Matsui went backstage to the prop room after starring in the opening performance of *Carmen*, carefully applied her make-up, then hanged herself with a kimono sash. Her death has often been interpreted as symbolic of the conflict between the aspirations of the age and the social realities underlying them.

IMAGES IN PAINT AND PRINT

Nihonga was both traditional and modern. Its aim was to reassert a Japanese identity through the recovery of its cultural past. To that end traditional genres and subjects were reinstated in the newer context of a more westernized Taisho Japan. Close to the spirit of the nihonga artists, the philosopher Watsuji Tetsuro advocated a retrieval of Japan's lost past and the creation of Taisho values more in keeping with an unassailably Japanese rather than western culture. These ideas were distilled into his influential book *Restoring the Idols*.

Within the nihonga school itself, Okakura Kakuzo, an advocate of the classical heritage and Buddhism, also emphasized the need for individual self-expression and innovation in art, a view shared by other late Meiji and Taisho cultural figures like Soseki Natsume and the sculptor Takamura Kotaro. Although western techniques were incorporated into this new style, artists were mainly interested in creating subjects that would reaffirm and renew beleaguered Japanese values. The conjunction of orthodox and progressive tendencies is evident in much Japanese art of this time. Like Edo-period woodblock prints, the themes in nihonga are often taken from everyday life.

Haunted by the sensual images and idealizations of both the Edo and Meiji periods, Taisho artists added deliberate touches of modernity to their *binjinga*, or "beautiful women" subjects: a casually held cigarette, a cocktail glass, a microphone stand, jazz dancers and bobbed hair. Taken in the socio-political context, the images are striking. The women in these prints have a physicality denied them by the more diaphanous, winsome treatment of the classic bijinga practitioners. Likewise, the vivid colour schemes are more assertive.

The subjects engage in a modern dialogue, one in which women were beginning to question society, and society to question women. While some artists chose themes that would aid their retreat into the past, others opted to eschew depictions of women sitting pensive before their mirrors or appraising their cosmetics in favour of subjects playing golf, stepping out of automobiles, or—unthinkable a decade earlier—staring back squarely at the artist. The impact at the time of these apparently minor innovations cannot be overstated.

Aesthetic innovation, political dissidence and the so-called "new women" were symptomatic of unprecedented enlightenment in the arts and society that characterized the few short years of Taisho and which met with equal measures of approval and opprobrium. The appearance of fashionably clad women in public, the compelling vogue for western habits and objects, aroused intense interest but also anxiety. As far as such things suggested privilege, this was acceptable, but implied independence was frowned upon. Rural elements in particular were severely critical of the social changes.

The Taisho period witnessed a vogue in everything from *enka* songbooks and new textile art to glassware, art deco furniture and ceramic figurines, reflecting the changing tastes and social aspirations of the times. The sudden popularity of ceramic dolls, often modelled on paintings of Japanese actresses and socialites, demonstrated the increasingly commercial character of society, with department stores emerging as unlikely venues for exhibitions.

The period also saw the emergence of a new mass, popular culture. Advances in communication, public transport, education, publishing and journalism, all parts of what was essentially an urban culture, were nowhere more in evidence than in Tokyo. Much of the cultural activity of the period was propelled by the wealth of the *narikin*, the nouveaux riches who had risen economically during the First World War. This newly empowered class was small, but helped to fill the gaping chasm between the working class and the unimaginable wealth of industrial oligarchs. With Japan on the side of the Allies during the war, its economy flourished as it took on the role of supplying goods that Europe's factories, focusing almost entirely on war production, were unable to manufacture. The same would happen again in the early 1950s and through the 1960s and 1970s as a lucrative procurement industry grew with the Korean and Vietnam wars.

The downside of the war, however, was that it created runaway inflation, which in turn led to riots over the price of rice. The rioting spread to Tokyo in mid-August 1918, when a well supported and initially peaceful rally took place in Hibiya Park. After predictably heavy-handed police methods, violence, looting and arson ensued and the rioters, now in the thousands, took their anger out on the police boxes and shop fronts of Nihonbashi, Kyobashi, Ginza and Shimbashi. A second wave of rioters, a crowd of roughly twenty thousand, closed in on Ueno and the Yoshiwara, inflicting more damage on the already declining fortunes of the pleasure quarter, where 69 houses were damaged. The riots brought about the downfall of the prime minister and also the formation of a government based on political parties. This turn of events symbolized for many people the beginnings of what became known as Taisho democracy.

With mass movements and mass production came mass consumerism, turning culture into a commodity available to almost everyone. What emerged was a modern "cultural life", one that continues to be at the heart of Japanese life today. The word *bunkateki* ("cultural") was now indiscriminately used to describe everything from "cultural cafés" and "cultural houses" to "cultural shampoo". Besides the large-scale expositions held in public parks, the new exhibition halls of culture were no longer restricted to the museum and gallery, but included that most "cultural" of Taisho-period institutions—the department store.

Though there were other flagships stores in Tokyo like Takashimaya and Shirokiya, Mitsukoshi had the greatest impact on the new urban consumer. Its first exhibition of paintings by the artist Ogata Korin had already been held in 1904. Three years later it established a permanent art gallery for both viewing and purchasing paintings and crafts by modern artists. Display windows and an in-house consumer magazine helped to promote its image as a conduit for art and literature. Art exhibitions and poster design competitions were part of its scheme for attracting and providing support to new talent.

With the proliferation of venues where one could eat, shop and seek cultural enlightenment, demand grew for stronger elements within the entertainment provided by magazines and floor shows. A taste for "the erotic, the grotesque and nonsense," truncated to *ero-guro-nansensu*, became the norm in even the most literary of magazines. Appropriated from late Edo-period literature, *ero* stood for the erotic taken to excess, though it also stood for the vitality and colour of the age; *guro* designated the deformations of the time, the beggars and homeless of a grotesquely depressed social order; while *nansensu* denoted the vaudeville-like fantasies, the political farces and mass consumerism built on the vagaries and uncertainties of capitalism. The three words combined and applied in real life represented an attack on orthodoxies.

If the Meiji era had been defined by nation building and the love of a good slogan like *wakon yosai* ("Japanese spirit, western awareness"), the Taisho period was characterized by the names of a number of art and literary movements. The New Print Group, one such movement, was active at this time. Under their rallying motto "Prints are for the masses," their dominant theme was the transformation of Tokyo in the aftermath of the great earthquake of 1923, and the life of the Low City, the districts of the *shitamachi*. The work of Shimizu Masahiro, a doctor in downtown Tamanoi, stands out for its focus on the ordinary lives of people in the Arakawa river districts.

Thousands of people crowded every week into the new department stores and public museums, stimulating artists to further experimentation. After the formation of the Japan Communist Party in 1922 proletarian posters strikingly similar to Russian socialist art began to appear. As the period moved to its denouement, the year 1925 saw a gathering of avant-garde artists under the banner of the Third Section Plastic Arts Association, a bold event featuring what must have struck many passers-by as a hideous apparition, the "Gate Tower" construction in Ueno Park. One evening newspaper ran a photo of the construction, made from salvaged waste materials, and its main creator, Okada Tatsuo, dressed in nothing more than a loincloth, with the headline "Naked and imitating a carpenter while glared at by the police." A partially visible section of an agitprop poster next to the structure reads: "the chains which bind ourselves... our own power... the workers... through workers' unions." Art and politics were about to engage.

KAFU'S TOKYO

The rapid physical changes to the city were noted in memoirs, city guides, gazettes and individual works of literature. Expressive of the intense sense of place that characterizes writers of the period, they provide a mass of observation and detail. This is how we know, for example, that not far from where the poet Basho lived, at the junction of the Sumida River and Onagi Canal, a fine old pine tree, gnarled but strong, survived until precisely 1909.

During the Edo period the Onagi served as an important route for the transportation of grain, rice, salt, and fertilizer made from pulverized fish to the storehouses of Nihonbashi and Fukagawa. By the early Taisho period steam-powered boats were beginning to use the waterway, polluting a river where boatmen lived with their families aboard ageing vessels. The feudal mansions and expansive gardens that lined the river had now been superseded by steel and flour mills, textile factories and gasworks whose belching chimneys could be seen for miles around. Writers like Shimazaki Toson and Tayama Katai, admirers of the natural features of the city, watched the transformation of their favourite spots with a mixture of fascination and unease. "The groves of trees I had known have all been cut to the ground," Tayama wrote in 1916: "the view of Meijirodai from the Suwa grove was once pleasant enough, but now large two-storied houses have been built."

Not everyone shared these sentiments, particularly when the subject was the development of more urban areas. Writing about Shinjuku, a former charcoal dealers' district close to the stockyards of Shinjuku station, Soma Aizo, the owner of the western-style Nakamura Bakery, noted in his memoirs: "In those days Shinjuku looked so miserable that there is nowhere to compare with it now. As for any notion of rustic suburban charm, it could not have looked drearier, and if you walked just a little way back, you would come upon open-air latrines." Better-class restaurants, fruit and clothes shops were to follow, clearing away most of the soot and grime from Shinjuku.

Nagai Kafu was among the first writers to mourn the loss of greenery and the bad air contaminating the city's once pastoral byways. By this time Kafu, a leading figure of the literary avant-garde known for his attempts to create a modern, western-style novel, had already begun to cultivate the persona of a latter-day Edo-period litterateur. It was typical of the writer that, at the moment the Taisho age was embracing everything new and novel, he should turn to nostalgia for a pre-modern age. In lamenting the passing of Meiji, Kafu, a master of threnodies suffused with remembrance of things past, was doing precisely the same thing he did during the latter years of Meiji, when he had written with longing about the Edo period. A contrarian by nature, he was a writer who took pains to remain outside the mainstream. When he did align himself with a movement, as when he associated himself with Mori Ogai and the anti-Naturalists, his position stood against the dominant trend of the times.

Gazing down at the arches of Asakusa's Azuma Bridge today, it is not difficult to imagine the ghost of Kafu, his slim figure shimmying over the oily water in trademark beret and horn-rimmed glasses. When he was alive the novelist was the unrivalled chronicler of the Tokyo *demi-monde*, a world that hardly exists now, but which can be strongly sensed from time to time by those familiar with the geography of his work.

Many of his perambulations around the old town were as much of a sexual nature as a literary one, although in Kafu's work the two pursuits intersected with remarkable success. If at times he saw himself as a gentleman scholar, it was the sort known as *bunjin*: intellectual but pleasure-seeking dilettantes accomplished, as Kafu was himself, in an assortment of minor arts that had flourished during the Edo period. It was a breed just as likely to be seen frequenting the gaggle of expensive teahouses at the mouth of the Kanda canal as the downtown *machiai*, or houses of assignation, for which certain parts of Tokyo were notorious.

Kafu generally preferred the company of women to that of men. For all its talk of progress and modernization, the Meiji Tokyo in which he was brought up was run almost exclusively by the male reformers, moralizers and meddlers whom Kafu saw as the worst despoilers of an older, more graceful city. What Kafu seems to have detested was the contemporary equation of civilization with modernization, much of it in the writer's view reckless. Even in his tirades against the architects of the new order, or the advent of the streetcar—a conveyance he nevertheless made liberal use of in his tireless explorations of Tokyo—Kafu was never a very stern moralizer. The main character of his story *Quiet Rain* is despondent that the young geisha he has set up in an elegant quarter of Akasaka is more interested in attending the movies in Asakusa or in meeting her friends at the Mitsukoshi department store than she is in perfecting her *shamisen* technique, and it is with sad but tolerant resignation that he laments that the younger generation "can read newspaper serials but not old novels" whose cursive styles are beyond them.

Kafu never uses the word "condemned" when referring to a house, building or district, but it hangs over most of his work. There is, in fact, barely an area of Tokyo left today that corresponds to his descriptions. A rapid process of decay, renewal and replacement must have been as much a part of Kafu's urban Tokyo as it is now. In *Coming Down with a Cold*, a short story published in 1912, the author describes the premises of the pleurisy-afflicted geisha Masukichi and her companion, a building that could hardly have been more than two or three decades old at the time, as "a third-rate brick tenement, a sort of relic, very shabby, of early Meiji". The opportunity to elegize a way of life, a condemned quarter of the old city or some fading custom or practice offered him a certain potential. Had the old city and all that went with it remained intact, it is doubtful that Kafu would have found quite the same muse that helped to make his name. "Buildings had to be decaying," Edward Seidensticker wrote, "cultures ill and dying, if not dead, before he could really like them."

Kafu knew the city at first hand having bought, rented or variously occupied premises in various locations from which he subsequently drew inspiration, such as Koishikawa, where he was born and raised, Yanagibashi and Asakusa. Some of these addresses found their way into the titles of his works, like *Azabu Miscellany* and *Commuting to Tsukiji*. Others, like Okubo, mused on at length in *Tidings from Okubo*, he was to temporarily abandon only to move back at a later stage. Many of Kafu's most delightful, random descriptions of out-of-the-way corners of Tokyo ("I feel quite satisfied if I can wander the streets aimlessly and scribble down whatever comes into my head," he wrote in his diary at the time) appear in his serendipitous 1915 collection of city vignettes entitled *Fair-Weather Geta*. Kafu was always keen to match human dramas with a physical location, a common enough technique among novelists, but in his case this characteristic is developed to an exceptional degree. It is this trait that has left us with highly vivid and detailed evocations of certain districts of Tokyo.

Kafu can always be relied on to sing the praises of places that give off a special aura, however sordid the milieu. He felt an affinity for the peculiar smells, sounds, and people that composed the texture and depraved Orientalism of New York's Chinatown during his year-long sojourn there. "I love Chinatown," he wrote in imitation of Baudelaire and other poets, mostly French: "It is a treasure trove of materials for *Les fleurs du mal*. I only fear that the so-called humanitarian charities may in the end sweep this special world from its corner of society."

Kafu underestimated the robustness of Tokyo's Low City tradition, and though the shadows cast across his beloved Sumida are more likely these days to come from office blocks and raised expressways than teahouses or the tenements of dissolute poets, the writer would recognize the essentials of present-day Asakusa. So too would Chokichi, the hero of his novel *The Sumida River*, who observes from the precincts of the great Sensoji temple "a moon... such as he would never see again." Sensoji is in many ways the spiritual centre of the area, its courtyards best approached after passing under the Kaminarimon or Thunder Gate, a weathered wooden entrance flanked by leering, twin meteorological gods and a magnificent red paper lantern with the character for "thunder" emblazoned across it. Asakusa has always been geared as much to the needs of the hedonist as to the incense-impregnated world of the priest and Buddhist acolyte. Just behind Sensoji, practically overlooking the little-visited abbot's garden, lies Asakusa's sprawling entertainment district. Lurid posters outside cinemas remind visitors of Kafu's novel observation in another work of fiction, *A Strange Tale from East of the River*, that "One can tell from the billboards what the general plots are, and what delights people so."

Kafu is often spoken of as the champion of Asakusa and similar entertainment districts, but from the publication in 1909 of his collection of short stories called *Bacchanals* a more critical writer emerges, one who, as Okazaki Yoshie has observed in his book *Japanese Literature in the Meiji Era*, "begins to express vehement resistance against the vulgar society which oppresses and destroys the aesthetic world." Despite the refined beauty and carefully crafted elegance intrinsic to the escapism many of Kafu's characters relish, the venality of teahouse owners, hired servants and the younger breed of new entertainers is faithfully recorded in order to hint at a more contemporary vulgarity. Here is the spectacle of the floating world transforming itself into a common flesh market where profit margins, account books and debit lists are displayed just as they would be in any run-of-the-mill business.

Kafu's Ginza, despite its veneer of a western shopping mall with its cafés, Italian restaurants and department buildings, is quite different from the one we know today. Kafu tells his contemporary readers (many would already have known as much), that most of the young women working in its European-style cafés, are prostitutes posing as waitresses. On the way to work in one of these cafés, pretentiously named the Don Juan, Kimie, the main character of his 1931 novella *During the Rains*, passes along an alley "just barely wide enough to let one person through." The alley is lined with enormous garbage cans, and "Even in the dead of winter bluebottles buzzed about, and at high noon ancient rats the size of weasels went about their business at will. When someone approached, they would splash up water from the puddle with their long tails."

Although Kafu spent frequent evenings in the company of Ginza waitresses, his writings express a preference for the more refined though increasingly embattled traditions of the nearby Shimbashi pleasure quarter. Here, all along the streets and alleys where geisha houses stood, fires burned in braziers outside entrances and lanterns were hung to greet the spirits of the dead during the O-bon, or All Souls Night festival, a sight that even in 1918, when Kafu's *Geisha in Rivalry* was published, seemed more reminiscent of a former age: "Somehow in this new world of telephones and electric lights," the narrator remarks, "the smoke of the welcome fires burning in front of the houses seemed out of place, and it gave things a pensive air." The Shimbashi pleasure quarter, the setting for *Geisha in Rivalry*, was, as Harry Guest has written, like the Yoshiwara, a "shadow-world of prostitution, shown to be symbiotic with that of the theater, recalling the prints of Utamaro and other great depicters of the Floating World."

Linking the disparate elements of the quarters Kafu favoured were the city's rivers and canals. Tokyo's waterways were already in a sorry state by the time he began writing about them. While paying tribute to them on the one hand, Kafu can be disarmingly realistic. The back canals of Tamanoi, the setting for much of *A Strange Tale from East of the River*, were no sweeter in Kafu's day than now. Their waters, tainted by industrial filth, provided the writer with just the right ambiance in which to suspend, momentarily, the flow of time: "the foulness of the canal, and the humming of the mosquitoes—all of these stirred me deeply, and called up visions of a past now dead some thirty or forty years." In the search for lost essence, O-Yuki, the prostitute in this tale of loss and fleeting retrieval, is "a skilful yet inarticulate artist with the power to summon the past." Though fictive, O-Yuki is almost certainly based on women the writer met in the quarter.

Not everything that Kafu wrote about in the Sumida area has vanished. The old boathouses and white-walled storehouses have long gone, but several of the canals are still there. Yanagibashi (the Willow Bridge) remains; so too does one of Kafu's old watering holes, the Kamiya Bar, on a street corner near the Azuma Bridge.

If Kafu's writings are about loss, they are also about discovery. In *The Sneer*, a serial he wrote for the *Asahi* newspaper between 1909 and 1910, he has his main character walking through Shiba Park, an area that has since been cleared away to make room for, among other things, Tokyo Tower, and stumbling for the first time on the mortuary shrines of the shoguns. The character's astonishment is genuine as he discovers that "in a corner of the vulgar, ugly, accursed city a place yet reserved for art, it was as if he had unearthed Pompeii." This sensation of coming across a thing of improbable beauty among the mediocrity of modern Tokyo is an experience as familiar in its own way to those who live in or explore the city now as it was to Kafu.

Kafu's reflections on the vestiges of an older Tokyo never succeeded in preserving any of the areas he wrote about, nor did his beautifully lyrical and analytical musings on women ever win him an enduring relationship. He was married twice, each time a failure due, most of his biographers and commentators concur, to his promiscuity, although we might give him the benefit of the doubt as a writer and put his divorces and countless affairs down to his insatiable curiosity about the life of females rather than to compulsive lust.

Kafu's opus is not a difficult one to read. His interest in the art and literature of the past and the social customs that had survived in many of the out-of-way corners of Tokyo never, to quote American scholar and translator Donald Keene, "penetrated very deeply because it was the surface, rather than the essence, that attracted him." Kafu has often been criticized for paying too much attention to location and neglecting character. The long and detailed descriptions of geisha houses, gardens, the merits of a certain kimono pattern and the changing seasons we find in his work, easily construed as digressions by western readers, are as important as the characters who inhabit his novels and stories. To some extent, they are the main characters.

"I have from time to time," the narrator of *A Strange Tale from East of the River* (Kafu's alter ego in a confessional frame of mind) tells us, "fallen into the error of emphasizing background at the expense of characterization." It is a literary shortcoming we can be very thankful for. Departing from Japan in the spring of 1955, Keene recorded that "On the plane I read Nagai Kafu's *Sumidagawa* (The River Sumida). I found that I was weeping, not because of the story but because of the beauty of the Japanese language and the evocations of the country I was leaving."

TANIZAKI'S NAOMI

Tanizaki Junichiro, arguably the finest Japanese novelist of his century, stood somewhat apart from the mainstream. Human desire and the primacy of the imagination were the focus for much of his work. Kafu and Tanizaki were equally preoccupied with women, but where Kafu's male characters earn the favours of women through patronage and longing, Tanizaki's gain their attention through humiliating episodes of erotic subjugation. The willing self-debasement of men in the cause of feminine beauty was one of Takizaki's central themes, but so was the by-now painfully manifest conflict between East and West. For Tanizaki, sex often stood as a metaphor for culture. Infatuated in his youth by western modernity and materialism, as he approached middle age he began to reassess the merits of traditional Japan, to retreat into the recent past. The clash between East and West, the domestic and the imported, is the main theme of his novel *Some Prefer Nettles*. But even here a degree of ambivalence lingers, as the narrator of the story, recalling a childhood oppressed by the "crassness of the merchant class" and the inability to "escape the scent of the market-place", observes:

He had grown up in the merchants' section of Tokyo before the earthquake destroyed it, and the thought of it could fill him with the keenest nostalgia; but the very fact that he was a child of the merchants' quarter made him especially sensitive to its inadequacies, to its vulgarity and its preoccupation with the material.

Embodying the cultural ambiguity of the "Modern Girl" (see below) was the heroine of Tanizaki's novel *A Fool's Love*. In this story, which both excited and disturbed readers, a young engineer, obsessed by the maturing body and sexuality of his child bride, is both gratified and bewildered. Naomi's overpowering desire, encouraged by her husband who compares her to screen idols of the day such as Mary Pickford and Gloria Swanson, is to look and act like a westerner. Bold and sexually subversive, her dabbling in cross-dressing and final entry into genteel ballroom society challenges existing class distinctions, gender and cultural practice. As Naomi's polymorphous persona, promiscuity and appearance are modified to fit a western lifestyle, her husband instinctively reverts to Japanese tastes and traditions of family and marriage. In the final scenes of the power play between the couple, Naomi has acquired the affectations of male speech while her husband, now thoroughly acquiescent to whatever demands she might make of him, adopts an increasingly infantilized mode of speech, a telling effect rather lost in translation.

A character like Naomi would have been inconceivable in the less tolerant Meiji era of just a few years before. The break with the past and a short-lived but very real permissiveness infused every aspect of the city. The period even saw a limited form of parliamentary democracy, with the first government cabinets drawn from political parties. Radical politics mixed with artistic experimentation to a degree not seen before. Cubism, Expressionism, Dada and Constructivism were explored. This was the day of the so-called "I-novel", realistic literary diaries painstakingly recording every detail and sensation of a character's life and mood changes. The final years of Taisho witnessed a blossoming of movements for various causes. There were campaigns for the liberation of outcast groups like the *burakumin*, a universal suffrage movement and a women's rights movement.

Greater pluralism translated into an increase in personal freedoms and a taste for frivolities and fads: dancing to jazz, staying up until all hours, drinking alcohol. The lyrics of one song, "Tokyo March", may have been trite in their requisitioning of neologisms like *jazu* (jazz) and *rikyuru* (liquor), but they capture the flavour of the times, the willingness to dabble and experiment. This was not entirely new. Even the Meiji period, stern in many ways, was not without its frivolities. Lafcadio Hearn noted the appearance in 1898 of a new variety of cigarette that, fitted with a paper mouthpiece, would produce a chemical reaction when lit, resulting in a photo perfect image of a dancing girl.

ASAKUSA: THE NEW HEDONISM

If you wanted to meet a real dancing girl, Asakusa was the place to go. The quarter provided a playground for the most intense sampling of the sensual, visual and gastronomic pleasures of the city. Asakusa Park had expanded in the Meiji era to include gardens, two ornamental lakes with roped walkways and a miniature Mount Fuji, the ascent of which could be made for a small fee. In 1903 the city's first cinema, the Electric Hall, opened. The theatres, street fairs, open-air sumo wrestling displays, women acrobats, archery galleries and cinemas that had sprung up just a block or two away from the Senso-ji temple had an immediate transforming effect on the area, drawing mass audiences to the district. While most people embraced the changes, some writers, like the playwright and novelist Kubota Mantaro, had their doubts. A native, he watched the effects wrought on his beloved Asakusa by the arrival of cinema with something like horror:

> It swept away all else, and took control of the park. The life of the place, the colour, quite changed. The "new tide" was violent and relentless. In the districts along the western ditch, by the Koryuji Temple, somnolence had reigned. It quite departed. The old shops, dealers in tools and scrap and rags, the hair dresser's and the bodkin and bangle places— they all went away, as did the water in the ditch. New shops put up their brazen signs: Western restaurants, beef and horse places, short-order places, milk parlours.

A shift towards brasher tastes and newer forms of entertainment could be seen everywhere one looked. Epitomizing the changes was the Hanayashiki (Flower Residence), a former aristocratic mansion to the west of the temple. The creation of landscape designer Morita Rokusaburo, the

Nakamise, the approach street to the Asakusa Kannon Temple

gardens were opened in 1853 in a part of the Asakusa Rokku district set aside for entertainment. Up to the first years of the Meiji period, the public enjoyed visiting the gardens at different seasons to admire flowering trees: late winter plum, spring cherries, camellias and autumn chrysanthemums. Haiku and *tanka* poets held parties there. By 1872 ersatz features began to appear in the garden: a small zoo with a real tiger and elephant, a merry-go-round and life-size dolls of the type that could be found during the Edo period in the requisitioned spaces near the city's river bridges. This was the same year that the prohibition on women climbing Mount Fuji was lifted. The garden provided a combination of amusement and religious pilgrimage for those who, for reasons of health or economic constraints, were not able to scale the real thing. The replica of the mountain erected in the park in 1887 was an instant success. Built of wood, covered with lime and painted an earthen colour, it rose to a height of a hundred feet. A woodblock print by Utagawa Yoshimori shows climbers following a spiral path to the summit, where telescopes were available to look at the real mountain. Funds from the ticket sales went towards restoration work on Senso-ji's five-storey pagoda, burnt in another of the city's fires.

By the Taisho era, any traces of the original gardens had, like the people of refined taste who originally visited them, totally disappeared, replaced by an amusement park. Tanizaki mentions the park in his unfinished novel *Mermaid*, giving us another view of Asakusa as it was in 1918: "... the Hanayashikki Amusement Park, the Twelve-Storey Tower, shooting galleries, whores, Japanese restaurants, Chinese restaurants and Western restaurants—the Rairaiken (a Chinese eatery), won ton, chow mien, oysters over rice, horsemeat, snapping turtles, eels, and the Cafe Paulista."

Asakusa spun like a kaleidoscopic orb, not always in the best of taste but guaranteed to dazzle. For Tanizaki it was a place that had everything. Two years later he was still singing the praises of the district with its intermingling of "innumerable classes of visitor and types of entertainment, and its constant and peerless richness preserved even as it furiously changes." The crowds and distractions, the sexually charged air enjoyed by both men and women, the nearby river lit by ferries and barges and the bustling pedestrian streets created a night scene akin to a Venetian masquerade. A character in another of Tanizaki's works, a short story entitled *The Secret*, suggests the possibilities of Asakusa at the dawn of the Taisho period, as it symbolizes the shift in the urban milieu from conservative social strictures to transgressive hedonism:

> Changing my costume every night so as not to be noticed, I plunged into the crowd in Asakusa Park... I enjoyed using a false beard, a mole, or a birthmark to alter my features. But one night, at a second-hand clothing shop... I saw a woman's lined kimono with a delicate check pattern against a blue ground, and was seized with a desire to try it on.

Hollywood was also a part of the Asakusa mix, with the faces of Claudette Colbert, Douglas Fairbanks and Lionel Barrymore hanging alongside huge billboards depicting samurai dramas with popular Japanese actors. Even the Marx Brothers had a place of honour in Asakusa, though a later film, *Duck Soup*, when it was released, was changed to *I Am a Duck*, an appropriation of Soseki Natsume's popular novel, *I Am a Cat*. There was a resurgent Japanese cinema too, and in Asakusa customers might have enjoyed a screening of "Thomas" Kurihara's *The Lasciviousness of the Viper*, or the Expressionist *A Page Out of Order*, for which Kawabata Yasunari wrote the screenplay. Audiences generally got value for their money. Reciters known as *benshi*, stars in their own right, provided the dialogue and provided embellished commentary on the action in the silent films, taking on both male and female parts. Some Asakusa picture houses even provided special effects, such as burning incense in the pits during funeral scenes.

The area was, and remains, the home of *Taishu Engeki*, a very shita-machi brand of popular theatre. A ticket for these low-brow dramas, full of the verve and earthy humour associated with this area, costs little even today. The cramped and intimate playhouses in which they are staged provide the explanation for the cost. Strong plots are the order of the day, and audiences, equipped with boxed lunches and cans of beer, attend per-formance that re-enact the destinies of star-crossed lovers, double suicides and tales of massively bloody vengeance. Appreciation is shown from the gallery by tossing money onto the stage.

GINZA CHIC

A tram ride to the south of Asakusa took you straight to the Ginza, its rival for the attentions of the public and another Tokyo zone that epito-mized the era. Tokyo's first subway opened in 1927, connecting Asakusa and Ueno. The mood along the Ginza had changed considerably since the final rather oppressive years of Meiji. Flapper girls in bobbed hairdos and Eton crops strolled under the willow trees of the boulevard in the company of foppish, lank-haired young men sporting bell-bottom trousers and round spectacles (*roido* eyeglasses) in imitation of the silent film actor Harold Lloyd.

Popular culture was personified in the newly confident image of the "Modern Boy" and "Modern Girl", abbreviated in spoken parlance to *mobo* and *moga*. The typical mobo was an office worker or student who af-fected to read the more serious western novels or, even more in tune with the radical chic of the day, Marxist literature. Long hair and western clothes were *de rigueur*. The tastes of his counterpart, the moga, were similar, though much to the distress of any relatives she might have in the countryside, she cut her hair short in a fashionable crop or spit-curl, or more stylishly had her hair shaped into a Marcel wave. The painter Kishida Ryusei commented on the physical transformation of the Modern Girl, aided by the new hair salons, fashion stores and cosmetic parlours, differ-

The Ginza Line, Tokyo's first subway

entiating her from her Meiji-era counterpart, in a series published in 1927 for the evening edition of the newspaper *Tokyo Hibi Shinbun*: "The face is that of a Japanese, but it is one which skilfully endorses western-style beauty. It is certainly not something translated nor futilely imitated, as in the Europeanization of just one period before..." While the dancing, smooching and smoking of the young habitués of Tokyo café society was a clear imitation of the practices spawned by the Jazz Age in America and Europe, there were other more local influences. Working in one of the new occupations created by a modern, expanding city, the literate urban young were able to enjoy an unheard of degree of economic independence.

The best place to spot the moga was the Ginza, which by the mid-1920s was Tokyo's indisputable fashion centre. When they could afford to, these shocking symbols of the new age frequented cafés, cinemas and theatres. If the Modern Girl was emblematic of a new style of female eroticism obsessively covered by the press, males became besotted with the Ginza waitress, a figure closely identified with the new promiscuity. Parisian-style cafés and German beer halls, frequented by writers and journalists, sprang up, their clientele representing the worlds of entertainment and the mass media. Cafés had been a feature of the new Tokyo for several decades. The first modern-style café, opened in 1888, was probably the two-storey Ka-hi Chakan in Shitaya. The famous Café Paulista and the Café Plantan, another favourite among writers and artists, soon followed. Ordinary coffee was priced at a half-sen, *café-au-lait* cost two sen. Customers could avail themselves of books, magazines and even billiards. Later cafés, like the Maison Konosu, which opened in the Koami-cho district in 1910, attracted a more literary set. A year later, the painter Matsuyama Shozo opened the stylish Café Printemps in Kyobashi. Its strong roasted coffee and salon-type interior attracted writers, artists and intellectuals, creating the kind of meeting place for creative people that is sadly wanting in contemporary Tokyo.

The Taisho café bore some resemblance to the Edo-period teahouse. The waitresses who worked in such places as the Lion Café were known, for a modest inducement, to be free with their favours. Kafu, always alert to the decadence mingled with longing that characterizes so much of his work, was a regular at the Ginza cafés and tea rooms, where the girls were as much a part of the attraction as the mugs of coffee and azuki bean cakes. On the topic of the Ginza waitresses, Kafu tells us that:

> Suddenly, from about the early twenties, they came into vogue and they held sway over the world, and along with movie actresses, took away the popularity of stage actresses. Today, however, a decade after the earthquake, the vogue of the café girls would seem to be passing. And their passing is the reason for my *During the Rains*.

More accessible to people like students and housewives were the milk halls of the 1910s and 1920s, where newspapers and magazines were provided at moderate prices along with mug-sized cups of coffee. As cafés competed with each other for customers, special features and novelties were introduced. The 1920s saw the emergence of *meikyoku kissaten* (music coffee shops), where male customers could listen to classical music in the company of young women. Other cafés underwent more extreme commercial alchemy in the search for a theme that often turned the ordinary into the erotic, foreshadowing the popular no-panties *kissaten* of the 1970s and 1980s, and the "maid" and "butler" cafés of today's Akihabara dis-

Frank Lloyd Wright's 1923 Imperial Hotel

trict, with their echoes of the old teahouse promiscuities of Edo. Certain types of nightclubs and dance halls provided taxi dancers for the benefit of single men.

Despite the self-conscious modernity, Tokyo was more of an Asian city in those days, with peddlers, mendicants and petitioners from esoteric religious sects entering cafés and circulating among the tables in a way that would be inconceivable today. In his later 1934 novel *The Eight Ginza Blocks*, Takeda Rintaro describes the scene as the door of a café opens:

> Everyone would look up in anticipation of a customer; but always there would be, and in considerable numbers, children selling flowers, and imitators of famous actors and singers, and mendicant priests with boxes inviting contributions to the Church of Light and Darkness, and violinists, and sketchers of likenesses, and lutists, and solemn-faced young men in student uniform selling pills and potions, and, with babies tied to their backs, women selling horoscopes.

Just around the corner in Hibiya, where Frank Lloyd Wright's Imperial Hotel stood, guests could take afternoon tea and munch on "Chaplin caramels".

BATHING IN THE RIVER

The intellectual and social vitality of the 1920s contrasting with the repressive climate of the late 1930s and early 1940s, the brevity of the Taisho experimentation represents a very real search for cultural identity, one that witnessed the advance of the women's movement, the growth of unions and the brief flowering of Taisho democracy. Sadly, innovations in style and design together with the mood of liberalism embraced by the cultured and wealthy, the two groups best placed to appreciate the changes, were not strong enough to resist the advance of freedom-crushing militarists. The aspirations of the era were real enough, but no match for insistent militarism. As for the "new woman", the champion of universal suffrage, she would have to go underground for a good two decades before re-emerging from the rubble of defeat.

The breakdown of social norms common under a dissolute leader had turned out to be little more than temporary. As the shadows of militarism lengthened, the fashions and tastes of a more liberal and generous age were increasingly viewed as subversive. With the military back at the helm and the new, more acquiescent Emperor Hirohito in situ from 1926, Japan reverted to a controlled society. Generals and officers were the new arbiters of taste, a fact evident even in art circles. By the late 1930s art institutions, bodies that set up and sat on their own selection committees, were reorganized to exert more state control over the art world.

Away from the political currents that were soon to wash over everyone, an older city, closer to nature and with gentler graces was still able to stir the imagination. Architect Maki Fumihiko grew up in the Tokyo of the 1930s and recalls a city where nature could still breathe fresh life into the streets:

> In the *yamanote*, or "upper town," where I lived, streets were often shadowed by big trees and were dark in the evenings. Small streets and narrow alleys were unpaved. After it rained, the smell of the earth and vegetation permeated the air.

水の上の

Houseboat life along the Sumida river

Life in the low-lying eastern parts of Tokyo, along the Sumida and the canals that flowed into it, could still evoke nostalgia for a former more languid age. It was no longer advisable to bathe in the river—though some families living on boathouses still did—but it was common enough to scoop up river water in buckets to make a hot bath. In Fukagawa a number of illicit gambling dens were located in old barges that also served as bath-tubs, fuelled by wood salvaged from the river. The families of boatmen would come to such places for an evening soak. One account, told by a former gangland boss fallen on hard times, recalls the scene, the easy-going dalliances that defined relations between people in an age that, as the storm clouds gathered, would soon be little more than a memory:

> ... the women and children took their clothes off right in front of you before getting in. And they'd sit there soaking with their towels on their heads, watching the men play. It was summer, so the doors were left open, and you could see the moon reflected on the surface of the river.

Chapter Seven
A TIME OF CALAMITIES
1923-1945

In the book dealer district of Kanda, the hands of the clock at the meteorological tower stopped at precisely 11.58 am on 1 September 1923, remaining frozen in shock for several weeks to come. The city had been expecting the sound of the noonday canon, which ever since 1871 had been fired regularly at that time. Instead, the earth shook with a series of violent convulsions. We know from records of the one seismograph at Tokyo University to survive the earthquake that over the next three days more than seventeen hundred shocks pounded the city.

The earthquake, registering 7.9 on the Richter scale, struck as people were preparing lunch on gas burners and charcoal braziers; fires then raged for three continuous days. Precise figures are difficult to confirm, but at least 99,000 people were crushed and incinerated, while over ninety per cent of the downtown area and nearly 45 per cent of buildings in the Tokyo metropolitan area were razed in what quickly became known as "the Great Kanto Earthquake". Whirlwinds of fire, several hundred feet high in some cases, engulfed the city. Compounding the destruction caused by fire were conflagrations caused by chemicals and electric wires. To the east, in Fukagawa and Honjo, the hardest hit and most densely inhabited areas of the city, 35,000 people fleeing to a nearby park with their bedding and cooking utensils perished as the flames devoured their belongings. Those who jumped into the canals were consumed by boiling waters. One man, arriving at Eitai Bridge, discovered that

> ... the whole area on the other bank, for hundreds of yards from Nihonbashi on to Asakusa, was like a roaring furnace. Looking back, we saw a cart being blown high up into the air. Bits of houses and roofs were being sucked up into the whirlwind too and were dancing about in the sky like leaves. A horse that had gone crazy was galloping about the street and finally jumped into the river.

Among the singed walls, burnt out electrical wires, charred tin panels, dead horses and heaps of dust and ash were extraordinary sights. The film director Kurosawa Akira, then a schoolboy, was led through the carnage by his elder brother: "No corner of the landscape was free of corpses. In some places the piles of corpses formed little mountains. On top of one of these mountains sat a blackened body in the lotus position of Zen meditation." Others saw equally bizarre sights. In her memoir of the city, *My Map of Tokyo*, Sata Ineko describes refugees walking along the tracks of the Keisei railway line:

> A man carried on his back the limp form of an injured Kabuki actor still wearing the red costuming of a young maiden. Hideously, the white makeup that thickly coated his face as it lay against the shoulder of the man bearing him had now taken on the appearance of a mask, suggesting that he had already breathed his last. The heavy hem of the red maiden costume was tucked up, exposing a man's slender legs, which dangled limply beneath it.

Elsewhere, builders in charge of restoring parts of the original Edo castle, where stones had been loosened in the quake, discovered the skeletons of men standing erect inside the walls, evidence of an ancient custom in which people were buried alive inside the foundations of bridges, river embankments and fortresses, in the belief that they would strengthen the buildings. These men, known as *hito bashira* ("pillar men"), were more often than not volunteers.

As shock turned to panic, wild rumours spread through the ruined city. A story concerning the existence of an earthquake-making machine, devised by a western country for the purposes of experimenting on Japan, began to circulate in the afternoon of the first day. While there were no incidents of violence against westerners, more lethal rumours developed during the ensuing chaos that Koreans were poisoning wells. These stories were exploited by the police, who authorized radio broadcasts warning that Koreans were burning down houses, murdering inhabitants and looting. The broadcasts urged people to "use all necessary measures" to protect themselves. The rumours were groundless, but civilian vigilantes and army reservists took to the streets, massacring thousands of Koreans before the bloodletting stopped. The police took advantage of an emer-

Asakusa's brick-built Twelve Storey Tower after the earthquake

gency ordinance and the climate of fear and disorder they had helped to foster by ordering the mass arrest of individuals marked down as socialists, political dissidents and radicals. Pandering to the murderous rage of some of the survivors, they encouraged the mobs to seek out anarchists, polemicists and social activists. Among those beaten to death, boiled in drums of oil or drowned in the Sumida river were the trade union official, Hirasawa Keishichi, and Osugi Sakae and his wife Ito Noe, put to death by police officers in their prison cells. One young man of letters, Kikuchi Kan, expressed the prevailing mood of nihilism when he wrote, "I came to know that the religion which teaches that there is a Being in the Universe greater than human beings who protects and reprimands men, is all nonsense... The Great Earthquake was, as a result, a social revolution. Property, status, and tradition utterly collapsed."

As the winds got up, the corpses of victims tossed from the upper floors of the twelve-storey Ryounkaku bobbed eerily in the shallow water of the Gourd Pond in Asakusa Park. Kawabata Yasunari was in the district within hours of the earthquake to inspect the damage. The reinforced steel frame and girders of the brick tower held up moderately well, with the first eight of the original floors left intact, but the top storeys had collapsed into the nearby pond. Army engineers dynamited the remains the following year.

Hundreds of geisha and prostitutes from the nearby Yoshiwara were burnt alive. Those who survived thronged the grounds of the Senso-ji temple, where the novelist found them flowing in "like a disordered field of flowers". The writer Akutagawa Ryunosuke, whose interest in the ghoulish was well known, accompanied Kawabata on a walk through the Yoshiwara, an event recorded in an essay published in 1929:

> The pond beside the Yoshiwara quarter was one of those horrible pictures of hell, which speak only to someone who has seen the real thing. The reader should imagine tens and hundreds of men and women as if boiled in a cauldron of mud. Muddy red cloth was strewn all up and down the banks, for most of the corpses were of courtesans. Smoke was rising from incense along the banks. Akutagawa stood with a handkerchief over his face.

According to Edward Seidensticker, who quotes from the article above

Tokyo devastated in the Great Kanto Earthquake

in his book *Tokyo Rising*: "The Taisho era needed a literary symbol, and Akutagawa was a good one, embodying (or so it is widely held) the sometimes neurotic refinement and intellectualism that were products of the great Meiji endeavor to encompass and catch up with the West. The common view has therefore been that his suicide, more than the death of the emperor, brought an end to an era."

His suicide, according to another account, had been foretold by the prostitutes of Tamanoi who, turning pale as they watched the tall, thin figure passing along their narrow lanes, had whispered to each other: "A ghost, a ghost!"

To everyone's wonder, the great Senso-ji, or Asakusa Kannon temple, where Kawabata and Akutagawa had walked, remained intact. According to local residents, its miraculous survival was due less to divine intervention than the ministrations of a statue in its grounds of the Meiji-era Kabuki actor Danjuro. Dressed in his role as the hero of the play *Shibaraku* ("Just a Moment, Please"), locals were convinced that he alone held back the advancing flames.

Frank Lloyd Wright's just completed Imperial Hotel survived less by miracle than method. The design was based on a system of foundations that would "float" on pilings just below the earth's stratum, preventing shocks from being directly transmitted into the building. It was not a totally original concept; there were other, older buildings in the city that had already applied the technique, and several of these also survived. Nor was the building as intact as some people have claimed. When the quake hit, the floor of the banquet hall dropped by two feet. Built near the site of the old Rokumeikan, with a lotus pond facing the main entrance, the hotel, though open to anyone who could afford it, had a similar cachet. Not everyone was enamoured of the building, though. The English writer Peter Quennell refused to join the chorus of praise, describing the structure, "built by an eccentric American architect," as a "queer façade, its pretentious squat asymmetry recalls a modernist chest-of-drawers in stone and brick, the stone used being of a repellently porous type, pocked with large holes like a Gruyere cheese."

In the ensuing crisis all government ministers resigned. A former Tokyo mayor, Count Goto, was charged with the task of overseeing the reconstruction of the city. The count immediately cabled an old acquaintance, Charles A. Beard, an American civil administrator and one time advisor to New York City:

EARTHQUAKE FIRE DESTROYED GREATER PART OF TOKYO. THOROUGHGOING RECONSTRUCTION NEEDED. PLEASE COME IMMEDIATELY, IF POSSIBLE, EVEN FOR SHORT TIME.

Beard's reply was equally swift:

LAY OUT NEW STREETS, FORBID BUILDING WITHOUT STREET-LINES, UNIFY RAILWAY STATIONS.

Beard rushed to Tokyo, where he acted as advisor to the reconstruction programme. Survivors of the earthquake were eager to begin the rebuilding of the "pride of civilization", as Tokyo had come to be referred to. Perhaps with the memory of the 1905 San Francisco disaster still within living memory, large sums of money were raised in the United States and sent to Tokyo's stricken citizens, along with food and clothing.

With the idea of the retributive catfish still lingering, the quake was widely interpreted as an expression of "the fury of the earth", divine punishment for the excessive materialism of the age. Mindful of the corrupt officials, profiteers and privileged elite who seemed to be assuming control of the city, one artist, the cartoonist Kitazawa Rakuten, depicted the spectral catfish on the front cover of the magazine *Jiji Manga* (Cartoons of contemporary events), the creature exclaiming, "Shall I shake them up one more time to really open their eyes?"

From the physical destruction and psychological trauma came a period of reflection and, eventually, renewal. Cataclysms in Japan, natural and human, have often resulted in surges of creative activity. Like fires, earthquakes, however terrifying, have traditionally been thought of as transformative, even numinous events. Woodblock images produced after the 1855 Edo earthquake also feature the giant, retributive catfish. Living beneath the surface of Japan, the creature was believed to stir, moving its tail and causing tremors at times of spiritual, moral or social crisis. A harbinger of material and human destruction, it was also an indicator of the need for spiritual transfusion, a liberating signal containing within the immediate calamities a promise of renewal.

Tanizaki Junichiro was in the mountains of Hakone south-west of Tokyo when the quake struck. Though fearing for his family left behind in Yokohama, he wrote: "Almost simultaneously I felt a surge of happiness which I could not keep down. 'Tokyo will be better for this!' I said to myself." Even Tanizaki's prediction that the city would be rebuilt within ten years proved an underestimate. Tokyo's reconstruction and recovery was complete in an astonishing seven years. Nobody, however, could have anticipated that its disaster-proof zones, new parks and generously proportioned streets would be inadequate for the populace that soon poured into the capital. And Tanizaki's vision of "an orderly pattern of streets, their bright new pavements gleaming... The geometric beauty of block towering upon block" was not to be.

No sooner had the ashes from the fires cooled than the reconstruction was underway. Tokyo and the city of Edo before it had experienced similar cycles of destruction followed by urban renewal. Department stores set up open markets, and street stalls appeared in places like Asakusa and the Ginza. There was even a popular ditty, *The Reconstruction Song*, to raise the spirits:

Completely burned out. But look:
The son of Edo has not lost his spirit.
So soon, these rows and rows of barracks,
And we can view the moon from our beds.

The "barracks" referred to the prefabricated emergency housing that went up in the days after the disaster. Though the scale of the earthquake was unparalleled, stocks of lumber floating in canals to the east of the Sumida were kept in readiness for circumstances like this. The reconstruction of Tokyo also acted, ironically, as an impetus to popular culture, provisioning the city with cafés, bars and other places of entertainment and refined leisure where the new, conspicuously modern generation could gather.

The turmoil was vividly depicted in a series of fourteen colour lithographs created by Ishikawa Shoten just one month after the disaster. The set, showing fleeing refugees, blackened buildings and people sucked into the air by cyclone-like fire twisters, was entitled a *Pictorial Account of the Great Tokyo Earthquake*. Prints, commemorative postcards and photographic collections marking the disaster and evoking the spectacle of poetic ruin were sold. The idea of the commercial postcard as documentary was a well established form in Japan. Photographers recorded new western-style buildings, trade exhibitions, railway stations, bridges, hotels, and families living on boats along the Sumida. Documenting the earthquake required a more forensic approach. It is still possible to come across postcards showing harrowing images of bodies floating in canals and ditches, or heaped into mounds that resemble Hindu funeral pyres.

The catastrophe was the subject of several songbooks. Collections like *Songs of the Great Earthquake* were written and performed by *enkashi*, songwriters who took their material onto the streets. In Japanese costumes topped with a bowler hat, the enkashi, accompanying themselves on violin, may have looked like gypsy minstrels, but their lyrical range and scope was strongly populist. Mixing music, illustration, news and political commentary, the songbooks were a new medium, offering an interesting window onto Taisho popular culture. When the title number from *Songs of the Great Earthquake* was first performed on the streets of Nippori, a traditional quarter of the city, the enkashi Soeda Tomomichi gathered a large crowd of people. In the song the earthquake, the ensuing fires and the struggles of victims to escape death are compared to Shura, the Buddhist hell.

Though shocked at the murder of leftist supporters and friends, members of the radical magazine *Mavo* responded to the devastation of Tokyo with creative verve. One of their most visible acts was the decorating of barracks, the prefabricated structures put up in the days after the quake to house the homeless. Much of this barrack design consisted of so-called *kanban kenchiku* ("signboard architecture") in which surfaces were painted and advertising boards for businesses created. Photographs of the two-storey Hayashi Restaurant in Hibiya show a highly expressive abstract façade that aspires to the level of public sculpture.

Murayama Tomoyoshi was the central figure among the avant-garde artists who ran the magazine. Newly arrived from Europe, where he had been exposed to Surrealism, Futurism and Cubism, it was the work of the German Expressionists that most influenced him. In the same year that Paul Morand's strenuously modern *Ouvert la nuit* was translated into Japanese, members of the Mavo committee declared their own intention of "denying things antique and inverting values."

Whatever traces of Edo persisted before the quake, including eastern sections of the city where much of Edo culture had sprung from, were almost totally obliterated in the quake. Another effect of the earthquake was the first diaspora of people moving from the Low City to western Tokyo and other districts deemed safer and more comfortable.

For some, the passing of an age and its physical attributes was too much to bear. The Taisho period still had a few more good years left, but the terrors of the earthquake had reminded people once again that nothing was assured. As a consequence of losing its past, Tokyo would henceforth become a city almost entirely fixated on the present.

Scarlet Gang of Asakusa

Soon after the earthquake, Kawabata stepped into the editor's seat of a new Tokyo magazine called *Bungei Jidai* (The Age of Literary Arts). Kawabata's exalted aim of re-examining the human condition prompted leading critics of the day to dub his group of like-minded artists the New Perception School. He would later abandon the group and found another one, the New Art School, which brought out a very capital-centric collection of stories and urban sketches entitled *Modern Tokyo Rondo*.

In Kawabata's younger days Asakusa was held to be the apogee of everything new, "a foundry in which all the old models are regularly melted down to be cast into new ones." Writers believed that the complexity of urban life, especially in Tokyo, could best be understood by revealing its multiform erotic and grotesque aspects. The first erotic revues were performed here as early as 1929, when the Casino Follies, on the second floor of an aquarium and next door to a museum with an extensive display of insects, put on a production typical of the *ero-guro-nansunsu* tastes that characterized the age. Kawabata described how the "girls of the Casino Follies passed the fishes in their tanks and turned in by a model of the sea king's palace to go to their dressing rooms," passing by "dusty cases of flies, beetles, butterflies, and bees" to get there.

Kafu enjoyed lurking in these dressing areas, the green rooms of the cabarets and revues where, as a famous writer and connoisseur of the *demimonde*, he was well received. The best-known artists of a former age like Utamaru and Saikaku, having an entrée to the interior life of the pleasure quarters and teahouses, could portray their subjects in persuasive detail. Kafu, with a similar pass to the back stages of popular Asakusa entertainments and the dressing rooms of the Shimbashi geisha, could observe the characters of this modern floating world at close quarters.

Asakusa's cultural mix—the fact that there was no perceived contradiction in patronizing the operetta, a sword fight play or one of the bawdy vaudeville stages—made it possible for the literati, and anyone else who felt like it, to imagine themselves temporarily *déclassé*. The variety shows spawned fashions like pencilled eyebrows, sailor suits and the Eton crops that resurfaced on the street. Along with the cosmopolitan mix of fashions, imported films and foreign-style variety shows were White Russians giving revue exhibitions, dancers from Finland performing at the Teikyo Theatre, Chinese acrobats and a never-to-be-heard-of-again American woman who, dressed like a seagull, jumped from a hundred-foot ladder into a small pond.

Women were highly visible in entertainment and shopping zones like Asakusa and Ginza, working in bars, coffee shops, go parlours, shooting galleries and the like, often offering services that exceeded their job descriptions. The great crowds in Asakusa attracted evangelists, anarchists, representatives of the workers' movements and unions, besides a good number of shady characters. Behind the glittering amusement centres were slum quarters where at night, as the lights went on in the dance halls and the plebeian opera houses, squalid hovels could be made out in the darkness.

Kawabata sought to create a modernist novel by merging the literary, vernacular and reportage in his hastily-written serialized work *The Scarlet Gang of Asakusa*. This not altogether successful experiment in the synthesis of forms resulted in something like a newsreel scrapbook compilation. It does, however, capture the breathless, freebooting mood of the times, the fondness for free association, dissonance and borrowed surrealism that was an element in the new avant-garde Japanese film that Kawabata was linked to, having written the scenario for Kinugasa Teisuke's deeply disturbing silent motion picture, *A Page Out of Order*, set in an insane asylum. The serialization of Kawabata's novel in the *Tokyo Asahi* daily paper, following the publication in the same slot of radical Marxist Hayashi Fusao's *City Hyperbola*, was typical of a practice followed by new and more established writers that had begun in the late nineteenth century, and continues to this day.

The young writer saw Asakusa, where he briefly lodged, as a more extravagant and lurid heir to all the pleasure quarters and resorts of the Edo age, where

> … the over-ripeness of the present era of capitalist corruption are thrown together in a forever disordered state. Or organized in a manner peculiarly like the place itself. Eroticism and frivolity and speed and comic-strip humour; the bare legs of dancing girls and jazzy reviews… Here the girls bob their hair and "bobbed-hair" so-and-so, wearing a red dress, plays the piano, deep in a narrow backstreet lane, with her knees exposed. Her rendezvous notes are scribbled on the back of the Goddess Kannon's written oracles.

Despite the lively patronage, Asakusa in the 1930s had more pawnshops and beggars than anywhere else in the capital. Kawabata maintained that the official figure of 800 homeless people sleeping in Asakusa Park was a gross underestimate. Exploring the grid of human existence in the early Showa-period capital, Takeda Rintaro's novels ignored the Jazz Age excesses of Asakusa, highlighting instead the squalor and penury that stood in contrast to the modern buildings and optimism of Tokyo. Starting as a socialist publishing proletarian novels, he turned his attention in what he called his "town stories", to the living conditions and social customs of real people living in the three-storey wooden apartments of Asakusa, or in the back lanes of Suzaki and Fukagawa that he and other novelists like him scoured for material.

THE DARK CORRIDOR

If the 1920s seemed to lean towards the left, the decade of the 1930s reoriented itself to the right. Idealistic civilians and young officers formed new organizations with ominous names like the Blood Brotherhood and the Cherry Blossom Society; assassination groups made it their responsibility to remove politicians and industrialists they felt were enriching themselves at the expense of the nation.

A promising trend towards democratization was reversed as the military assumed a more dominant role in the affairs of the state. With the resurgence of militarism in the mid-1930s, the environment, whether in politics or the arts, became increasingly repressive. The economic depression, like the disasters that had followed the appearance of Perry's black ships and the Great Kanto Earthquake, seemed further proof to many that the deities were displeased, that the time had come for a return to the simpler, purer virtues of a different age.

It did look as if parliamentary democracy had a sporting chance during the early Taisho period. By the late 1920s, however, a series of laws aimed at suppressing political dissent saw party politicians speaking out in favour of crackdowns on not only the radical left, but social democrats. In the place of free speech and a healthy national debate came propaganda urging national unity and emperor worship. Any lingering hopes that "Taisho democracy" as an idea might still have a future were dashed.

A city that had been so in step with the times found itself at odds with a brisk new military rhythm. Military music gradually replaced jazz, and trumpet players who had blown their horns in Jazz Age ecstasy on the stages of Asakusa found the musical score changed, the trumpet replaced with the bugle. The marching songs of the new age went by names like "Military Spy Song" and "The Imperial Army Marches Off". If the songs that dominated the airwaves and dance halls of the early 1930s were Japanese recordings of hits like "Sing Me a Song of Araby" and "My Blue Heaven", by the latter part of the decade there were more edifying dirges

海軍大演習之壯觀

Japan prepares the hardware for war

like "The Bivouac Song" and "March of the Warships". Lovers of ballet were reduced to productions with titles like the "Decisive Aerial Warfare Suite".

The partygoers of Asakusa and Ginza might turn up their gramophone players a little higher when they returned home, but the jazz ditties failed to drown out the growing fear that the 1930s were turning into a decade of insurrection and political terror. By 1936 dance halls, revues and cafés were under surveillance. Even *rakugo*, never more than lightly scatological, attracted the attention of the Japan Arts and Culture League, a government body empowered with drawing up guidelines of acceptability even in the humble popular arts. Badgered into re-examining their stories, rakugo representatives keen to avoid the wrath of the authorities drew up a list of 53 stories that would be "voluntarily" dropped from their repertoires. A stone memorial to rakugo was erected by a group of "mourners" in the grounds of an Asakusa temple. After the war, rituals were conducted at the site to restore the 53 banned stories.

Escapist entertainment was still sought in the *ero-guru-nansensu* world of dance halls and all girl revues. Even the most literary magazines of the day provided temporary oblivion from the new realities. Filmmakers continued to test permissible limits, though under more constraints than before. Mizoguchi Kenji's 1929 *Tokyo March*, a leftist film that proved a box-office hit, spurred the director to make *Metropolitan Symphony* the same year. This film ran into more problems. On location in the shitamachi district of Fukagawa, the director, cast and crew spent much of their time avoiding the attentions of the police, who were already trying to ferret out dissidents. Mizoguchi's team resorted to dressing as labourers and concealing their cameras under workmen's clothes. The director had a similar experience when he took his crew to Tamanoi in 1931 to film *And Yet They Go On*. It was still possible as late as 1931 to explore themes of social inequality, as two films released in that year, Ozu Yasujiro's *I Was Born, But...* and Naruse Mikio's *Flunky, Work Hard*, proved. Both were set in the gritty Tokyo distict of Kamata. Tokyo cinemas were still able to offer escapist relief from the combined effects of the Depression and militarism. Comedies and erotic farces fitted the need for distraction. One of the decade's big hits was a Naruse film called *Uproar over the Aphrodisiac Dumpling*.

The Manchurian Incident of 1931 and the China War, which broke out in 1937, accelerated the suppression of personal freedoms in Japan, strengthened the government's hand and brought about tighter censorship. The Tokyo newsstands soon began to offer a predictable diet of nationalist rhetoric. Women's magazines celebrated the war effort, running profiles of war widows, battlefield narratives and pieces on how to budget on food and clothing during the emergency.

Many nihonga painters of the period began to resurrect Japan's ancient myths as subjects. At the same time, the Taisho- and Showa-period intellectual Kuki Shuzo helped to restore the partially discredited culture of the Tokugawa and Meiji eras in his 1930 work, *The Structure of Iki*. Here he presented what he believed to be evidence of the uniqueness of Japanese aesthetics and spirit. Literary quality was one of the first casualties of militarism. Those who still retained enough reason to feel a profound unease with the expansionist ambitions of the military were shocked to read the anti-war poet Yosano Akiko's new work *Citizens of Japan, A Morning Song*, with its recycled imagery of falling cherry blossoms, glorifying the death of young soldiers whose scattered bodies were "purer than a flower".

PATRIOTIC INSURRECTIONS

On the afternoon of 15 May 1932, a group of young naval officers stormed into the offices of the prime minister and shot him dead. Memories of police torture and the murder of anarchists and left-wing activists and sympathizers under cover of the chaos following the 1923 earthquake, the activities of the so-called Special Higher Police, the suppression of the Communist Party in 1928 and the quashing of agitprop art and art groups by 1934 must have sent a clear message that the containment of ultra-nationalism and military expansion was unlikely.

An ill wind blew through Tokyo in the bitter winter of 1936. In the early morning of 26 February, a month that saw the heaviest snowfall for thirty years, junior Imperial Way officers went on strike. It was a day as beautiful as the one on which the 47 *ronin* had carried the head of Lord Kira through the snow-shrouded streets of Edo. In the attempt to take over central Tokyo, a feat accomplished by 1,400 rebel troops for a period of four days, assassins struck at key government officials including the finance minister. Prime Minister Okada narrowly escaped with his life when his brother-in-law was mistakenly murdered in his place. Okada, who promptly resigned from office after the incident, had been the leader of a government energetically promoting emperor worship and its accompanying theory of a mystical *kokutai* or "national essence". The fact that his assailants wished to target him for his lack of zeal is an indication of how extreme the young renegade officers were.

The attacks were orderly, highly focused and not without a touch of tradition. As a token of respect, the rebels burned incense beside the bodies of their victims. Emperor Hirohito, astutely seeing the coup as an attack on the central establishment that supported his own position, refused to endorse the aims of these insubordinate young officers, who made their last stand in the grounds of the Sanno Hotel near Hibiya Park. The walls and bridges that led to the palace just across from the park, symbols of imperial rule, were the setting for pseudo-samurai suicides by some of the failed officers, though most were executed by conventional means.

Shocking as these developments were, the violence should not be exaggerated. Unlike Germany in the 1930s or the contemporary political climate in communist Russia or Kuomintang China, there were no mass atroocities in Japan. The government did not make a practice of liquidating its opponents, nor did political rivals in general assassinate each other.

Dissenters remained for the most part free, restricted in their public utterances or, in the case of politicians, required to renounce office.

Mishima Yukio glamorized the officers' insurgency in a story, *Patriotism*, which appeared in 1961. Mishima portrays a double suicide, set in the upper room of a dismal rented house in the Tokyo Aoba-cho district of Yotsuya. Excluded by his closest colleagues from taking part in the uprising because of his recent marriage, loath to bear the shame of his friends being branded as traitors and afraid that he may be ordered to shoot them, an imperial army lieutenant, after a scene of protracted love-making, ritually disembowels himself in the room. He is followed by his wife, who thrusts a knife into her neck. The suicides are described in highly realistic detail. If the story had been published in 1936 rather than 1961, it would have undoubtedly delighted the authorities. Mishima leaves us in no doubt about where his feelings and inclinations lie when he writes, "The last moments of this heroic and dedicated couple were such as to make the gods themselves weep." The writer, eager in his own words, to "restore the sword" to Japanese culture, had previously written about the event in his *Voices of the Illustrious Spirits*, where he stated that, "I admired the heroic posture of the rebels, their unmatched purity, their determination, their youth and their death. They seemed to be mythological heroes." The combination of sex and death, so beloved of Mishima, reached its climax here and in the film Mishima made of the story. Casting himself in the role of the doomed officer, it may have been a dress rehearsal for his own death several years later.

IMPERIAL METROPOLIS

The violence against politicians by fanatical army officers was reflected in the actions of the authorities themselves, as communists were arrested, left-wing sympathizers and dissenters marginalized and rigorous censorship imposed on writing that was not overtly patriotic. The government issued authors with subjects to write about that would inspire students to volunteer for military service, while the reading habits of the public were carefully monitored. Works of fiction like Kafu's *A Strange Tale from East of the River* and Hayashi Fumiko's *First Journey* were disliked by the authorities for their failure to address the war effort.

Although he was never a political animal, the nationalist drift stupefied Kafu. As the nation began to revaluate its traditional culture under the spell of an increasingly effective indoctrination campaign, Kafu was openly critical of government policy and the debased culture that was helping to create it. While the rest of the nation, with the exception of a few notable dissenters, embraced the new doctrine of *Nihon kaiki* or "Return to Japan", Kafu pointedly dissociated himself from the current. Rejecting the values of the military government, he refused to cooperate with the authorities for the war period. His dissent is clear from a reading of his *Dyspepsia House Days*, the diary he kept from 1917 to 1959.

Tanizaki was another passive dissenter in the field of literature, as were Maruki Toshi and Maruki Iri in art, but they were few and far between. Few writers, film directors, painters or journalists hesitated in their support of the government's push to establish its Greater East Asia Co-Prosperity Sphere, its scheme to spread Japanese cultural hegemony alongside the iron grip of its military. Creative people in all media rushed to praise the invincibility of the Japanese spirit, the courage of its soldiers and the need to make the Japanese language a mandatory part of school curricula in the occupied countries. Although giants of literature like Tanizaki and Kafu were mostly left to their own devices, those who actively resisted could face harassment, imprisonment, even torture.

More wholesome than Kafu's work, at least in the government's view, were the war diaries written by Hino Ashihei, respectively entitled *Troops among Barley*, *Troops on Bare Earth* and *Troops among Flowers*. Published in 1938 and 1939, these tributes to Japan's divine mission to free the Asian mainland from colonial rule by the European powers were instant best-sellers.

POLAR CITIES

Families brought their conscripted sons to the moated area surrounding the Imperial Palace to photograph them in their new uniforms before they were dispatched to Manchuria, and later to the Pacific war zone. Bands played military marches and flags were waved with a singularly Japanese blend of decorum and passion on 10 November 1940 when parades celebrated the 2600th anniversary of the founding of the imperial line. Rising from the imperial moat, Fushimi Tower, Nijubashi (Double Bridge) and the walls of the palace became symbols of a mystical patriotism. Passengers in trams passing along this stretch of the outer moat would rise from their seats, steady themselves and bow deeply towards the palace. Pointing cameras in the direction of the imperial residence was strictly forbidden.

Even the architecture of the city was affected by the times, the 1938 Daiichi-Life Insurance Building reflecting in its austere, Bauhaus-style lines tastes closer to Berlin than Tokyo. The design preferences, the transplants of an earlier age, were still in evidence. The 1936 design for the second National Diet building, modelled on one of the ancient world's seven wonders, the Mausoleum of Halikarnassos, was an example of the severe hybridization of many Tokyo buildings. A slightly earlier design, the Honganji temple in Tsukiji, is another striking example of architectural eclecticism. Designed by Ito Chuta in 1934, it is a curious blend of Indian, Chinese, Javanese and the prevailing Tenjika style, a Japanese Buddhist form of the Edo period. To their credit, though, both the temple and the Diet building have shown their durability. Symptomatic of the decline were more vulnerable buildings. Takami Jun wrote that by 1938 many of the best-known Asakusa venues had been abandoned, including the Casino Follies, now "in a state of advanced neglect, the subject of weird stories. Late at night, it was said, you could hear the sound of tap dancing on the roof."

On Halloween Night 1940 the government closed down all Tokyo dance halls and banned jazz performances. The neon lights of the Ginza were extinguished, women were forbidden to style their hair or to wear smart western clothes. In the same year daily commodities like salt, sugar and rice were rationed. The Tokyo of 1920 was poles apart from the city of 1940. Where the former was experimental, an urban laboratory of dance halls, tattoo artists, union leaders, poets and print-makers, the latter was now a stage for political assassination, censorship and summary arrest, a terror camp run by an ascendant military class.

In the remaining days before Pearl Harbor a haunting stillness overcame the city. Martin Cruz Smith's novel *December 6* recreates the mood of those hours before catastrophe struck. Distrusted by the Japanese police, spurned by his own embassy and abandoned by friends, Smith's main character, Harry Niles, watches as the city stiffens itself for war. Passing the inner moat of the Imperial Palace, with its fairy tale bridges "patrolled by a few guards with white-socked rifles," he muses that even "on the eve of war, the emperor's tranquillity was maintained. Either the palace was a sinkhole in the middle of reality, or the rest of the world was the emperor's dream."

Emperor Hirohito in military uniform

Although a small number remained open throughout the coming years of war, all the large cinemas were closed down by the spring of 1944. Travelling Kabuki troupes kept performing in front of small audiences, but the main Kabuki-za theatre was closed down. The Shimbashi Embujo fared a little better, reopening towards the end of the war. Both theatres were thoroughly gutted in air raids during the closing months of the war. Large theatres like the Nichigeki and Imperial Theatre were requisitioned for the production of incendiary balloons. One of the more harmless failures of the Japanese military, the balloons were supposed to float across the Pacific, igniting firestorms over American cities.

If geisha establishments were required to close by eleven, they were not completely shut down until the spring of 1944. The patronage of the civil bureaucracy, police and military may explain their reluctance to close them down. Individual geisha houses, affiliated with branches of a power structure riddled with mutual mistrust and suspicion, served in their traditional role as disseminators of information, intelligence and carelessly uttered confidences.

Kafu, savouring one of the city's last chorus line shows, described the backstage scene at the Asakusa Opera in *The Decoration*, one of his last stories, written in 1942. What first caught the eye, he noted:

> ... was not the violent jumble of colours, or even the faces of the girls as they sprawled about on the floor and then sat up again. It was the powerful flesh of the arms and legs... it called to mind the earthen hallway of a florist's shop, where a litter of torn-off petals and withering leaves is left unswept and trampled into shapelessness.

Most of the dance hall girls and other members of the entertainment quarters, including geisha, would soon be coerced into working in factories to support the war effort. Kafu's story centres on the figure of an old man who earns a little money bringing the girls their food. Boasting of his military record in the 1904 Russo-Japanese war, he is asked to bring in one of the medals that he won. The girls get him to pose for a photograph dressed in a military stage uniform. When the image is developed, it is seen that the medal appears on the right-hand pocket of the uniform, not the left. To "make things seem in order," the photographer reverses the negative. Kafu's commentary on the manipulation of truth and the emptiness at the core of militarism was not published until 1946.

THE WASTELAND

If Britain had painted its colonies dark red on the world map, Japan's chosen colour was a lighter, bloodier version. As China was sliced open, the stain spread. In early 1942, at the height of its expansion, *Dai Nippon Teikoku*, the Great Japanese Empire, had its foot soldiers planted at all points across the Asian compass, from the northern Aleutian Islands to Southeast Asia, from interior China to the islands of the mid-Pacific. It was to be the briefest of empires, the optimism a delirium soon referred to by the Japanese themselves as "victory disease". Overstretched resources and a far more powerful America meant that Japan's holy war, predicated on the notion of an invincible, emperor-centred national polity, was doomed from the very onset, though such was the public's euphoria that few had the vision to see that.

Only six months after Pearl Harbor, the country suffered its first major defeat in the Battle of Midway. A year later, with the annihilation of its forces on Attu Island, in the Aleutian Archipelago, the by now increasingly irrational military high command began using the term *gyokusai*, an ancient Chinese word with the literal meaning of "a jewel shatters," but with the applied sense of "dying gallantly" rather than surviving ignominiously.

The first US aerial attack on Tokyo, an experiment in long-range bombardment, was carried out in April 1942, a warning of worse to come. With the destruction of munitions factories no longer the main priority, attention was turned to heavily populated areas of major cities. Mock-ups of Japanese houses were built at Florida's Elgin airbase, where they were subjected to attack by incendiary bombs. While the results were considered adequate, a more realistic test was considered necessary before major air raids could be made on civilian areas. On 25 February 1943, just before 3p.m. on a snowy afternoon, 130 bombers took off for a trial raid on Tokyo. In all, 25,000 buildings were destroyed and several hundred people killed, a result that was deemed satisfactory.

B-29 Super Fortresses under the command of the cigar-chomping Major General Curtis E. Le May, were loaded with incendiaries aimed at destroying tightly packed residential areas of Tokyo. Unnerving the capital and weakening the resolve of the government to continue a hopeless war by causing heavy damage and loss of life were the main purposes of the coming raids. The attacks were also intended to shatter the morale of the Japanese, their faith in leaders who had led them to the brink of disaster.

Robert Guillain, correspondent for *Le Monde*, captured the mood in the days before the storm:

> Tokyo, which had never been a beautiful city, had now become a dirty city... The capital woke up each morning a little more sordid, as if tainted by the doom-laden night in which it had bathed....The raids had still to begin, and yet, night after night, an obsession gripped the city plunged into darkness by the blackout, an obsession that debilitated and corroded it more than even the appearance overhead of the first enemy squadrons was able to do...Tokyo was a giant village of wooden boards, and it knew it.

Tokyo still continued to go about its business, but in a climate of fear, knowing it was only a question of time before the cataclysm. Fatalism and an inability to grasp the full capacity of US air power resulted in the delay of emergency procedures like evacuation. Nets and webbing were used to camouflage the Diet building, but the majority of structures were exposed. It was a time of inadvisable stalling and strange connections. Government offices were only evacuated after the situation became sufficiently serious for the authorities to have the lions in Ueno Zoo destroyed for fear that they would roam free after the raids. Next to the zoo, the lotus-covered water at Shinobazu Pond was drained and turned into a vegetable patch.

"If the flavour of the city must go," a 1944 entry in Kafu's diary reads, "I would like to go with it." His wish almost came true when his house burned down in the air raids a year later. Kafu, who was more attached to ideas and the past than to people or even property, never really minded the excuse to change address, and the burning of this particular house seems to have been less important to him than the loss during the air raid of his library of 10,000 books.

In all, Tokyo suffered 102 raids, the most intense between 1944 to March 1945. The most devastating raid, on the night of 9-10 March, began around 10.30 p.m., with hundreds of B-29 Super Fortress bombers offloading thousands of tons of incendiary and fragmentation bombs onto the most densely populated working-class districts east of the river. Three hundred and thirty-four B-29s, each loaded with up to six tons of oil, napalm, jellied gasoline and phosphorous, swooped over Asakusa. Some 2,000 tons of incendiaries were dropped on the quarter, a twelve square-mile area where the population density was 103,000 per square mile. Residents recall that the gasoline-filled bombs were dropped concentrically, to make sure there were no avenues of escape. The planes then turned to target the wards east of the Sumida. Napalm, a substance that would be used extensively in a much later Asian war, needed to be tested, and Tokyo provided the perfect killing laboratory. According to eyewitness accounts by pilots and journalists travelling in the B29s, the fires could be seen from 150 miles out in the Pacific. The fuselages of the planes that returned to their base in the Mariana Islands were covered in soot from the inferno.

From a military perspective the operation was an overriding success. Le May was to record in his memoir that 80-100,000 people were "scorched and boiled and baked to death." The general elaborated on his position when he stated that, "There are no innocent civilians, so it doesn't bother me so much to be killing innocent bystanders." For good measure, an extra four thousand tons of flammables were dropped on residential areas of north-western Tokyo on 26 May.

The extreme nature of the bombing, though generally supported by US planners, did have a small number of detractors. Brigadier Bonner Fellers, MacArthur's military secretary, a well-read Japan scholar, condemned the bombings as "one of the most ruthless and barbaric killings of non-combatants in all history." An estimated two-fifths of the city was burnt down in the horrors of that spring. Aerial photos of the devastation reveal most of the bridges across the Sumida intact. Perhaps because of their future usefulness for the occupiers, they were spared. Mirroring Tokyo's obliteration were large incinerated tracts of neighbouring Kawasaki, an industrial area, and the port city of Yokohama.

The sense of helplessness, breeding inertia and fatalism, is captured in *Sumida River*, a fictional account of those days by Shimamura Toshimasa:

> Already, crimson flames were rising in the sky to the east of Tokyo. It was obvious that the B29s were bent on attacking Tokyo east of the Sumida River. The dark forms of the planes caught in the searchlights were heading, one after another, straight into the conflagration, scorching the night sky… Against the backdrop of the crimson sky the gigantic silver bodies of the B29s shone eerily as if bathed in blood. Some flew surprisingly low as they crawled through the sky. I watched feeling utterly powerless to do anything.

Some Tokyo residents, naming the incendiary cylinders that were dropped to mark the target spots "Molotov flower baskets", claimed to find a terrifying beauty in the resulting fires and in the blue sprays of spark that fell from bombs that accidentally exploded in mid-air. This was doubtless part of the mood of collective derangement, the scrambling of the senses, the descent into hallucination springing from a combination of trauma and malnutrition.

The main character of Sakaguchi Ango's 1946 story *One Woman and the War* is heard to claim:

The war really was beautiful. It was a beauty you could not anticipate; you could only glimpse it in the midst of your terror. As soon as you were aware of it, it was gone. War was without fakery, without regrets, and it was extravagant. I didn't begrudge losing my house, my neighbourhood, my life to it. Because there was nothing that I was sufficiently attached to that I would begrudge losing.

And then, on the air raids:

If I were asked what about the night bombings was the most magnificent, truth to tell, my real feeling, more than anything else, was one of pleasure at the vastness of the destruction. The dull silver B-29s too, as they suddenly hove into view amid the arrows of the searchlights, were beautiful. And the antiaircraft guns spitting fire, the droning B-29s that swam through the noise of the guns, and the incendiary bombs that burst in the sky like fireworks. But only the vast, world-destroying conflagration on the ground gave me complete satisfaction.

Literary critic and essayist Takeyama Michio, was also mesmerized by the poetics of death, describing one air raid in unabashedly lyrical terms:

It was the third or fourth time that B-29s had appeared in the skies over Tokyo. In the clear early winter air, they floated calmly, violet and sparkling. Shining like a firework, a Japanese plane approached like a shooting star and rammed a B-29. Then, spinning and giving off black smoke, it fell to earth. Drawing long white frosty lines, the B-29s faded slowly into the crystalline distance.

Describing the March 1945 bombings of Tokyo that resulted in the extermination of tens of thousands of civilians in a single night, Mishima Yukio told a later audience: "it was the most beautiful fireworks display I have ever seen." Two months after those raids, Mishima witnessed another air strike from a shelter on the outskirts of the city, where a group of men were watching from inside a warren of caves: "The workmen were particularly vociferous. The sound of hand-clapping and cheering rang out from the mouths of the scattered tunnels as though in a theatre... It seemed to make no essential difference whether the falling plane was ours or the enemy's."

Mishima, who could always identify a redeeming aesthetic even in the midst of ruin, expressed his personal feelings when he wrote of the incident and others like it: "The air raids on the distant metropolis, which I watched from the shelter at the arsenal, were beautiful. The flames seemed to hue to all the colours in the rainbow: it was like watching the light of a distant bonfire at a great banquet of extravagant death and destruction."

The young Mishima managed to publish his first book of short stories in October 1944, in "a modest attempt to preserve the literary tradition of the empire." This was no mean feat as Tokyo began to burn, and paper supplies with it. In the months after the spring attacks more than three million people left the city. Many felt consternation when the annual May sumo tournament was moved to an outdoor setting and reduced to a week after two of its highest ranking wrestlers, Matsuragata and Toyoshima, were killed in the raids and the main arena partially damaged. The same month, a large section of the Imperial Palace was destroyed. The structure, dating from 1884, had been built of the very best cypress wood. The bombs devastated the main building, its copper roofs collapsing on exquisitely painted screens, ceilings and chandeliers imported from Europe. The same night the Meiji shrine was obliterated.

The disillusionment of ordinary people with a holy war gone horribly wrong grew during these months. By the summer of 1945 anonymous letters calling for the end of the war were being received by newspapers, though none were printed. Contempt for those in charge manifested itself in graffiti scrawled over walls and lampposts, reading "Overthrow the Government," "End the War," and "Kill the Emperor." It was time for the government to confront the truth, to rouse itself from its martial dreams and imperial myths. All but the leaders of the army were now reconciled to the inevitability of defeat.

Discontent with the direction of the war was exacerbated by severe food shortages. Most families had long been reduced to a daily diet of barley and potatoes, but now even that was in short supply. People were encouraged to supplement mineral deficiency with rose petals, re-used tea leaves and seeds, their lack of starch with peanut shells, acorns and sawdust. A shortage of protein could be made up by consuming grasshoppers, snakes, worms and moles. Properly cleaned and prepared, the authorities ventured to suggest, there was little difference in taste between rats and small birds.

Families who possessed heirlooms of any value walked or clambered into congested trains that took them into the countryside, where their precious lacquer ware, pottery, gold, and cherished silk kimonos, objects that might have been in the family for generations, were traded for a meagre sack or two of rice or sweet potatoes. Reduced to virtual refugee status, many people found themselves with, quite literally, only the clothes they stood in. Memories are fading, but elderly Japanese who remember those times still bear simmering grudges against the farmers of prefectures surrounding Tokyo, like Chiba and Saitama, who gained so much in those trade offs.

After these excursions into the farms on the periphery of the city, many would return to Tokyo only to find that their homes had vanished. Survivors tell of a city scattered with "green stones", an allusion to the glass lumps formed after bottles had melted in the fierce heat from the incendiary bombs. A neighbour of mine, who fled her home in the district of Honjo, recalled the difficulty she and her family experienced in locating the charred outline of their former residence. The molten remains of an iron teapot set, a gift from relatives living in one of the northern prefectures, were the only means of identifying their plot.

Voice of the Crane

At 10.30 a.m. on 14 August, the emperor took the unprecedented step of addressing the nation on the radio. The broadcast was made in what was termed the Voice of the Crane, meaning an imperial command whose resonance, like that of the bird, could still be heard in the sky after the crane's passing. Fosco Maraini, an Italian held in custody along with fellow countrymen suspected of anti-fascism, recalled the summons to listen to the broadcast: "The Emperor made his speech (in which he actually did announce the surrender), but none of the Japanese around us could understand him. The text was, in fact, in a language that was only known in court—it was so different from everyday speech that you had to be a philologist to make sense of it."

Once understood, the message in which the emperor exhorted his people to "endure the unendurable," was meekly accepted. A number of the more fanatical army officers, unable to bear the thought of defeat, marched to the parade grounds in front of the palace and disembowelled themselves with their swords. For those like Mishima, who worshipped the more muscular gods of death, this was an incomparably beautiful act, the ultimate sacrifice to a shattered idol; for the majority of Japanese, this act of atonement for the loss of the country's military honour symbolized the misguided values that had led to calamity in the first place.

In February 1944 the population of the capital had stood at 7.3 million. By November 1945 death and evacuation had reduced the city to 3.5 million inhabitants, the majority weak from hunger. A quarter of a million residents had died. Three-quarters of a million houses had been razed, three million people made homeless. The normally indigent, the day labourers and rag pickers, people who had always been there, now seemed more visible.

The physical damage was astounding. Half the city's houses had vanished, along with the great Senso-ji temple and Meiji shrine. The five miles of downtown Tokyo that stretched from Hibiya to Shibuya was little more than a charred plain. People called cities like Tokyo *yaki-nohara* ("scorched fields"). The once glittering district of Ginza was now a wasteland of rubble and twisted metal. Tramcar tracks had sprung from their casings and melted. The "city of civilization" was a ruin. No longer obscured by buildings, the majestic cone of Mount Fuji could once again be seen on the horizon above the ash-covered landscape as it had in the woodblock prints of Hiroshige and Hokusai.

Five out of seven million Tokyo residents had left the city by the war's end. They now began to drift back. With 65 per cent of all homes destroyed, the spectre of massive homelessness loomed. Shantytowns sprang up overnight, makeshift hovels constructed of foraged wood, chicken wire, tarpaper and debris. War widows and orphans resorted to finding shelter in burnt-out buses, tram cars, underground subway tunnels of large stations like Ueno, bomb craters and caves dug out of rubble. Where enough hovels were huddled together to form something resembling a community, occupants took turns in bathing in oil drums.

The English poet Edmund Blunden, who came to Tokyo shortly after the war to teach, was less shocked perhaps than many of the young American soldiers who drove for the first time into the scorched city, observing that "It has been the fate of my generation to become habituated to the ruining of cities." The writer's comparative perspective came from the fact that he had been here before: "The Tokyo which I formerly knew was ruins, after the earthquake and the fire, though some districts had been spared; and now I was coming again to a desolated and incinerated city."

Chapter Eight

TOKYO REDUX

1945-1970S

On 15 August 1945 the filmmaker Kurosawa Akira was summoned to his studio in Tokyo's Setagaya ward to listen to the emperor's radio announcement. In his book *Something Like an Autobiography*, he recalled the day:

> I will never forget the scenes I saw as I walked the streets that day. On the way from Soshigaya to the studios in Kinuta the shopping street looked fully prepared for the Honourable Death of the Hundred Million. The atmosphere was tense, panicked. There were even shop owners who had taken their Japanese swords from their sheaths and sat staring at the bare blades.
>
> However, when I walked the same route back to my home after listening to the imperial proclamation, the scene was entirely different. The people on the shopping street were bustling about with cheerful faces as if preparing for a festival the next day. I don't know if this represents Japanese adaptability or Japanese imbecility.

The "Honourable Death of the Hundred Million" was a reference to General Tojo Hideki's February 1944 "emergency declaration" in which, as prime minister and head of the military cabinet, he had called for *ichioku gyokusai*, "one hundred million shattering like a jewel." Japan's population at the time was seventy million, Koreans and Taiwanese would also have been included in the order for mass suicide in the event of defeat. Whether the "hundred million hearts beating as one", as the propaganda of the day put it, would actually have gone through with a mass suicide is questionable, but the Japanese, prepared for the worst, had, to quote scholar Tsurumi Kazuko's chilling term, been effectively conditioned in a collective "socialization for death".

Many people have commented on the alacrity with which the

Japanese are capable of certain kinds of change. Even so, the extraordinary turnaround in sentiment was baffling, even for the Americans. John Dower, in *Embracing Defeat*, his matchless history of the occupation, explains:

> The Americans arrived anticipating, many of them, traumatic confrontation with fanatical emperor worshippers. They were accosted instead by women who called "yoo hoo" to the first troops landing on the beaches in full battle gear, and men who bowed and asked what it was the conquerors wished.

After all the horrors they had experienced, the Japanese wished for nothing more than to re-emerge reborn from the flames, purged of the past. The Americans, it turned out, were just the right people to help them achieve their purpose. And there were a few things that the occupiers, from the savagery of their own campaign in the Pacific war zone to the atom bombings of Hiroshima and Nagasaki, were disposed to forgetting themselves.

General Douglas MacArthur's aircraft touched down at Atsugi naval aerodrome on 30 August 1945. It was a carefully rehearsed performance. The general was a seasoned public relations figure, a ham actor perhaps, but one who understood that the times required drama and presence, not subtlety or finesse. Known in his earlier chief of staff days for flaunting military conventions by wearing a Japanese kimono at his desk when the whim took him, MacArthur brought all his tried and tested acting props along with him to Japan that day. Emerging at the top of the steps, the commander thrust his corncob pipe between his teeth, surveyed the conquered land before him through military issue dark glasses. It was a well practised pose that had already become his trademark, but one that was calculated to impress the uninitiated Japanese. The general held the pose just long enough for the press photographers to get some good shots.

It was not long before the Japanese, observing MacArthur's imperial manner and almost ritualistic public appearances, were calling him, with a touch of reproof but mostly awe, the "blue-eyed shogun". Tellingly, the general had installed himself along with his staff in the Dai-ichi Insurance Building, just across the moat from the Imperial Palace, earning him another epithet from the Japanese: "the emperor outside the moat". The term SCAP (Supreme Commander of the Allied Powers) was to refer to both MacArthur himself and his bureaucracy. The building that served as its headquarters has been remodelled in recent years, but still stands, MacArthur's office and furnishings left untouched. The spot became quite well known over the coming years as the building stood near the Hibiya Crossing, an intersection with the palace moat on one side, the entrance to Hibiya Park on the other. The crossing was a landmark of sorts, with two uniformed policemen directing the little traffic that existed in those days. One of the policemen was Japanese, the other American. They appeared to move in perfect synchronization, choreographed as if designed for each other, but looking closely one would notice that the Japanese officer was carefully watching out for the next move from his American counterpart before following suit. Things would be like this for some time in Japan.

Censoring Culture

In SCAP's estimation the Japanese soul was infested with obscurantist values and misconceived notions of loyalty, many of these ideas promulgated in the arts and culture. In the light of Japan's recent history, culture itself would have to be re-examined and remodelled. Dower has described the occupation as a "neocolonial military dictatorship", a crusade by Christian zealots.

> Unlike Germany, this vanquished enemy represented an exotic, alien society to its conquerors: non-white, non-Western, non-Christian. Yellow, Asian, pagan Japan, supine and vulnerable, provoked an ethnocentric missionary zeal inconceivable vis-à-vis Germany.

The Kabuki theatre, with its suicide scenes and loyal samurai retainers, was regarded as a malign medieval remnant. Plays were banned or heavily censored. These included the classic *Chushingura*, which was accused of glorifying the feudal-martial mentality that had put Japan on the road to war. Samurai films were completely banned. In 1946 a performer on the Tokyo vaudeville stage sang a song containing the lines, "Everybody is talking about democracy. But how can we have a democracy with two emperors?" Getting wind of the show, SCAP quickly moved to ban the song. Satirical cartoons questioning occupation policies were forbidden. Newspaper articles, books and documentary films on the bombings of Hiroshima and Nagasaki were strictly banned, as were the many less than edifying stories of rape and prostitution involving GIs. As a symbol of Shinto worship, Mount Fuji was singled out as another negative cultural symbol. SCAP could hardly have the sacred mountain removed, but it could excise its image from Japanese films, which it proceeded to do. At the same time as these measures were being introduced and the Japanese were being lectured on the benefits of free speech, civic rights and women's suffrage, any criticism or even mention of censorship was itself censored. As Dower observes: "The overall censorship operation eventually came to entail extensive checklists for taboo subjects, and in the best Orwellian manner these taboos included any public acknowledgment of the existence of censorship."

A similar list of prohibited subjects was drawn up for filmmakers. As none of these short-lived strictures could begin to compare with the restrictions of the years under Japanese militarism, few people voiced serious complaints. Although the occupying forces practised their own form of strict censorship, to their credit they set about abolishing the more irksome Board of Censors, releasing writers and Marxist intellectuals from prison. Rule by fiat may have hinted at white supremacism over a vanquished race, but it is difficult to imagine how, given the age and circumstances, it could have been much different.

Many modernist writers, former avant-garde poets and proponents of radical change in the arts tried to conceal their wartime collaborationist activities with the militarists, or transform their work into something more appropriate for the times. Many showed a remarkable facility in adapting, causing one Japanese artist, Uchida Iwao, to comment, "Those who just a month ago disavowed culture, and wanted to organize attack battalions on our own soil are now going around yelling about culture, culture."

A committee of leftist Japanese critics and writers, as self-righteous as any of the fascist censors who had preceded them, began compiling a list of "literary war criminals". Ono Masuji, the central character in Ishiguro Kazuo's novel *An Artist of the Floating World*, is a painter who specializes in scenes from Tokyo's *demi-monde*. With the rise of nationalism in the 1930s, he becomes an official artist, turning out propagandist work that wins him several prestigious awards. Wandering through the ruined districts of the post-war city, he belatedly ponders the futility of imperialism. Willing to atone but without the means to do so, he encounters unrepentant former colleagues who are relieved to see that the Americans, satisfied with token trials of the more conspicuously guilty, have little interest in probing down to the lower ranks. In the "June, 1950" chapter of the novel, a former acquaintance speaks his mind:

> "Army officers, politicians, businessmen," Matsuda said. "They've all been blamed for what happened to this country. But as for the likes of us, Ono, our contribution was always marginal. No one cares now what the likes of you and me once did. They look at us and see only two old men with their sticks."

Fujita Tsuguharu was an artist whose reputation in Japan never really recovered from his enthusiastic support for the military government. Although nothing came of it, and in the event no artists were ever indicted, there was talk of him being classified a war criminal because of his wartime propaganda works. SCAP eventually got round to confiscating 153 Japanese war paintings, a fraction of the real number produced, which were then shipped back to the US, where they stayed out of the news for a few decades. The paintings were eventually sent back to Japan on "permanent loan" after pressure from the Japanese for their return. In 1977 Tokyo's National Museum of Modern Art, where the paintings were stored, planned to hold a large exhibition of the works, but cancelled the show at the last minute. The official reason given was that the paintings would provoke criticism from Asian nations under former Japanese occupation, but a likely concern was the reaction from the divided ranks of the Japanese themselves. Though single paintings occasionally appear in exhibitions, the collection remains in the museum in Ueno Park, away from public view.

Through the ministries of MacArthur, who regarded Hirohito as essential to the stability of post-war Japan, the emperor had been spared from trial and possible execution for the very real part he had played in the war. Right from the start of the occupation, Brigadier Bonner Fellers also went against the prevailing mood for punishment and revenge, counselling the victors that "Hanging of the Emperor to them [the Japanese] would be comparable to the crucifixion of Christ to us." Their view prevailed.

A few days after surrendering to the Allies, the emperor had expressed his unrepentant position in a short allegorical *waka*:

Under the heavy snow of winter,
The pine tree bends,
But does not break,
Or change its colour.
People should be like this.

If the emperor managed to evade both the noose and the judgment of his own amnesia-prone subjects, others were appalled at the collective memory loss descending on the country. In Osaragi Jiro's aggrieved novel *The Journey*, an examination of the impact of the American occupation on Japan, a character remarks on the subject of war guilt and responsibility:

"I can think of quite a few people who could do with a bit of shock treatment. To begin with, all the members of the Diet and the Cabinet—those fellows certainly need it once in their lives… they must be made to remember that there's such a thing as shame in this world. They're all suffering from chronic amnesia."

People could not bear to be reminded of the war, and yet there were reminders wherever they looked. In 1946 and the following year 800,000 repatriated troops flowed into Tokyo alone, where as visible proof of Japan's defeat and shame they were coldly received. Many of the men who returned were in worse shape than they should have been. MacArthur had pressed for a swift repatriation of soldiers after Japan's broken army was dissolved. Britain, eager to exploit the troops as cheap conscript labour, refused. The sting of humiliation over Japan's easy victories against British forces at the beginning of the war, and the appalling treatment of British POWs were still fresh in the mind. With the tables turned, the British treated their Japanese captives as barely human. Living on only half the stipulated prisoner-of-war diet and forced in many cases to kneel and beg for their food, almost 9,000 of them died from malnutrition or from untreated diseases. The last to return from "Operation Nipoff", as the prolonged detention was spitefully called, did not arrive home until 1948. Among those who returned many were maimed, ending up on the street as beggars wearing their tattered military fatigues. The occupiers may have been trying to cheer the populace up, but the sight of former Imperial Army soldiers dressed in white, clutching their begging bowls outside stations with speakers blaring American boogie-woogie, was profoundly shaming.

AMONG THE RUINS

The Japanese paid a high price for their military adventures in Asia. With the fabric of the city blown apart, living conditions were deplorable. Children, many of them orphaned, lived in the ruins, in train stations or under overpasses, making out as best they could by selling newspapers, recycling goods, shining shoes, dealing in illegal food coupons or working as pickpockets and beggars. Abandoned dogs, with a newly acquired taste for human flesh, ran in packs at night through the city like wolves. Rats and crows found rich pickings among the ruins. The use of rivers and canals as toilets exacerbated the incidence of typhus and cholera.

Aerial views of Tokyo at the time show mainline stations and major river bridges mostly intact, but all the surrounding areas are wasteland. Even the American personnel seeing the city for the first time, were shocked at the extent of the destruction. Russell Brines, the first foreign journalist to enter the incinerated city, noted how everything had been flattened: "Only thumbs stood up from the flatlands—the chimneys of bathhouses, heavy house safes and an occasional stout building with heavy iron shutters." The bathhouses had been targeted because American bombers mistook them for small factories. The American translator Edward Seidensticker, recalling the Tokyo of the 1940s, remembered some of the old Tokugawa tombs in Ueno, covered in weeds and neglected, but easily accessible if one was prepared to clamber over broken down fences. "All by myself," he wrote, "I spent hours exploring the graves, and melancholy testimonial they were to the evanescence of glory. They were very beautiful, with the especial beauty of ruinous monuments."

The ruination was corroborated by Donald Richie, who wrote in his journals:

> February 28, 1947, Winter—cold, crisp, clear—and Fuji stands sharp on the horizon, growing purple, then indigo in the fading light. I stand at the main crossing on the Ginza, nothing between me and the moun-

Bombed and incinerated areas along the Sumida river

tain. It is clear because there is no smoke, few factories, no fumes because the few cars are charcoal-burning, Fuji looks much as it must have for Hokusai and Hiroshige... And it is dark, this Ginza which had once been a fountain of light. Now it is lit only by the passing headlights of Occupation jeeps and trucks, and the acetylene torches in the night stalls.

Standing at this main crossing of the Ginza, where the curving Hattori Building had miraculously been spared, Richie reveals a documentary eye for detail. The open panels in the walls of the city, blown away by showers of ordinance, would soon close up again. Although what he saw was "a burned wasteland, a vast and blackened plain where a city had once stood," there was already a hint of renewal in the air, "the yellow sheen of new wood" between the few brick and stone buildings that remained standing.

In the shuffling, traumatized crowds, something was beginning to stir. The charred bodies had been removed and the living were coming back to re-inhabit the city. Richie walked through a world where the past was up for grabs, streets in which, perhaps with more relief than regret, an entire way of life—or at least its outer forms—was being auctioned off. In wonderfully drawn vignettes, the young Richie observes "the products of a dead civilization" laid across tables and stalls: "There were wartime medals and egret feather tiaras... bridles and bits and damascene cufflinks. There were old brocades and pieces of calligraphy, battered woodblock prints and old framed photographs." In a city where the division between the urban and rural, between street and paddy, had been temporarily dissolved, Richie glimpsed the oddest of sights, "braces of oxen on the Ginza".

The old entertainment quarter of Asakusa was gradually getting back on its feet. Braving Allied occupation signs reading "NO FRATER-NIZATION WITH THE INDIGENOUS PERSONNEL", Richie, in an essay for *Time* magazine, recalled taking the Ginza line subway to its terminus in Asakusa, surfacing "into this sexy stratum, redolent of oysters over rice and camellia hair oil, cotton candy and underarm sweat." The observation tower at the top of the subway restaurant tower building provided him with a full view of the flattened city. (The building had replaced the taller twelve-storey Ryounkaku after it snapped in half during the 1923 earthquake.) Finding himself in the company of Kawabata Yasunari, Richie seems to have experienced an affinity of feeling with the older writer about "a place that allowed anonymity, freedom, where life flowed on no matter what, where you could pick up pleasure, and where small rooms with paper flowers were rented by the hour."

It was still possible to find reminders of pre-war Tokyo, relics of an older culture. In the immediate post-war period Asakusa still had its street traders, soothsayers, hypnotists, mountebanks selling potions made from preserved vipers, and one straight-faced gent offering to sell an angel in a glass bell jar. Among purveyors of the mystical were spokesmen for the new religious cults that were springing up from the ruined city.

The speed with which Asakusa rebuilt its entertainment district was remarkable. The need for novelties, escapist performances and titillation within a theatrical context produced among other phenomena tightrope strip shows, and the mildly erotic *Onna Kengeki* ("women's swordplay") dramas. Asakusa's two ponds were filled in, the iconic Senso-ji temple rebuilt. Asakusa's archery galleries ceased to exist, but the old licensed quarters of the Yoshiwara, Shinagawa, Shinjuku and Susaki prospered in the post-war years.

Open soliciting took place in the park and on the riverbanks of Asakusa. Kafu's story, *Azuma Bridge*, describes women importuning passers-by. One of the women, leaning against the railing of the bridge, evokes the beauty and forlorn sadness of the scene:

> The water was illuminated by a neon sing advertising Asahi beer that shone in the sky on the other side of the river and by the flickering lights of the unending succession of trains that ran back and forth across the Tobu railway bridge. She could clearly make out not only the figures of young men and women rowing boats they had rented, but also melon rinds and discarded *geta* floating amongst the refuse carried along by the current.

While the Japanese starved, "Little America", as the residential sections of the city that had survived the bombings to be requisitioned were known, went shopping. A steady stream of occupiers and their families could be seen entering the well-stocked PX stores. One colonel's wife described the Japanese onlookers outside, "watching the customers come in and out, flattening their noses against the show windows, gazing in silent awe at the display of merchandise: the souvenirs, candy bars, cameras, milkshakes, shoes, wool sweaters, silk kimonos and guaranteed curios of the Orient."

Japan's overseers were probably no worse, and in many cases a good deal better, than their equivalents among the masters of the subject peoples of the European empires, but SCAP staff's privileged existence and absolute authority over the defeated must have been provocative in the extreme. George Kennan, a vocal detractor of SCAP policies, wrote that the Americans in Tokyo were indulging in "everything that smacks of comfort, elegance or luxury" and that the wives of MacArthur's staff were behaving as if the sole purpose of the war was to furnish them with "six Japanese butlers with the divisional insignia on their jackets".

BLACK MARKETS

It was on the scorched wastelands encircling major railway stations that, in the first months of stunned defeat, demobbed men and displaced persons would come and, spreading a towel, newspaper or piece of cardboard on the ground, place a saucepan, iron teapot or worn kimono in the hope of finding a customer. Literal proof of the alchemy of change, of the expression "turning swords into plough shares," could be seen in pots and pans made from ex-servicemen's helmets and kitchen utensils forged from military issue blades.

These were the tentative beginnings of Tokyo's black markets. A large market, optimistically advertising itself with the slogan *Hikari Wa Shinjuku Yori* (Light Shining from Shinjuku), opened towards the end of August 1945. Under the circumstances, the wares displayed on the wooden crates were of a remarkable variety: electrical goods, sandals, tea, cooking oil, rice and a surprising amount of military clothing and equipment. Most of the items for sale were contraband goods spirited away from a secret stock prepared to equip and mobilize a large home defence corps in the event of invasion. With nobody apparently in charge, military depots were broken into all over the country, their goods "liberated". By September the market had acquired over a hundred electric light bulbs, their illumination helping to dispel some of the gloom that had descended on the dark city.

Most of the black markets were run by underworld gangs, each with their own turf that they fiercely, sometimes violently, protected. There were Chinese and Korean operators too, men forced into serving in the Imperial Army who now found themselves classified as *sankokujin*, "third-country persons". As the markets grew, so did the quality and range of their goods. Though they failed to get the markets closed down, police swoops were common. The black market at Ueno, a veritable emporium of re-tailored clothes, soap, cigarettes and kitchen utensils, is fondly remembered for its sweets. Many of the goods, originally from the PX stores, were sold to stall holders by the *pan pan,* prostitutes who served American forces. Dozens of stalls were set up in the warren of lanes and houses between Okachimachi and Ueno stations on the Yamanote loop line, giving rise to the name Ameya Yokocho, Confectionary Row. Many of the sweets were made from potato but satisfied the craving for sugar. Scenes of the large black market at Ikebukuro feature in Hayashi Fumiko's 1951 novel *Floating Clouds.*

Another area of prophetically lively commerce was Akihabara. Akihabara's post-war black market developed into an area of stalls under the railway tracks, selling spare parts for radios. Stolen and recycled American provisions—everything from powdered milk and drugs to inner tubes—helped to get several new enterprises off the ground in the early

post-war years. Black-market items like radios and walkie-talkies were assiduously cannibalized for their parts, often by near-destitute students
from the Kanda-Hongo university quarter who found building radios a
more profitable sideline than selling matches and peanuts on street corners.
Rajio Kaikan is the site where the original spare parts salesmen were
housed after their operation became too sprawling for the streets. Provision
was made in 1951 for dealings to take place under the tracks of the Sobu
line.

If the black markets provided desperate, enterprising and occasionally unscrupulous men with a way of making ends meet, the post-war phenomenon most strongly associated with the activities of women on the
margins of Tokyo life were the so-called *pan pan* girls. The etymology of
the name is obscure, but may refer to a South Pacific island term for available women picked up by American servicemen. There was nothing new
about Japanese women consorting with foreigners for gain. Financial
arrangements had been made in the mid-nineteenth century for certain
women to become the mistresses or temporary "wives" of foreigners living
in the treaty ports, and near the foreign settlement in Tokyo's Tsukiji district a licensed pleasure quarter, exclusively for the use of westerners, had
been set up. Yet what struck people as new and shocking about the pan pan
was their frankness, even defiance of social conventions, which dictated
that paid sexual relations should be conducted discreetly. The sight of the
heavily made-up pan pan smoking on street corners beneath railway overpasses at stations like Yurakucho, or even worse, the sight of these women
hanging from the arm of their swaggering GI partners, constituted a
painful affront to male national pride. In his book *Meeting with Japan*
(1959), Fosco Maraini witnessed the reaction to "the shameless *pan pan*,
painted like harridans, with huge heels and misshapen legs, who shout,
smoke, spit, chew gum, and call out 'Hey, Johnnie!' to passers-by." An
even greater affront in the eyes of some Japanese was the habit of some
GIs of tossing their used condoms into the waters of the moat surrounding the Imperial Palace, where the emperor resided. The offending objects
were removed once a week with the aid of a large wire scoop.

While the pan pan girls were generally treated with contempt by
society, others were attracted by their brazen sexuality and open-minded-
ness, recognizing a modern counterpart to the women of the old pleasure
quarters whom Saikaku and others had written about. In a magazine in-

terview on the topic of the newly democratized Japan, the well-known scholar and critic Tatsuno Takashi went so far as to suggest that pan pan were the most liberal elements in contemporary society, the people who best "transcended racial and international prejudice." Inevitably, the pan pan entered into the literature of the time.

THE DECADENTS

In conditions like these, men and women with barely enough food to eat drank themselves into oblivion. When it came to profit, the black marketers had few scruples about selling concoctions that were near lethal. One particularly vicious blend was a mixture of artificial sweetening and an alcohol base stolen or otherwise acquired from aircrafts, where it was used as an engine lubricant. Not much better was *kasutori shochu*, a truly repellent drink that left most people comatose by the third glass. Those who made a regular habit of it risked blindness.

This was the drink of choice among a group of young artists, writers and barfly intelligentsia who were making a virtue, even a movement, out of nihilism and degeneracy. With the endorsement of some genuinely talented figures, *kasutori bunka* (kasutori culture), centred around erotic entertainment, pulp fiction, sleazy bars and clubs, could seem like an authentic counter-culture. Embracing the world of black marketers and pan pan, it was wilfully nihilistic and iconoclastic,

More talented writers, while affecting an air of fashionable nihilism in both their work and lifestyle, fused moral decay and eroticism with the idea of ascendant individualism and the repudiation of traditional, authorial values. In *On Decadence*, a highly influential, passionately argued essay published in the spring of 1946, Sakaguchi Ango drew a parallel between the unreality of the war years and the post-war experience, seeing the former as a baptism of fire, the latter as an intensification of a degeneracy that, forced to breaking point, might yield hope. Dismantling three sacred icons at once, Ango asked:

> Could we not say that the kamikaze hero was a mere illusion, and that human history begins from the point where he takes to black-marketeering? That the widow as devoted apostle is mere illusion, and that human history begins from the moment when the image of a new face enters her breast? And perhaps the emperor too is no more than illu-

sion, and the emperor's true history begins from the point where he becomes an ordinary human.

In Sakaguchi's view, the Japanese had gone along with the war because it offered them the rare comfort of not having to think for themselves. Another writer who epitomized the kasutori culture was Tamura Taijiro, a former foot soldier in the Imperial Army, who confronted his disillusionment with the war years in a series of novels and essays extolling the physical reality of the individual over the dangerous abstractions of the militarists. The best-known of these novels of exploratory debauchery was *Gate of Flesh*. Published in 1947, it portrays the lives and ethics of streetwalkers living in the wrecked dockyards of the Sumida.

The relative freedom of expression enjoyed by writers under the occupation was tempered by a sense of dislocation and unease most clearly embodied in the work of these so-called *burai-ha* or "dissolutes". The burai-ha, viewing the world as an existential void in much the same way as their less emotional French counterparts Sartre and Camus struck out against what they saw as the double standards, duplicity and self-illusions of the age, the ill-fitting, hybrid values promulgated by the occupation authorities and their Japanese counterparts.

The most notorious representative of this new school of literary *louche*, a past master of self-cultivated neurosis and carefully affected dissoluteness, was Dazai Osamu. Born into a wealthy landowning family in Aomori prefecture, in 1930 Dazai entered Tokyo University, where he involved himself in the left-wing student movement, a means to atone for the privileged social position in which he was born. Like his fellow literary aspirant, Sakaguchi Ango, Dazai had affected the life of a literary vagabond in the pre-war city. His descent to the lower depths of Tokyo life, the suicide and double-suicide attempts, the hospitalization to recover from self-poisoning, his troubled first marriage and subsequent divorce from a geisha all provided him with the raw material for books like the 1935 *Retrogression* and the collection of linked novels, *Eight Views of Tokyo,* which would gain him literary recognition.

Dazai's characters, much like the writer himself, attempt to reignite the efforts of the late Meiji- and Taisho-period proletarian writers to secure, as Dazai put it, "an admission ticket for the rooms of the people." From the start of 1947 through to 1948 Dazai wrote with an extraordinary passion and clarity. *The Setting Sun, Villon's Wife, Cherry* and *No Longer Human* were produced during this short period. In *The Setting Sun*, Dazai tells the story of an aristocratic family's decline in the post-war years. The family scion, bearing a remarkable resemblance to the author himself, declares:

> "I wanted to become coarse, to be strong—no, brutal. I thought that was the only way I could qualify myself as a 'friend of the people.' Liquor was not enough. I was perpetually prey to a terrible dizziness. That was why I had no choice but to take drugs. I had to forget my family. I had to oppose my father's blood."

Few works capture the mood of demoralization and dream with as much accuracy as this novel. Dazai's trademark instability together with drug and alcohol addiction led to four pre-war attempts at suicide. In one tragically botched attempt with a barmaid, she perished while he survived to shame his family and despise himself even more. Dazai made his personal demons work for him in a series of deeply flawed but brilliant works, until inevitably, they overpowered him. His fifth attempt at self-destruction in 1948, a double suicide with another mistress, involved tying themselves together with a kimono sash, then plunging into the Setagaya reservoir at the edge of Tokyo. A successful suicide, it terminated his life at the age of thirty-nine and left behind a wife and three children. His illegitimate daughter, Tsushima Yoko, born a year before his death, is a well-known fiction writer living in Tokyo. The romantic self-annihilation of these writers still resonates with the Japanese. There would be more suicides of writers to come in later decades. The "terrible dizziness" experienced by Dazai's characters captured one of many complex post-war moods. That theories of decadence and hedonism could co-exist with lingering malnutrition was one of the more disturbing paradoxes of the time.

Kafu addressed the moral decline, the dog-eat-dog attitudes all too easily justified by necessity, in one of his last stories, *The Scavengers*. Scouring the countryside outside Tokyo for food, two women manage to exchange towels and shoes with a farmer for rice. Overcome by the heat and exertion, the older woman dies. Making sure she is not observed, her companion robs the corpse and, once over the next hill, sells the rice at a good profit to another scavenger.

Disinclined to continue living in the post-war era, Kawabata Yasunari declared in a short essay in November, 1945: "I have the strong, unavoidable feeling that my life is already at an end. For me there is only the solitary return to the mountains and rivers of the past. From this point on, as one already dead, I intend to write only of the poor beauty of Japan, not a line else." Most of his best work would appear in the following decades, as would the Nobel Prize for Literature. The desire for death would also be satisfied, but not until 1972.

PULP CULTURE

On the premise that the opposite of war is not, as one poet put it, peace but civilization, Tokyo set about remaking itself into a city of culture. After ten years of repression and silence, imprisoned writers, along with those who had gone into hiding, began pouring into Tokyo, renewing old ties, writing with a new fury, founding dozens of new publications. Pin-up magazines, pulp fiction and strip shows were part of the new culture. Pulp fiction revived the *ero-guro-nansensu* (erotic, grotesque, nonsensical) fad associated with the 1920s and early 1930s. *Kasutori zasshi* (kasutori magazines) with titles like *Buinasu* (Venus), *Oru Ryoki* (All Bizarre) and *Neo-riberaru* (Neo-liberal) were quick to exploit the urge towards rebellion and carnality and to provide the escapist illusion that authority had been abolished once and for all.

The big hit of 1948, the year Dazai's alcohol-sodden body was retrieved from the Tama river reservoir, was a jazz ditty by the name of "Tokyo Boogie Woogie":

Tokyo Boogie-Woogie
Rhythm. Wowie Wowie.
My heart goes pit-a-pat. Tick-a-tack.
A song of the world. A happy song.
Tokyo Boogie-Woogie.

It was like the 1920s all over again. So was the re-emergence in the coffee shops and university campuses of Marxism and the politics of the left. An older school of established writers, the *bunkajin* or "people of culture", notably Kawabata Yasunari, Nagai Kafu and Tanizaki Junichiro, novelists who had withdrawn into dignified, largely unmolested silence during the war years, choosing to neither actively resist nor endorse the military, resumed working as if nothing had happened.

Their main theme, the primacy of the individual, was well suited to the times, though Kafu's continued peregrinations through the twice-razed, increasingly modernizing neighbourhoods to the east of Tokyo were a doomed search for traces of Edo and Meiji culture. Contenting himself with graveyards, mouldering tombs and carved deities, Kafu has a character in one of his later stories comment, "A certain cemetery in Minowa, north of Asakusa, was about to be moved, and there were tombstones that I desperately wanted to have pictures of before they disappeared." Offsetting the prevailing nihilism and the unexamined embrace of all things western were themes springing from the rediscovery of Japanese culture. Two postwar works in particular, Osaragi Jiro's *Homecoming* and Tanizaki's *Some Prefer Nettles*, are outstanding examples of this counter-tendency.

Despite a paper shortage (a flourishing black-market commodity) publishing went into overdrive in the immediate post-war years. Over a thousand books, many of them serious, well-considered works by authors who had been suppressed during the war years, appeared even before the end of 1945. Given the shortages, this was a remarkable achievement. Magazines in particular were sold out as soon as they appeared. It was a common sight in those days to see book retailers pressing into the offices of popular publishers with rucksacks on their backs filled with vegetables and other foods, commodities needed to supplement cash. The market was insatiable. As the writer Nakamura Mitsuo put it: "People were hungry for art and culture as much as they were for food. As they ate meat, fish or anything so long as it was palatable, anything that looked like literature or had the form of literature was satisfactory for healing the dissolute mind."

Publishers responded to the thirst for words by bringing out everything from translations of foreign writers to trenchant critical journals, books and essays promoting left-wing ideologies, and cheesy pulp magazines. "What a race of readers the Japanese are!" Edmund Blunden wrote after a visit at this time to the bookshop district of Jimbocho: "it is almost a national vice, this appetite for printed matter." A photo taken by a photographer with the *Asahi Shinbun* newspaper in July 1947 supports this view. The image depicts a long line of customers sleeping outside the Iwanami bookstore in the Kanda district, patiently waiting to buy copies of the collected works of the Japanese philosopher Nishida Kitaro. The queue, which had begun forming three days before the publication date, grew to over two hundred people.

Ten years later, Edward Seidensticker could portray a fully awakened city, a pullulating urban mass with little to offer in the way of beauty but steeped in atmosphere, a place where the newcomer:

> ... must walk the streets until he sees for himself. The roar about him is not just the roar of trains and taxicabs. It is also the roar of sinews and blood. A good Buddhist, in the days when the species survived, might have described Tokyo as smelling of meat; Walt Whitman might have said that it had the fine, clean smell of armpits. Tokyo is a stewing mass of people, and there are no beautiful, dead surfaces to distract one from the vitality once it is known.

Many foreign writers without Seidensticker's more nuanced view of Japan continued to fixate on its more exotic aspects. Even Arthur Koestler, on a visit to "Lotus land", described his first sensation of the country as evoking "an atmosphere with an erotic flicker like the crisp sparks from a comb drawn through a woman's hair."

RAZING THE YOSHIWARA

That old affliction, the need for western approval, resurfaced in the pre-Olympic years (Tokyo was chosen in 1958 to host the 1964 Games of the XVIII Olympiad). One of the first items coming in for a public drubbing was the old Yoshiwara pleasure quarter. The Yoshiwara of the print masters and poets had long vanished. The elegant old teahouses, where a certain amount of protocol was maintained, had been replaced with ersatz western confections, forerunners of some of the more fanciful love hotels that appeared in the 1960s. The soft glow of red and orange lanterns had given way to neon signs advertising beer, jazz and girls. A tourist could go there to buy a table napkin decorated with an Utamaru print or a teacup with a quote from Saikaku. Laws were introduced in 1949 to abolish the quarter. A counter-campaign was launched to preserve the Yoshiwara, but it was too late. As the sentimental Koestler put it: "Old guard sensualists fought in rage and bitterness to save the Yoshiwara... For nine years the old guard, the ancient rakes, the men with memories of better times and wilder joys fought the government. But puritanism had come in with TV, coke and stretch pants."

With the official outlawing of prostitution on April Fool's Day 1958, the Yoshiwara breathed its last. Naturally, the law itself was toothless, having little effect on the profession itself, with the more marketable women of the Yoshiwara simply relocating to hostess bars, night clubs, massage parlours and other water trade venues—places that were unlikely to leave much of a cultural legacy or be celebrated in art or literature.

For the indentured women of the Yoshiwara, those whom the moats and walls were meant to keep in, the reforms intended to liberate them were in any case too late. Jokan-ji, a sad little temple in the district of Minowa, not far from the old site of the Yoshiwara, is also known by the name Nagekomi Temple. *Nagekomi* means "thrown away"; it was here that women who died in the Yoshiwara were, quite literally, tossed over the walls of the temple for the priests to cremate and dispose of in unmarked graves. J. E. de Becker, in his exhaustive 1899 study of the Yoshiwara, *The Nightless City*, gives us a memorable account of the temple:

> Here the whole surface of the earth is damp and humid, and a dismal grave-like smell of mouldy earth pervades the locality. Probably the sunshine has never penetrated to this spot for centuries. The dead leaves of the *e-no-ki* trees have been allowed to lie as they have fallen year after year, so they have piled up, crumbled, mouldered, and rotted on the dark ground, and from the purulent mildewed soil have sprung into being myriads of weird uncanny poisonous toadstools and foul fungi fearful and horrid in shape and strangely ghastly in colour. Ah! what a desolate uncanny appearance the place has! Persons visiting it soon experience a deep sense of commiseration and sympathy, and feel as if they had entered a chilly under-ground vault. In this gloomy dismal place lie the bones of the courtesan who only up to yesterday resembled a beautiful butterfly or lovely blossom when seen in all the glory of her gorgeous apparel, with her glossy black hair ornamented with gold and her snowy-white body clad in rich brocade robes now exchanged for the cerements of death.

It is still a lugubrious place, the air smelling of incense and mildew. Kafu's wish was to be buried here in an ignominious plot beside the decaying headstones of the Yoshiwara women, but it was not to be. When death came in 1959, his brother, always a stickler for the social proprieties, had his ashes interred in a plot alongside those of his parents in Zoshigaya cemetery. He did at least get his way with the inscription on the headstone, which reads: "The Grave of Kafu the Scribbler". He was far more than just a scribbler, and unquestionably knew as much himself. There is a small stone marker to Kafu though, in front of the memorial to the women who were disposed of at Jokan-ji. It contains his false teeth and one of his writing brushes.

A FILM VIEW OF THE CITY

In the 1950s and 1960s, the coffee shops and bars of Shinjuku emerged as the centre for a new type of intellectual life, one grounded in the literature and cinema of the day. The Chikyu-za was the first cinema in Japan to start showing European and Russian films. By this time the Japanese were once again making their own films. Rather than resorting to a dictated or imported style, this was an indigenous school of cinema.

Earlier films, like Naruse's 1935 *Wife, Be Like a Rose*, and Mizoguchi's even older *White Threads of the Cascade*, contain interesting location shots tracing Tokyo's changing skyline. Kurosawa's early post-war films are bleakly realistic and ironic studies. *No Regrets For Our Youth*, a political film released in 1946, concerns the persecution of liberals in the repressive early 1930s; *Wonderful Sunday*, which appeared the next year, follows two young lovers through the bombed ruins of Tokyo; his *Stray Dog* (1949) has the great Japanese actor Mifune playing a detective searching through the grimmer parts of Ueno and Asakusa for his stolen pistol. Imai Tadashi's 1951 *And Yet We Live* was also shot in the vicinity of Ueno Station, using hidden cameras and a crew who blended in with real crowds and street scenes. Gosho Heinosuke's *Where Chimneys Are Seen* (1953) looks at the creeping industrialization along the banks of the Sumida river.

Films concentrating on the plight of women were also common. Naruse's *Mother* (1952) depicts the life of a young widow in a depressed suburb of Tokyo. Mizoguchi's semi-documentary *Red Light District* is a sympathetic look at the world of the Tokyo prostitute on the eve of the ineffectual banning of that trade. A widowed daughter-in-law turns out to be the most sympathetic character in Ozu Yasujiro's 1953 classic, *Tokyo Story*, when elderly parents visit their children, only to find them too busy with their new lives to take care of them.

Oshima Nagisa's film, *Diary of a Shinjuku Thief*, was made in the 1960s. The dimly lit bars and jazz coffee shops that sprouted up in the almost bohemian milieu of Shinjuku epitomized Japan's version of the alternative culture of the 1960s, attracting a lively mix of radical students, novelists, poets and experimental playwrights like Kara Juro, Terayama Shuji and Suzuki Tadashi. Among the circles of writers were beatniks, hippies and Vietnam-bound draftees in the US army, and a few deserters too. A centre of free love and art movements, the district also attracted its fair share of ruffians, drug peddlers and *yakuza*—Tokyo's violent mafia connected to the black market.

GROWTH AND RESURGENCE

Remnants of the feudal city, at least the parts that had survived the bombings, could still be glimpsed a decade or so after the war. Architect Charlotte Perriand described Tokyo at the time of her visit as a compress of ancient looking wooden buildings in the shadows of new colossi: "Tokyo 1956: modern buildings, small glass and cement fortresses, one after the other, housing the most unbelievable complexes: railway stations, metro, department stores, restaurants, theaters. At their feet a city of eight million inhabitants built from paper and wood."

All of that was about to change, though not everyone had the prescience to see it. In 1957 the respected Japan scholar and future US ambassador to Japan, Edwin O. Reischauer, gloomily observed, "The economic situation in Japan may be so fundamentally unsound that no policies, no matter how wise, can save her from slow economic starvation and all the concomitant political and social ills that situation would produce." How utterly wrong he was. Japan was already moving towards an economic resurgence that would astonish the world. By the beginning of the 1960s, its GNP was the fifth largest in the world. By the end of the same decade it was second only to that of the United States. On 27 December 1960 Prime Minister Ikeda Hayato initiated an ambitious ten-year plan to double incomes by the end of the decade. The target was reached in just seven years.

Japan's rapid post-war progress is often dated from the Korean War (1950-53), when the country benefited from a massive procurement trade, producing goods for American military forces. The infusion of funds from the Korean and later Vietnam War, when Japan once again became a supply depot and staging post for US forces, spurred investment in industrial plants and equipment and boosted Japan's confidence in competing in the international marketplace. In a supreme irony, Japan's former, very recent enemy, was now providing the country with a flood of contracts to supply goods for new Asian wars.

Exogenous events like the Korean War may have stimulated the economy, but the roots of the economic miracle were in the Meiji era, when the country began a massive industrialization programme, one that was largely destroyed in the Second World War. That programme was driven by similar factors to those of the post-war revival: an ability to adapt and innovate, a thirst for progress, determination to catch up and surpass the West, a skilled labour pool, prodigious amounts of hard work, astute planning and a long tradition of entrepreneurship. Tokyo, the ideal engine for the economic resurgence, had always been a thoroughly commercial city. The Victorian traveller Isabella Bird noted the fact with some distaste when she wrote in 1880 that "a bald materialism is its highest creed and material gain its goal."

TOKYO OLYMPIAD

In 1964 Tokyo invited the world to come and take a look at the new Japan. The year of the Olympic Games was to be Japan's *annus mirabilis*, its re-entry into the international community as a fully functioning democracy.

It also provided another economic turning point. A staggering eighty per cent of expenditure on the Olympics went on public works projects. Most visible were the complex overhead system of expressways, the expanded subways, gigantic apartment blocks, gleaming new hotels and the city's plans for skyscrapers. On 1 October of the Olympic year, the new "bullet train", the world's fastest, left Tokyo Station for the 300-mile trip to Osaka. Joining a long list of rousing slogans and refrains dating back to the previous century came a new one, freshly minted for the times: "Prosperity in Peace Time".

The area facing Omotesando-dori, the "Outer Approach Road" to Meiji Shrine had been requisitioned by the occupation forces after the war and turned into housing quarters for military personnel and their families. The site remained in US hands after the occupation ended in 1952. The land the barracks stood on, renamed "Washington Heights", was now handed back to the Japanese government after Tokyo was selected as the host city for the games. The barracks were turned into a temporary village for athletes. Author Norma Field recalls in one of her books that in the decade or two before the transfer, "there was a scary spot under a set of train tracks where Japanese veterans dressed in white and chained to a wall played accordions and thrust out tin cups on a hook." The same tracks would soon run alongside the concrete pavilions of the Olympic structures.

Ichikawa Kon's documentary *Tokyo Olympiad*, scripted by the poet Tanikawa Shuntaro, was a visual masterpiece that failed to impress the Olympic Organizing Board, which seems to have had something grander and more heroic in mind. In the uncut version of Ichikawa's film, the camera pans across the faces of the spectators, capturing not only the victories of the Japanese participants, but also the human moments of exhaustion and defeat. Sadly, many scenes from what Donald Richie has described as "the most beautiful, attentive, and moving sports film ever made," have never been publicly screened.

The foreign media declared the games an unconditional success, however, some going as far as saying they were the best organized Olympics in living memory. In addition to the flawless organization, was the impressive Olympic architecture. The location for the Nippon Budokan, venue for the martial arts events, close to the great stonewalls and moats of the Imperial Palace, reinforced the link between tradition and modernity. Constructed of ferro-concrete and steel, the octagonal floor plan, with a roof and orb similar to a sumo wrestler's topknot, were designed to evoke the wooden Hall of Dreams, part of Horyu-ji Temple near the ancient city of Nara.

The standout designs, however, were the work of Tange Kenzo. The architect's National Yoyogi Sport Centre, sweeping and curving tent-like rooflines of tensile steel, won the Pritzker Prize for architecture in 1967, reinforcing the pride of the Japanese, for whom the Olympics were a celebration of Japan's democratic revival. The postwar period of humiliation and poverty was finally over.

REMODELLING TOKYO

The fever of construction leading up the Olympics remodelled the city almost beyond recognition. Disinterred from their graves in the already much reduced grounds of Zojo-ji, the embalmed bodies of the Togugawa shoguns were examined and probed by historians and scientists before being reburied in a much smaller graveyard behind the temple. The original tombs stood in the way of development and plans to build a new hotel, golf club and the construction in 1958 of Tokyo Tower, built for the purpose of transmitting radio and television signals. The seizing of temple land by the authorities, begun in the Meiji era, resumed in earnest in the post-war period. In Tanizaki's final novel, *Diary of a Mad Old Man* (1961), the narrator muses:

> The bones of my grandmother and grandfather have been disturbed twice: once when their temple was moved from Fukagawa to Asakusa because the whole neighbourhood had become industrial, and again, after the temple burned down in the great earthquake, to the Tama Cemetery. So graves in Tokyo have to be constantly shifted to escape destruction.

Dozens of new hotels followed, including the super-modern Hotel New Otani. The spacious new hotels were, quite literally, eating into the past. The Australian writer Hal Porter revisited in 1967, remarking on how

> ... the authorities of Hie Shrine have sold an area of their rocks and moss and elderly gingko trees to the Hilton. I learn that this has become a common practice. Other gigantic structures, the Tokyo Prince Hotel and the Tokyo Tower for example, now occupy former shrine grounds once forlorn with lichened *torii* (shrine gateways), gangling stone lanterns, and raven-sullied cryptomerias gloomy as Pluto.

Wooden stalls were removed from the streets, new subways and a monorail built and a terminal for the world's fastest train system constructed. The utilitarian concrete buildings and drab cookie-cutter apartment blocks that were springing up beyond the Olympic pavilions and the grounds of luxury hotels were less impressive. Ian Fleming's secret agent took a swipe at the utilitarian city in his 1964 novel, *You Only Live Twice*: "Bond waved at the cluttered shambles of the Tokyo suburbs through which they were tearing at what seemed to Bond a suicide speed. 'Doesn't look the most attractive city in the world. And why are we driving on the left?'" Interestingly, the title of Fleming's book comes from a little known haiku by Basho:

You only live twice:
Once when you are born
And once when you look death in the face.

In the rush to put up elevated freeways with sound-protective steel barriers, entire canal systems were filled in with concrete. Systems that remained were often noisome in their levels of pollution. People still remember the waters of the Kanda river bubbling and reeking with gases. The end result of all these efforts at breakneck modernization were lost on many foreign observers. To quote once more from Hal Porter, that sternest critic of all things Japanese, Tokyo was

A city built too late for feudalism and too early for democracy, it remains makeshift and confused, a freak weed sprung from a crack in history, and drenched by a fertilizer that makes it monstrous but not mighty, immense but immoral, overgrown and undercivilized.

Porter preferred the ruined city he knew during the years of the occupation, and its more submissive, defeated people. In the years since his earlier visits the Japanese had become more self-assured and assertive. In demonizing the city as "groaning, shrieking, roaring, clashing, squealing and thundering like a satanic factory," he was also, in the company of many other foreign writers and observers who inspected the new Tokyo, demonizing the new Japanese.

One of the saddest casualties of the Olympics was also one of the most enduring symbols of the city: the Nihonbashi Bridge. At the congested heart of Edo, this important span was rebuilt several times after fires devastated it. On one occasion its wooden supports had given way under the weight of the crowds, resulting in the deaths of over a thousand townspeople. The present bridge, a graceful granite structure guarded by four bronze lions of Chinese provenance, four seated unicorns and two obelisk-shaped bronze light standards, dates from 1911. Photos taken at the time show a purposefully durable European structure standing among a sea of perishable wooden houses, shacks, barges along the quays of Tokyo's main fish market.

In one of the city's famously reckless drives towards modernization, the authorities decided in the run up to the Olympics to build a system of expressways to relieve Tokyo of its traffic congestion. The ready-made corridors of rivers and canals were co-opted as the obvious choice for construction of a ferro-concrete nexus. One of these routes, an eight-lane freeway, ran right over the top of Nihonbashi, consigning the bridge not to destruction but perpetual shadow and the rumble of motorized traffic.

Assuredly reflecting his own feelings on the subject, Tanizaki's main character in *Diary of a Mad Old Man*, declares: "I suppose it doesn't matter where they put you once you're dead; still I dislike the thought of being buried in a place as unpleasant as Tokyo, a place that has lost all meaning for me." Referring to the city as "that overturned rubbish heap of Tokyo", the narrator pursues the theme of defilement when he asks:

> Who made Tokyo into such a miserable, chaotic city? Weren't they all boorish, country-bred politicians unaware of the good qualities of old Tokyo? Weren't those the men who turned our beautiful canals into muddy ditches, men who never knew that whitebait swam in the Sumida River?

Tanizaki had written about shadows of a different order: textured, subdued lighting, full of the cultural fermentation of a different age. The catchphrase that came to best express the aspirations of this altogether different city, a neon and fluorescent western derivative, was *akarui seikatsu*, the "bright new life".

Chapter Nine

DREAM MESSENGER

1970s-

On 4 October 1970, the author Mishima Yukio sat down and wrote a letter to the young British journalist Henry Scott Stokes, in which he concluded, "Finishing the long novel makes me feel sometimes as if it will be the end of the world." The next month he was dead.

This was no ordinary death. Mishima and members of his private army known as the *Tatenokai* (Shield Society) had entered the office of General Mashita at the headquarters of the Self-Defence Forces in Tokyo's Ichigaya district and, in a scene thoroughly documented by the media, Mishima had made a speech from the balcony appealing for the restoration of imperial sovereignty. Having failed to win over the troops assembled for his speech, much of which was inaudible above the commotion below, the author returned to the room and, in the tradition of the samurai warrior, committed *seppuku*, ritual disembowelment.

By the time Stokes jumped into the taxi that took him to Ichigaya amidst the din of helicopters circling overhead and revving police motorbikes, it was all over. Mishima's hungry ghost, though, has never really been laid to rest, the image of his death never quite brushed under the bloodstained carpet of the general's office.

Before completing his last work, *The Decay of the Angel*, the coda to his tetralogy *The Sea of Fertility*, Mishima had organized a retrospective of his life and work at the Tobu department store in Ikebukuro, in which he divided the exhibition space into four contiguous sections: The River of Writing, Theatre, Body, and finally The River of Action. To the astonishment of visitors, the hall was draped in black curtains similar to *maku*, the hanging textiles used in Japanese funerals to delineate boundaries. In pride of place and impossible to ignore was the sword that Mishima's companion in death, student Morita Masakatsu, would use to decapitate the writer the following month.

Invited to Stokes' home for dinner just two months before what the media would term "The Mishima Incident", the usually voluble author turned solemn: "I made the steaks for us and underdid them," Stokes notes: "Put off by something in Yukio. Steaks had to go into the pan again, bloody red. After dinner he struck his pessimistic note again... used an odd image: said that Japan was under the curse of a 'green snake'."

"I thought you were warriors," Mishima berated members of the Self-Defence Forces gathered below the general's office: "If so, why are you safeguarding the Constitution that denies your existence? Why are you so obsequious?" If Mishima wished to put the steel back into Japan, it was because, as Marguerite Yourcenar wrote, he was "a writer revolted by the flabbiness of his times."

Another Mishima biographer, John Nathan, argues convincingly that the writer's life might be seen as a paradigm of the struggle experienced by the nation itself in the years since the arrival of Perry's black ships, "to find an authentic *self* by reconciling two disparate and often irreconcilable cultures—one native, inherent and grounded in tradition, the other foreign and intractable." Right up to the moment of his suicide, Mishima conducted his search for that "authentic self" on a public stage. The public were by turns transfixed and appalled by this very un-Japanese exhibitionism and baring of the soul.

In *Streams and Rivers*, the poet Iijima Koichi reflects on the meaning of Mishima's sacrifice and his efforts to somehow align himself with the irretrievable past:

He did live in a gorgeous western-style house,
But that was imitation West;
Even his military uniform was fake.
He was always feeling inferior
To the absolutely genuine elitism
Of the Meiji poet Ogai.

That uniform was on display at an exhibition I attended some years ago at Kanagawa Museum of Modern Literature in Yokohama. Mishima's physical form, the way he wished to be perceived, dominated the exhibition. Almost the first exhibit was one of the author's well-cut, pinstriped suits. Measurements never lie, but like the diminutive samurai armour displayed in museums and castles, the squat outline and pinched shoulders of Mishima's suit belied the real stature of the figure that once filled it.

It was an exhibition rich in imagery. Mishima was never camera shy, posing for the lens whenever the occasion presented itself, believing perhaps that if enough moments in time could be frozen, they might assure his immortality. I can think of few Japanese authors who have courted quite so much attention. Mixed in with the family, publishers and news images were more carefully staged shots, among them the famous re-enactment of St. Sebastian's martyrdom: Mishima in loincloth, hands bound, an oiled chest bristling with arrows, all done in a Tokyo studio. Some of the most remarkable prints were from Hosoe Eikoh's photo homage, *Ordeal by Roses*.

Mishima's physique had grown powerful by the time these later images were taken, the author having subjected himself to a punishing body-building regime at a Tokyo gym, one that would, quite literally, turn stringy arms and a concave chest into iron-clad plating. In this transformation there was no doubt something of the samurai notion that one should always be ready for death, that the warrior should not only be mentally prepared but physically presentable. A well-known eighteenth-century Japanese document advised followers of *Bushido*, The Way of the Samurai, to always "carry rouge and powder," especially when going to battle as they should look beautiful in death. It was common practice when respectfully displaying the heads of illustrious enemies for the victors to have the faces beautified with rouge.

The latter part of the exhibition featured a statue of the author cast in bronze. Mishima, one remembers, was inordinately fond of the ancient classical world and its muscular statuary. A photo of the house in the Tokyo district of Magome, which Mishima built in 1959, shows a prominent replica of Apollo Belvedere in the garden. The most striking feature about the Mishima statue was the author's physique, notably his height, which appeared to have grown by a good head. In the end it was Mishima's tailor who carried the most authority. The author's cleanly pressed uniform, undeniably life-size, stood near the exit, draped over the shoulders of a headless mannequin. Mishima's real stature as both a writer and major figure of our times has never been in question.

As a novelist, playwright and essayist, Mishima was, however, aware of the limits of even his prolific output, something that may have tempted him back to the once complementary traditions in Japan of literature and the martial arts. In Mishima the two disciplines would combine, achieve critical mass and then self-destruct. A militarist in the imperialist mode, he stood for everything that Japan was trying to forget. It was as if the emperor, the Voice of the Crane, having declared himself human, Mishima would make himself superhuman. He ended up instead as an acute embarrassment to the Japanese public, a people who saw themselves engaged in a different kind of heroic endeavour: the transformation of a discredited nation into an industrial giant and pacifist model. Where the majority of Japanese viewed the post-war period as an opportunity for moral cleansing and regeneration, Mishima saw only torpor and decay, a poisoning of the very ground water that had nourished the national spirit. He believed perhaps that only an act of calculated violence could forestall the corruption, force stagnation and inaction back into a strong, mainstream current.

It was already too late. Mishima, whose punishing training schedules had driven his body to its intended physical peak, had no intention of growing old gracefully. His ritual disembowelment, besides its nationalist symbolism, was also the destruction of Narcissus, the sword crashing into the mirror of beauty before it could transmit back an image of decay.

Before it was all over, Mishima sought one final, quintessentially Japanese touch to the beautification of the body. A little over a week before his carefully conceived death Mishima, seized by the idea of having the illustration of a lion-dog and peony engraved on his back, contacted the tattoo master Owada Mitsuaki, better known by his professional name Horikin. As a final flourish to Mishima's stage-managed suicide, in keeping with his obsession with Japanese culture, it was a very Edo-period touch. If Mishima had known a little more about tattoos, however, he would have realized that such works of art cannot be undertaken at such short notice, accomplished in just a few days.

TRACES OF EDO
On close inspection the headless body, floating like a swollen flower against the embankments of the Sumida river, appeared to have no fingertips, leaving the Tokyo police with no obvious clues to identity. Except one. Covering the back of the naked torso was the upper section of a full-body tattoo, its main feature a lion-dog and peony.

Indelible proof of an underworld connection, the vivid, recently completed design, described at length by the Tokyo newspapers, was of such fine quality that it could only have been executed by one of the few surviving masters of the art. It was only a question of time before the victim's identity and gangland affiliation were established.

Strongly associated in the general public's mind with members of Japan's criminal underworld, those who display tattoos, however discreetly, run the risk of incurring social exclusion and ostracism. In Japan, where affiliation still counts for a great deal, it is only natural in highly organized, semi-secret groups like the yakuza, where rigid codes, ceremonies, initiation rituals and special rites of passage are integral to its traditions, that tattoos have been important membership credentials.

Especially among the working-class people of the shitamachi, however, tattoos have not been simply the exclusive reserve of gangsters. They were popular with quasi-feudal groups and guilds like carpenters, fairground hucksters and sushi chefs. Even now, as John E. Thayer has written, "there is still the young dump truck driver who, like his Edo artisan forebear, spends all his free time and salary having a genuine work of art engraved upon his back."

Tattooing became closely connected with the Japanese woodblock print in its design, colouring and techniques, and the popularity of artists like Kunisada and Utamaro, who all vigorously depicted the figures of tattooed actors, courtesans and gods, and whose work had enormous appeal at all social levels, coincided with the blossoming of tattoo art among the masses.

The firemen of Edo, colourful characters who might almost have stepped out of fiction themselves, may have been the first to sport the full-body tattoo, a work that covered everything bar the hands, feet and head. Fire-fighting groups displayed different preferences in their designs, but all of them wore a protective water symbol of some kind, usually a carp or water dragon. Although tattoos were still regarded with suspicion by the authorities and condemned as "deleterious to public morals", a newly affluent middle class, enthusiastic patrons in all fields of art, was showing a lively appreciation of the practice.

In the search for symbols that embody strength and sagacity, various Buddhist sub-deities have been inducted into the repertoire of popular tattooing. The two best-known figures are probably Fudo, the Guardian of

A man with traditional tattoos at the Sanja Festival in Asakusa

Hell, an awesome deity clutching a burning sword and a length of rope, and Kannon, the sensual, consoling Goddess of Mercy. Figures from popular folklore with whom wearers of tattoos generally like to identify include the angel Hagoramo, who appears in a popular Noh play, the voluptuous female Shinto deity Benten, the bare-breasted Tamatori-hime, a diving girl who is on good terms with submerged dragons and, among the male figures, Kintaro, a boy who is strongly identified with the virtuous, ever popular carp. The gentleman thief Benten Kozo and Benkei, the Japanese Hercules, are also popular figures.

Love and religion seem to have been the main inspirations for early Japanese tattoos. Lovers, courtesans and lowly prostitutes often had the name of a loved one written in Chinese ideograms along the inner portion of the arm. Tattoos to deify an amorous experience or affair were rarer by the twentieth century. A notable exception comes to mind: that great chronicler of the Tokyo *demi-monde*, Kafu, who is said to have had a tattoo drawn in the likeness of a geisha named Tomimatsu, with whom he was infatuated for a short time until he lost her to a wealthier patron. Whether in a spirit of romanticism or because of the stubbornness of the inks used in the process, he seemingly carried the image to his grave.

In Tanizaki's exquisitely written 1910 story, *The Tattooist*, the story of a woman strangely empowered by the work of a master tattoo artist, Edo is transformed into a heightened realm of the senses, a world of striking brilliance and illumination:

> People did all they could to beautify themselves, some even having pigments injected into their precious skins. Gaudy patterns of line and colour danced over men's bodies. Visitors to the pleasure quarters of Edo preferred to hire palanquin bearers who were splendidly tattooed; courtesans of the Yoshiwara and the Tatsumi quarter fell in love with tattooed men. Among those so adorned were not only gamblers, firemen, and the like, but members of the merchant class and even samurai.

Tattoos worn by women, apart from functioning as badges of affiliation with institutions like the old licensed pleasure quarters or specific yakuza organizations, have also been worn as amulets to impair malevolent spirits and as symbols of inner strength and parity with men. In Japanese literature, tattoos have even been used as devices to demonize women, the tools of the tattooist's trade serving as surgical instruments in an operation to transform not only the woman's body but her personality. Tanizaki's story concerns a tattoo artist who is searching for the perfect woman to double as a canvass for his art. Once he has found the ideal subject, a young, rather inexperienced geisha, he drugs her in his studio and sets to work. When she regains consciousness she finds that her back is covered with the figure of a giant, black spider, whose legs "with each shuddering breath... stirred as if they were alive." With such an image, the tattooist tells her, no man will be able to resist becoming her victim.

With the opening of the country during the Meiji Restoration, fresh efforts were made to suppress the practice. Increasingly marginalized, displays of tattooing grew rarer, occasionally surfacing in the form of bizarre displays, faintly risqué sideshows for the delectation of tourists and those with a taste for the eccentric. James Kirkup, in his 1970 book *Japan Behind the Fan*, describes attending a "special show" in the working-class Sanya district of Tokyo, featuring a tattooed sailor whose body was covered in a frondescence of leaves, grasses and ferns supporting a sumptuous visual menagerie including lizards, spiders, fox cubs and snakes. The centrepiece, a beautifully composed figure of Kannon in a tiara and swirling robes, "stood with lissom feet upon a sevenfold lotus flower." By flexing his back muscles, this iconographic mass came to life, "the drapery of the Kannon seeming to stir gently in a breeze from Nirvana."

Although official disapproval of tattooing was discontinued in the postwar years, many of the old masters had already retired, passed on their skills to less gifted practitioners, or simply given up the ghost. Though tattoos continue to remain living documents, transmitting and codifying for us colourful elements from the popular culture of the past, the fact remains that one would be more welcome in a public bathhouse wearing a necklace of shrunken skulls than a tattoo.

SUMIDA FIRE FLOWERS

Before it became a great event on the city's cultural calendar, the *kawabiraki* ("river opening") was conducted in the hope that it would repel malign spirits responsible for the outbreak and spread of cholera. The first official fireworks display was held in 1733, the year that famine and plague killed almost a million people nationwide. The shogun Tokugawa Yoshimune lit the fuse on the first *hanabi* (literally "flower fires").

Following another exorcism tradition, the shogun released dozens of *mukaebi* (floating lights), believed to guide souls back to earth during the summer Obon festival. The scouring of the riverbanks seems to have worked, and the fireworks were so popular they remained.

Fireworks were red at this time. By the time Clara Whitney observed the display, chemical flaming agents had been added. Noting in her early Meiji-period diary the inseparable association of summer with watermelons, sake and fireworks, she described the river during the night of the display, a setting "alive with lanterns of every colour and shape, and musical with the notes of the samisen." Besides standard Roman candles and rockets were fireworks depicting "a Fuji, a lady, umbrellas, dogs, men, some characters, and other things, which I could not make out."

The extravagance of burning things for pleasure might seem antithetical to an older Japanese ascetic of frugality, but there were other considerations involved in the display. Mishima Yukio's 1953 short story, *Fireworks*, a tale of power, politics and the underworld, is set in a high-class geisha restaurant in Yanagibashi, one of the most coveted spots in those days for watching the summer display along the river:

> Boats already moved about on the Sumida River, and a number fitted with fireworks racks sat in midstream. On shore, people with chairs and stools brought from home began to gather, and on every building rooftop, at each window, heads jostled with one another for space. There were policemen assigned to crowd control, tents erected here and there by the neighbourhood associations, the incredible confusion of people coming and going, and above it all, the relentless booming of fireworks, invisible in the light of day, rending the lowering sky that once again began to let fall a spattering rain.

The fireworks in Mishima's story have names like Pentachromic Necklace, Five Flowers of the Ascending Dragon and The Dance of the Blossom-Vying Geisha, which the narrator finds "absurdly gaudy and abstract".

Angela Carter was an English writer who lived in Tokyo in the 1970s. The setting for one of the stories in her collection, *Fireworks*, is less ostentatious. The main character rides "the train out of Shinjuku for an hour to watch one of the public displays which are held over rivers so that the dark water multiplies the reflections." On the banks of an unnamed river that bears a strong resemblance to the Edogawa in the eastern reaches of Tokyo, the writer gives us a touching description of the scene, one that has changed little:

> ... mothers had scrubbed and dressed up the smallest children to celebrate the treat. The little girls were especially immaculate in pink and white cotton kimonos tied with fluffy sashes like swatches of candyfloss. Their hair had been most beautifully brushed, arranged in sleek, twin bunches and decorated with twists of gold and silver thread. These children were all on their best behaviour because they were staying up late and held their parents' hands with a charming propriety. We followed the family parties until we came to some fields by the river and saw, high in the air, fireworks already opening out like variegated parasols.

Today's revived river pageant, with pleasure boats floating around Ryogoku bridge as vendors along the banks sell watermelon and beer to an impossible crush of spectators, crackles with a vitality the townspeople of Edo would surely recognize.

RIVER CHRONICLES

Edo's wealth and culture were founded, at least partially, on water. The majority of Edo's theatres were built near rivers and canals. Playhouses and red-light areas developed simultaneously along the water's edge. A detailed painting called the *Illustrated Screen of Edo Landmarks* depicts the Nakabashi theatre district between Nihonbashi and Kyobashi, where *Kabuki* was presented for the first time in the city. Boats crowd the waterways leading to puppet, acrobatic and Kabuki theatres surrounded by a vibrant mix of archery galleries, street vendors, bathhouses and louche teahouses. All the major temples and shrines in the Low City were oriented towards water. Like the Benten Shrine at Shinobazu Pond in Ueno, many inland places of worships were built facing or cantilevered over a large pond.

The water's edge was where the energies of the city were concentrated. Even today, Tokyo claims some 1,300 miles of rivers, canals and other watercourses spanned by nearly 6,000 bridges. The natural rivers and manmade canals of the Low City formed an ideal network of channels for transporting goods. Aqueducts brought water from the west in the Edo

The Sumida river

period, but a surprising number of people in the Low City still depended on wells, even though many of them were foul and brackish. Those who could afford to bought fresh water from vendors.

People are fond of waxing lyrical about the qualities of the old Sumida, but by the Meiji industrial period the condition of the river, awash with the human sewage of its aquatic population and those whose homes and shacks backed onto its waterways, can hardly have been pleasant. The realities of living along the river, softened by literary references to fireflies on its banks and assignations by boat at dusk, were more hazardous in real life. Taisho-era families who made their living from ferrying people across the river or transporting goods often lived on boats along the mouths of canals that washed into the river. However hard they may have worked, they remained trapped in their poverty, washing their clothes in the river, lighting cooking fires with coal scrap, their homes polluted by smokestacks from recently built factories. These squalid conditions were visible to any passer-by.

The Sumida has also known its fair share of tragedy. The shogun Ieyasu seems to have more or less treated the river as an outer moat for Edo castle. The Senju-ohashi was the only bridge permitted to span the waterway during his regime, a security obsession that led to tragedy when the Furisode Fire of 1657 struck, stranding people in the most intense fire zone. Other memorable tragedies associated with the Sumida were the Great Kanto Earthquake and the incendiary bombings of 1945 when the river, into which hundreds of people had plunged, turned into a sheet of fire. Of the first event, film director Akira Kurosawa, a witness to the aftermath of the earthquake, wrote:

> ... the Sumidagawa was dyed red, but it wasn't a blood-red. It was the same kind of light brownish red as the rest of the landscape, a red muddied with white like the eye of a rotten fish. The corpses floating in the river were all swollen to the bursting point...

Floods were a constant threat. The river could be expected to break its banks on average once every three years. A tidal flood in 1959, which left 5,000 dead, prompted the construction over the following decades of concrete retaining walls. Floodgates and walls were built after two major typhoons in 1947 and 1949 inundated the area between Edogawa and Arakawa. With the concrete walls, promenades disappeared overnight, diminishing intimate contact with the river and the pleasure of strolling its banks at will.

In Kafu's writings from the first half of the last century we have the impression of a more leisurely waterway, supporting a riverine population more in tune with the seasons. "From the new two-storey house with willows at its gate," the narrator of *The Sumida River* observes, "came the sound of a shamisen, and the masters of the low houses along the canal were beginning to emerge half naked from latticed doors to enjoy the evening cool."

Kafu's river, however, is a lightning rod for the changes being carried out in the name of progress. In his latter work the river and its canals are already choked by industrial waste. In Kafu's day, whole families lived on boats. Clay stoves for cooking rice were found on the sterns, laundry hung out to dry over sculling oars, and in the early Meiji period it was still possible to take water from the river to rinse vegetables. Canals began to be filled in during the late Meiji years as the city turned from water-borne to motorized pleasures. After the 1923 earthquake and again in 1945 during the air raids, canals were used to dump rubble and cinder. Many of these were eventually filled in and turned into roads.

Although Tokyo's premier waterway remains a symbol of the city, its literary associations forming a rich body of lore, by the post-war years most of the old ferries that once enjoyed a brisk trade across the river had been replaced by bridges. The painted girders, shackles and bolts of the older bridges that have survived, structures like Umayabashi, and Kiyosubashi, with their sweeping arches, stone stanchions and wrought-iron lanterns, are reassuringly durable presences that have not been overshadowed by the triple-layered expressways that slice the river overhead a short distance away.

Tokyo's Sumida provides the setting for what is possibly one of the most interesting concentrations of bridges in Japan. Strong nostalgia is still attached to them, and Tokyoites continue to celebrate their existence in songs, films, and novels. The painted girders and bolts of the older bridges that have survived earthquakes, air raids and intense volumes of traffic remain little altered amidst the accelerated confusion of today's city. Although a commentary in the 1933 *Almanac of Greater Tokyo* asserting that "Tokyo is now recognized in particular as a 'capital city of bridges'... in its number of bridges, it is surely first in the world" may be a forgivable exaggeration, these constructions still retain the power to both charm and transform our view of the city.

Although one would be hard pressed to find peony gardens, vegetable plots or the earthen walls of a former age in this section of present-day Tokyo, the river is enjoying a revival of interest. Claude Lévi-Strauss, surveying the compressed sprawl of its living and working quarters in the 1980s, judged that the city's future lay along the banks of the Sumida. Low-hulled *choki-bune*, operated by single oarsmen, have long gone, but in their place have appeared conventional pleasure boats, fishing sculls and *yakata-bune*—roofed vessels hung with lanterns, a section of the deck pleasantly *tatami*-matted—which resemble older craft.

Waterfront developments that would have turned the river into a construction corridor have, mercifully, been scaled back or scuttled altogether with the evaporation of funds. In tandem with this new, mandatory moderation, environment groups have scored some commendable successes, including the cleansing of the river so that fish may return. The river banks at Hakozaki, Shinkawa and the strip between Asakusa and Sakurabashi and other spots are being reclaimed from their vertical, concrete encasements, planted with grass, saplings and bushes, the embankments remodelled with graduated slopes to create new pedestrian zones. Stands of pampas grass grace the riverbanks in front of one apartment block near Eitaibashi. Among the unintended beneficiaries of this largesse have been the homeless, for whom lavatories, water spigots and easy access to roads and the overflowing bins of nearby convenience stores provide an alternative to cramped city parks, and subway entrances.

Downriver, the residents of Tsukuda-jima, an artificial island near the mouth of the river, were originally brought from Osaka to Edo in order to supply the shogun's kitchens with whitebait. The first residents also worked as spies and informers for the castle, keeping an eye on shipping movements in the bay. A few descendants of the original islanders still work in nearby Tsukiji fish market. Experts at drying, curing and preserving, the islanders created a nourishing concoction made from seaweed and shellfish, seasoned with salt, soy and sugar. The result, known as *tsukudani*, is still made there.

The north portion of the island, known as River City 21, has been aggressively developed, and its taller buildings cast the remnants of the older town into growing obscurity. Several older houses remain, however, especially those in the vicinity of Sumiyoshi Shrine, an old tutelary shrine for fisher folk. This cluster of houses is in fairly good shape, with well-finished features that include black ceramic roof tiles, oxidized copper finials of an aged, green patina and seasoned wood walls. Until 1964, when a 750-foot bridge was completed, the island's only direct connection with central Tokyo was by ferryboat. On 27 August 1964, without the slightest fanfare for the passing of an era, the last ferry to cross the Sumida made its journey into the watery reaches of the city's notoriously short memory.

THE INVISIBLE GODDESS
Strongly associated with Edo life, Asakusa's spiritual centrepiece, the current Senso-ji Temple, was rebuilt after Allied bombs destroyed the former structure, itself a reconstruction of a fire victim. Above the sombre beauty of the altar, incense burners and flickering candles, the ceiling of the temple is distinguished by a large dragon painting, the creature holding a jewelled orb. A symbol of Fate, the dragon is said to have risen

from the seabed to the heavens with the object, representing human aspirations, firmly in its clutches. The *ryu* is a symbol of good luck; those born in the year of the dragon are considered gifted, wise and blessed with boundless energy. Before Tokyo rose to block out the building, it was said that if you gazed across the Sumida towards Asakusa, you would see a silhouette that strongly resembled that of a giant dragon. When the temple was rebuilt in 1958, a dragon dance was held to celebrate the event. The golden dragon dance continues to be held twice a year, in March and October.

Such is the attachment to the sacred grounds at the centre of the city's profaner pleasures that Kawaguchi Matsutaro could write, "The Asakusa Kannon Temple is home, so to speak, to all those who inhabit downtown Tokyo. An Asakusa native need only step onto the temple grounds to feel he is treading his native soil."

The most celebrated object in the temple remains an enigma. According to believers, the golden image of Kannon-sama, the bodhisattva of mercy trapped in fishing nets by the Hinokuma brothers all those centuries ago, is enshrined here. While some scholars and historians subscribe to this interpretation, others have questioned the very existence of the image. Japan is as rich in religious relics as it is in legends. A satisfactory explanation remains elusive, as the key evidence, just two-inches tall according to the temple, is shielded from human eyes.

The official version of the story claims that the reliquary holding the statue decayed centuries ago, requiring others to be built over it. The statue, despite being removed time and again to escape fires, remains at the heart of the temple. During the Meiji period a group of minor government officials demanded to see the object under threat of punishment. The statue was taken from its sanctuary by priests who bowed their heads respectfully low, but also in order to avoid casting their eyes on the image. This was strictly in accordance with the wishes of St. Shokai, the original founder of the temple, who received a divine injunction in a dream, commanding him to preserve the image from human gaze. It seems that the officials, all of whom subsequently died under mysterious circumstances, were the last mortals to see the golden statue. It is just the type of story that people, more interested in the essence of a tale than its historical veracity, appreciate. Never seen nor verified, its presence is truly mystic, for it exists on faith alone.

IN GHOSTLY TOKYO

For all the city's modernity, the spirit world is never far away. Scratch the surface and old beliefs come bubbling up. Strong folkloric elements associated with rural societies saturate this post-industrial city.

When Edo was built, shrines and temples were situated to ensure the correct flow of *ki*, or spiritual energy. *Kimon* (devil's gates) were positioned to block or divert malign forces and promote beneficial currents. Redevelopment projects and the demolition of many of these gates have upset the old balances, weakening the protective barriers. According to traditional geomancy, the north-east is the direction from which malevolent spirits enter the city. Two temples positioned in the north-east, Kanne-ji in Ueno and Senso-ji in Asakusa, still function as spirit barriers.

The geomantic concerns of Edo were planned by the priest Tenkai with full consideration for the most propitious flow of ki. Subsequent buildings and subways were constructed in accord with *feng shui* principles. A notable exception is the Oedo subway line, completed in 2000. Disregarding the plan, the line passes under Aoyama cemetery, disturbing the spirits resting there and sending currents of destructive ki west towards the entertainment and commercial district of Roppongi. With no shrine positioned to send the flow back, the area, with dozens of misaligned buildings, has suffered an unusually high outbreak of private and corporate crimes and malfeasance over the years. Passengers expected to use the line, with reduced commuting time to districts like Shinjuku, have failed to materialize. In other instances, measures have been taken in advance to avert the effects of negative energy fields. Bad ki at Nogi Shrine, built to enshrine the spirit of the general who entered a suicide pact on the site along with his wife, obliged the Defence Agency headquarters to relocate.

The bronze surface of a seated cow at Ushijima Shrine near the eastern banks of the Sumida is worn smooth. This supernatural statue, like many others in the city, is believed to have the power to cure illnesses. Stroke the part of the cow's body that corresponds with the area that is troubling you and relief will soon come. *Inari* shrines are the most visible expressions of a world where strange spells and transmutations are common. Nominally part of Shinto religion, these shrines feature an astounding number of stone foxes with red bibs tied around their necks that serve as messengers of the gods. Capable of taking on human form, they properly belong to the animist world. The oldest Inari shrines are located just at

Devotees washing the auspicious Togenuki Jizo statue at Kogan-ji temple in Sugamo

the foot of the high ground of the Yamanote hills, often at the point where they drop to the flatlands. Appearing in the gardens of feudal mansions and in the back streets of almost every block in the city, their number increased dramatically in the 1770s and 1780s, decades with a particularly high incidence of natural disasters.

Fox possession was a grave problem. There are countless shrines around the city bearing the names of people who erected them in the hope of exorcising the spirit. The place where a victim was possessed would often draw large crowds, creating, as markets and cult followers sprang up around the spot, a near millenarian atmosphere. In the quiet residential district of Hakusan is an eerie fox shrine called Takuzosu-Inari. Shoehorned into its pinched precincts are rows of *torii* gates, Jizo and Kannon statues and fierce-looking fox messengers. This is not a place to venture much after twilight. A flight of stone steps descends under blackened trees that seem permanently damp to a spirit cave called the *Oana*, its dank rock-face the home, it is believed, of the resident white fox.

Credence is lent to its existence in an account by Kafu who, in his short story *The Fox* relates how his father spotted the bushy-tailed messenger here one afternoon.

Basil Hall Chamberlain, one of the most astute observers of frantically modernizing Meiji Japan, recorded a supernatural tale told of the metamorphosing powers of the fox. The account was

> ... widely circulated and believed of a fox having taken the shape of a railway train on the Tokyo-Yokohama line. The phantom train seemed to be coming toward a real train which happened to be running in the opposite direction, but yet never got any nearer to it. The engine-driver of the real train, seeing all his signals to be useless, put on a tremendous speed. The result was that the phantom was at last caught up with, when lo and behold!—nothing but a crushed fox was found beneath the engine-wheels.

Tanizaki remembered that his mother and grandmother "had often told me how a badger kept appearing at the foot of the Ogibashi bridge in Fukagawa, playing tricks on the unwary residents." Residential areas, even in downtown parts of the city, were still dark during the late Meiji-period night. Tanizaki recalled his childhood reluctance to venture even to the washbasin that stood beside the yard of his house:

> My fear at such moments focused not so much on robbers, but on the thought that a ball of flame, the soul of the dead, might come flying by, or that a badger or fox, transformed into something terrible, might suddenly appear... I was terrified, most of all, by the story that badgers sometimes assumed the form of giant bald-headed monsters. Two or three times, I actually heard in the distance the sound of badgers drumming on their bellies. Some adult nearby had always made sure to confirm it, saying "That's the sound right there."

Venerated tattoo artist Horiyoshi III recalled seeing a figure walk into his studio while he was working. When he turned to offer a greeting, it disappeared into black powder. Consulting a psychic, he was told that during the Meiji era there was an execution ground on the site of the present studio, so that even now there were many ghosts wandering around his neighbourhood. The story, like an incident from the Edo-period broadsheets, was told to a Tokyo reporter in the summer of 2007.

Noh dramas, Kabuki and the *Bunraku* puppet-dramas have repertoires swarming with ghosts and unquiet spirits. The Kabuki play *Yotsuya Kaidan,* regularly shown in film versions on television, provides a cold frisson much appreciated in the torrid summer months, especially August, when homes set out revolving lanterns and festivals of *bon-odori* dancing are provided for the ghosts of the departed as they return for the few brief days of the Bon Festival.

Phantoms lurk in the western district of Mejirodai, where a temple and graveyard once existed. Only the slope remains, but its name, Yureizaka ("Ghost Slope") marks the place where apparitions are occasionally seen. The towering Sunshine 60 and City buildings in Ikebukuro, on the western stretch of the Yamanote line, were built on the grounds of the notorious Sugamo Prison. The authorities hanged their criminals here before the war, and then the Americans executed Japanese convicted of war crimes during the years of the occupation. Ghosts in full military regalia are said to stalk the corridors of the sixty-storey skyscraper.

When Kakuda Nobuaki, a martial arts master, was interviewed by a newspaper in the autumn of 2007, he asserted that "Ghosts are real, so I always protect myself. I carry good luck charms at all times. When I fly, I put a necklace on, but keep my most powerful amulet hidden as it might be too strong for others. It is a stone from the Emperor's grave."

RITUALS, CULTS AND PORTENTS

On a day in November 1990, 37,000 policemen were deployed to close off the normally busy streets of central Tokyo for the coronation of the new Emperor Akihito. The marionette personage of the emperor was dressed in a loose, dark brown dressing gown; on his head a black cap finished off with a three-foot tall plume added to the unreality of the costume drama. Beside him, the Empress Michiko, a slightly built woman, stood stock still under the oppressive weight of a sumptuous five-layered kimono. The imperial tableau stood on the Takamikura, a lacquered purple stage whose canopy held the figure of a golden phoenix, symbolizing Mount Takachiho, site of the Sun Goddess Amaterasu Omikami's placement of her grandson, the first in an unbroken line of emperors descending from the goddess.

An even more extraordinary scene took place ten days later with the ritual known as *Daijosai*, the "great food-offering ceremony". Having taken a purifying bath, the emperor walked along a carpet representing the bridge between heaven and earth. He then entered a bedchamber in the company of two women priests, where he made the first rice offering of the season to the Sun Goddess. Although the ceremony was conducted in the utmost secrecy, scholars agree about what happened next: the emperor lay on the bed and had simulated sexual intimacy with the Sun Goddess, before being reborn as a living god.

For most Japanese, these esoteric enthronement scenes might as well have been taking place on a different planet. What could have passed for scenes from the intergalactic court of some Japanese science fiction *manga*, were interpreted by some observers within the world's most technologically advanced nation to symbolize a reversal of the renunciation of divine status taken by Hirohito in 1946 under duress from General MacArthur, and as an attempt to restore the imperial institution to its former glory and status.

In the winter of that same year, 1990, the writer Murakami Haruki witnessed an oddly unsettling sight not far from his Tokyo apartment:

> Day after day strange music played from big lorries with sound-systems, while white-robed young men in oversized Asahara masks and elephant heads lined the pavement outside my local train station, waving and dancing some incomprehensible jig.

Nauseated by a sight reminiscent perhaps of the antics performed by the millenarian cults of the 1850s, the writer could never have imagined the horror and chaos that the Aum Shinrikyu (Sublime Truth Sect), a mix of Buddhism, Hinduism and apocalyptic cults, and its central figure, Asahara Shoko, would wreck on the Tokyo subway system five years later. Under the influence of their half-blind leader, educated young members of the cult, many from elite Japanese universities, dropped plastic bags of deadly liquid Sarin gas onto the floors of carriages on five subway lines during the busiest rush hour time. Before leaving the trains, they punctured the bags with the sharpened ends of their umbrellas. Of the 5,000 commuters who inhaled the gas, many suffered vomiting, convulsions, and in some cases blindness. Twelve passengers died as the emergency services, stretched and unprepared, tried to deal with the number of victims.

Murakami, whose 1997 book *Underground* consists of a series of interviews with the victims together with commentary and vivid portraits, was convinced that there were deep fault lines in Japanese society and historical precedents for the unchecked insanity of the attack. While researching the 1939 Namonhan Incident, an aggressive incursion by Japanese forces into Mongolia, Murakami noted:

> The more I delved into the records, the more aghast I became at the recklessness, the sheer lunacy of the Imperial Army's system of command. How had this pointless tragedy been passed over in the history books? Again, researching the Tokyo gas attack, I was struck by the fact that the closed, responsibility-evading ways of Japanese society were really not any different from how the Imperial Japanese Army operated at the time.

HALL OF DREAMS

Although corrupted by gain themselves, cults were partly a reaction to the febrile consumerism of the times. Sweeping political and economic reforms after the war had cleared the way for the adoption of a market driven modernization that existed in a vacuum without a great deal of reference to traditions, customs or aesthetics. It introduced among other things the phenomenon of the Japanese "salary man", stereotypically a workaholic whose personal goals were material prosperity, comfort and security in a corporate world free from the restrains of historical and cultural heritage. The success of the economy depended upon the commitment of its participants, their willingness to embrace the prosperity offered by new ideas and technologies, to forego any reservations about the ill effects of progress.

Economic growth was a national phenomenon, but the majority of the financial and industrial centres were massed in the Tokyo area. A population standing at a little over one million at the end of the nineteenth century had exploded to thirty million in the greater Tokyo area by the 1980s. At its peak, before the hall of dreams dissolved, Japan was theoretically capable, according to Christopher Wood's *The Bubble Economy*, to "buy the whole of America by selling off metropolitan Tokyo, or all of Canada by hawking the grounds of the Imperial Palace."

The country that emerged into the early days of 1989, just months before the steam went out of the bubble economy, was second only in wealth to the United States, with financial assets of $7 trillion, roughly fourteen times that of Britain. A country that owned the four largest banks in the world, stood at the cutting edge of futuristic technologies, and whose industrial clout had made companies like Sony, Toyota, Mitsubishi and Fujitsu household names, still basked in its own superlatives.

Japan's over-accelerated development accomplished what even the worst natural disasters had only partially succeeded in doing: to change forever the face of Tokyo. A society now accustomed to disposing of goods with unseemly haste applied the same practice to buildings. With building values only a small fraction of the asset value of land, offices and commercial complexes were reduced to advertising organs or consumer objects, remorselessly torn down and replaced as if they were film sets. Japanese construction firms, referred to as "the richest powerhouses of advanced technology in the world", transformed the appearance of the city. Over half of its buildings today date from the 1980s.

It was inevitable that in a city flush with capital, where shopping for brand goods had become elevated to an art form, a novel like Tanaka Yasuo's 1980 *Nantonaku, Kurisutaru* ("Somehow, Crystal"), should have appeared. As much a consumer lifestyle manual as novel, 400 notes accompanied the text, referring readers to detailed descriptions of chic Tokyo retail districts, brand clothes and accessory dealers, even to cafés and restaurants where the "crystal life" could be lived. Tanaka's novel showed how the structure and formation of personality and identity had become increasingly dependent on the choice of districts in which consumption and social life were conducted.

Even Ayukawa Nobuo, a poet of immense integrity, much of whose work was concerned with war guilt and remembrance, felt compelled to address the hollow ring of the economic miracle and the insatiable urges it induced:

Fighting in the sordid world of profit and loss,
your friends, good at mimicry, sing in chorus:
These are bad times.
They complain to a hostess in a lonely bar
that water doesn't turn into wine,

that desire doesn't turn into more
consumption.

The English-language work that best captures the mood of febrile 1980s consumerism is Donald Richie's experimental novel *Tokyo Nights*. The antithesis of the 1940s Ginza captured in his journals, a place of fire-blackened buildings and malnourished ghost-crowds, is the same district observed forty years later. Here is a metropolis wallowing in wealth. Strung with brand names and expensive baubles, the Ginza district represents a modern mega-city stiff with money and commodities. Those who re-member that singular decade will recall the novelties of bars serving sushi rolled in gold leaf, of toilet lids finished in mink.

In the bubble years Nihonbashi was where much of the wealth was created, the Ginza, centre of the bubble era's commodity fetishism, was where it was spent or squandered. Habitués of the district still remember a man walking around the Ginza each night with a suitcase stuffed with money. He would only hail a taxi home when he was satisfied the suitcase was empty. The Ginza has always been associated with a degree of opu-lence, even decadence. The Australian journalist Richard Hughes fre-quented the area in 1940, in the days before Japan became an ally of Germany. In *Foreign Devil*, his account of reporting from the Far East, he wrote about entering the Rheingold, a Ginza restaurant-bar run by a genial Bavarian expatriate, where "the Nazi community was drinking *steins* of good Japanese draught beer, with their arms around the waists of the bargirls. There was a piano behind the bar covered with a swastika flag."

The Organic Maze

From the roof of one of its corporate monuments or culture towers and through the soft focus of humidity and pollution, Tokyo looks a little like a clay swamp, its surfaces and horizons choked with concrete ramps, con-struction piers and high-rise jetties. In a city where the longevity of build-ings is measured not in epochs but decades, where architectural co-ordination is rarely sought, Tokyo often strikes the outsider as hardly a city at all in the western sense, but rather a metamorphic environment perpetually responding and adapting to change and the expediency of the moment.

A case might be made for calling Tokyo a Taoist city, conforming as it does to that philosophy's doctrine of submission to constant flux and transformation. For a people less prone to agonizing over the disjunction between the old and the new, it is the ideal city. Comparing the megalopolis to European capitals and their depopulated cores, architect Ashihara Yoshinobu comments: "the heart of Tokyo—and most of Japan's cities—remains vital. This is the result of a healthy—if somewhat hypermetabolism." Ashihara, in a passage from his book *The Hidden Order*, extends his analogy between the architecture of Tokyo and living organisms that are capable of constant adjustment to changing usages. He writes of this fluid, self-regenerating city:

> At first glance, Tokyo looks chaotic. But if we consider that there is an invisible order, a random-switch mechanism through which each level of the whole structure tolerates some haphazardness so as to respond to changes in the environment—rather like the action of genes in the development of a multicellular organism—then we begin to see an order in the city structure.

The fragmentation of Tokyo and its subsequent mutation into a number of internal cities with different functions began in the 1950s. This was when decentralization plans aimed at the transformation of the city into its present form were implemented by creating multiple centres like Shinjuku, Ikebukuro, Shibuya Ueno, Kameido and finally, with space running out, artificial landfill islands in the bay.

Given the concentration of sub-cities and facilities contiguous with the circular Yamanote train line, the original urban design of Edo remains remarkably intact. Temples and sanctuaries erected according to Taoist dictates to protect the city against malign forces have survived, as has the division of the city into its high and low quarters. The emperor and his family continue to live in the imperial palace, the former site of Edo castle. Roland Barthes, in his *Empire of Signs* writes: "Tokyo presents this amazing paradox: it does have a centre, but this centre is empty... Every day, with their rapid, forceful motion, taxis speed by like bullets, avoiding this ring, whose low rooftops—visible forms of the invisible—conceal its sacred nothingness." The core of the original citadel, a cobweb of roads, sunken expressways and overhead traffic lanes superimposed over the outer boundaries of the castle, is a visible legacy of Edo and its centre of power. Yet many of the clues to Edo's original grid, the radials and energy lines of an ordained structure, have been erased by floods, fires, earthquakes, typhoons and air raids, visited upon the city with an almost Old Testament force. What has grown out of the countless reconstructions is an astonishing mishmash of structures. Right angles do not last long among the fluid lines and superimposed vistas of this polyglot cityscape, the planet's largest concentration of steel and concrete.

The perception of what makes a city worth living in is fundamentally different from that of the West. Interest is aroused and attachments made to specific buildings or segments of the city, taken one by one. The city begins to make more sense when it is seen as a series of panels, only one or two of which can be taken in at any one time. This piecemeal vision of Tokyo is confirmed by Maki Fumihiko, who has noted that very few people "have a distinct image of today's megalopolis in its entirety. The image that most residents have of the city is only a diagram... on which is plotted the knowledge of the very few parts of the city with which they are familiar." Hiroshige emphasized the idea of picturesque sites that were autonomous rather than subordinate to a city whole in his woodblock series, *One Hundred Famous Spots in Edo*. *Meisho Sugoroku* was a popular Edo-period game, where players moved around a board marked with famous places (*meisho*) in a way that made them feel they were travelling around the city. Each site was presented as a single point of interest. Connecting the points or filling in the spaces between was not required. In this kind of city, each building is enjoyed in its own right; integration is not sought. The result is a layered complexity that seems to go its own way, obeying organic rather than structural codes.

The freedoms offered by this flexibility have attracted prominent foreign architects: Josiah Conder in the Meiji period, Frank Lloyd Wright in the 1920s, Bruno Taut in the 1930s, Le Corbusier and Charlotte Perriand in the 1950s. A large number of renowned European and American architects worked in the city during the 1980s and 1990s, among them Peter Eisenman, Cesar Pelli, Hugh Stubbins, Steven Holl and Richard Rogers. Among designs for the twenty-first century, the Swiss firm Herzog and de Meuron's Prada Aoyama Boutique is a fine example of design responding to the constrictions of space. The surface of this six-storey, triangular chrysalis of light consists of diamond-shaped transparent glass panels that seems to function as optical devices, moving as the building is circled.

In his short story *Jacob's Tokyo Ladder* Hino Keizo writes about a city that over-stimulates, where ensembles of buildings have the power to transmit messages and sensations. Hino's story is firmly rooted in the architecture of Tokyo's Marunouchi business district, its daylight rigidity of "massive parallelepipeds, constructed with absolute straight lines and planes" mutating via the uneasy perception of the story's narrator into dark, organically active surfaces. There is one building, he observes, with "massive walls, all a dark taupe, making it look as if the whole edifice had been carved out of a mountain of volcanic rock."

SURFACE TENSIONS

In submitting itself to repeated sessions of radical surgery, allowing the scalpel to slice away and dispose of its loose tissue, Tokyo's remodelled surfaces always seem youthful, to have somehow escaped the ageing of European capitals. Despite its colossal building projects, however, Tokyo can seem inchoate, even incorporeal, a massive jellyfish of cement and light. At twilight, solid forms make way for liquid states, semiotic codes replacing the function of architecture, pixels of light replacing concrete and glass. Electronic information flows across the city, giant screens, LED images and neon traceries, the paraphernalia of a cybernetic city replacing the old waterways of Edo as the medium of flux, of instant, virtual communication. At night, buildings recede into darkness as single, digitally alive blocks turn Tokyo into a flat, multi-dimensional screen, its surfaces acting as conductors for all the dreams, fantasies and yearnings of commercial messaging. In the shift towards an information-based economy, its buildings have become sounding boards, global-age transmitters. One can almost see on the surfaces of these buildings, the alternating currents of the economy.

Materials such as glass tubing, gleaming metallic adjuncts, raw concrete, oxidized aluminium plates, translucent screens, and fibre canopies are the order of the day, representing perhaps a new form of deconstructivism, or at least a disposition towards exterior surfaces that can be dismantled and replaced at will. This flexible system of choreographed space is achieved with high-tech materials like LC glass, perforated metal and stainless steel sheets. At their most successful, these new surfaces and the

floating contraptions surrounding the core of the buildings create an illusion of depth and space. This tendency is visible in the use of lighter, non-
durable, hi-tech industrial materials. The merits of insubstantiality are
highly visible in the work of contemporary architects, whose constructions are routinely sheathed in floating membranes, perforated panels and
light-reflecting surfaces. Maki Fumihiko has noted: "The days when there
was an immutable style are past... any work of architecture that, in a sense,
internalizes the city and functions on its surfaces as a mechanism of trans-
mission will symbolize today's image of the city."

Expedient to a fault, the city has moved through rapid facial changes
as fresh ideas and materials became available. Wood and clay walls have
given way to clapboard panels, copper sheeting, mortar, ferro-concrete and
tile, as convenience and cost have dictated. In William Gibson's 1996 sci-
fi novel *Idoru*, a work set almost entirely in Tokyo, skyscrapers in the
Shinjuku district, covered in organic building substances, appear to "ripple,
to crawl slightly... a movement like osmosis or the sequential contraction
of some sea creature's palps."

THE SCRIPTED CITY

In acquiring the added function of advertising props Tokyo buildings have
been transformed into surfaces of running commercial text and scroll. In
the street, a pre-eminently commercial environment, pedestrians rarely see
beyond the side of a building that overlooks the street. Views are flattened
into two-dimensional planes. Urban geographer Paul Waley has observed
that: "Space in the Japanese city is conceived only in the context of the immediate visual field. This gives it an episodic quality." If each panel is vi-
sualized as a story frame, it is one in a narrative set on constant replay, or
re-write, the text as fresh and as shallow, as urgently produced as an advertising script.

If the world's largest city is unclassified in its particulars, the details left
unnamed, commercial advertising inscribes Tokyo in a deliberate, expressive manner. The textual quality of Japanese cities, from their daylight advertising to night-time electro-graphics, permits urban spaces to be
scanned and read. Like the city itself, this commercial script can only be
digested piecemeal, in lines of haiku length or even just a few syllables.

Where a former age delighted more in the texture and tone of walls
and other urban exteriors, in contemporary, space-depleted Tokyo utility

dominates the use of walls and surfaces. The result is a proliferation of panels hung with a forest of signage. ("In this country the empire of signifiers," wrote Barthes.) Text is not confined to walls, daylight or neon. A common sight in the city is the address panel attached to a lamppost, accompanied by adhesive advertisements. Electric utility poles, similarly plastered with colourful commercials, often look like totem poles. Strings of image and text undulate from street level down steps and corridors into the tunnels of subways, reappearing inside the train itself as concave strips along the upper walls of carriages.

In an age of information and consumerism, the transformation of walls into message boards was perhaps inevitable. This is not, however, an entirely new thing, but rather a development of practices dating from the Edo and Meiji periods. Lafcadio Hearn wrote in his 1894 work, *Glimpses of Unfamiliar Japan*, that, "To the Japanese brain an ideograph is a vivid picture... the whole space of a Japanese street is full of such living characters—decorating everything, even surfaces of doorposts and paper screens." William Faulkner, passing through Tokyo in the summer of 1955, took in the forest of Japanese syllabaries and Chinese ideograms with the dutiful awe of the foreigner who assumes that there must be profound messages and codes in the incomprehensible signage.

Boards, vertical banners at right angles to buildings, even square rooftop signs, were a common feature of eighteenth-century Edo. Old postcards from the Taisho period show streets in the Asakusa district strewn with entertainment boards and banners, the wall already a lively vector for information and advertising. Signage in Japanese cities has developed since then to such an extent that in some instances the entire building may be obscured by hanging objects and structures. Many are liquid constructions, façade-scale TV screens so carefully aligned and affixed that they appear as a seamless part of the building itself. If billboards and hanging banners fix the message in an eye-catching static form, electronic screens represent the flow of time. At night conventional lighting is secondary to pools of neon in which, as writer Michael Ross has put it, "light varies from a supergraphic word to an entire building." There is no equal in the western world to the complexity and density of detail embedded in Tokyo's kinetic surfaces.

The main character in another William Gibson novel, *Pattern Recognition*, steps into an electric twilight with "some different flavor of hydrocarbons to greet her as she exits Shinjuku Station." She gazes from the crepuscular calm of a Tokyo taxi onto:

> ... a remarkably virtual-looking skyline, a floating jumble of electric Lego, studded with odd shapes you somehow wouldn't see elsewhere, as if you'd need special Tokyo add-ons to build this at home. Logos of corporations she doesn't even recognize: a strange luxury, and in itself almost worth the trip. She remembers this now from previous visits, and also the way certain labels are mysteriously recontextualized here.

Are such liquid dreams the shape of things to come? For some, these seductive transmissions, like panels of disposable manga, are, quite literally, the writing on the wall.

Manga Metro

The Edo woodblock artist Hokusai Ando is attributed with first coining the term *manga* in 1814 with his *Hokusai Manga*, a fifteen-volume collection of whimsical sketches and drawings. The highly contemporary subject matter of manga, its vitality and the relative speed of production bear some comparison with the ukiyo-e woodblock print, illustrations regarded at the time as products of a mass culture rather than high art. Japan is the first country to have really taken the comic book seriously, to have experimented on a mass scale with the medium as a new form of literacy.

Today's comic books and magazines have direct links with eighteenth- and nineteenth-century picture books like the kibyoshi or "yellow-jacket books," and the even earlier aohon, the "green books" that were already making use of synthetic and kinetic lines and panel organization. With the emergence of a money economy among the merchant class, the demand for inexpensive, mass-produced art, not for art's sake but as pure entertainment, increased. Written largely by members of the samurai class with literary aspirations and a need to make some easy money, kibyoshi were mainly read by merchants and low-ranking samurai frequenting the city's pleasure quarters.

The mass-produced woodblock printed books of the Edo period involved a production process and division of labour similar to that existing among modern manga artists and their assistants. There are also parallels in the method of serialization used in kibyoshi and manga, as well as in content, which was expressed in a visual-verbal comic book format. Drawings produced in blocks were combined with text to form running narratives and illustrated panels not unlike modern comics. Like today's manga too, many were published in serial form. As entertainment, their unique visual aesthetic is easily traced to the popular mass art of the Edo period, in which stylized violence, deformation and exaggerated sexuality were an accepted part of the common culture of the time.

A flood of newspapers and magazines during the Taisho period helped to popularize the work of illustrators like Okamoto Ippei. Sometimes called the "father of manga", Tezuka Osamu is credited with adapting cinematic techniques to the cartoon strips he produced in the late 1940s. Manga took off in the still poverty-stricken early to mid-1950s, satisfying a hunger for cheap visual entertainment. Tezuka's cartoons of humanoids and androids, making their appearance as early as 1946, provided a fantasy world for war-weary readers. By the early 1960s, TV sets were no longer beyond the dreams of ordinary people. The two forms announced the primacy of the visual.

The production of comics on a mass scale in the 1950s helped to expand readership among teenagers and adults. Lending libraries spread the word still further. Television and animated films, rather than sounding the death knell of the form, helped to influence the creation of manga as visual novels, resulting in many fruitful TV-manga tie-ins.

Tokyo's cycles of destruction and renewal are reflected in *anime* films, which routinely show cataclysms being visited on the city. Otomo Katsuhiro's manga and anime work *Akira* has Tokyo convulsed by a powerful psychic explosion. From the dust a fresh city emerges and is christened "Neo-Tokyo". The city is saved by the inner resilience and the hardened fatalism of its residents, their ability to sustain periods of almost Buddhistic non-attachment and an unshakeable optimism, the belief that a better world follows naturally upon destruction. Catherine Russell has written, "It is a surprisingly short distance from the narrow streets of old Edo to the cybernetic space of contemporary *anime*."

Mishima Yukio is said to have been an admirer of the more violent, hyper-realistic forms of manga practised by illustrators like Hirata Hiroshi, of whom Mishima wrote a lengthy defence. Although there is no discernible manga influence in Mishima's writing, his own blood-spattered ritual suicide would sit comfortably in the frame of a Hirata comic strip.

Many writers who were weaned on manga and anime have used the structure and pacing of comic books and films for their novels. This particularly applies to women writers who emerged from the world of pop culture like Tokyo author Banana Yoshimoto, who has developed the introspective nature and exploration of psychology that characterize women's manga for her own work, citing manga artist Oshima Yumiko as an influence. Yoshimoto has said that comics provided her with the inspiration for characters in works like *The Kitchen, Lizard* and *Amrita*. Severed from any links to social institutions like family or the work place, her characters console themselves by creating their own constructs that are simulations of family and social networks. The anomie of Tokyo, where almost all the country's important writers reside, feeds the romantic longing of Yoshimoto's readers as well as those of many authors. Anomie as a characteristic of the city, rather than a failing, is evident in Abe Kobo's novel, *The Ruined Map*, where the coordinates of Tokyo are impossible to locate. Literary critic Maeda Ai has noted that place-names in Murukami Haruki's works have been almost completely expunged, transforming the city into an abstraction.

ANOTHER NEW TOKYO

If Tokyo has lost anything from its attachment to development and change, it is the evocative corners of a city once tinged with an aching, poetic melancholy. Witness Kawabata's "On rainy nights, carrying large oiled-paper umbrellas, the street-walkers come out of the flophouses in Honjo to solicit bums who stand under the eaves of the theatres and along the earthen walls of temples." A little of this atmosphere can still be sensed in the back alleys of the city, where ghosts and elderly buildings exhale their musty breath, but it is muted, a far cry from the ambience-soaked city described in Okamoto Kanoko's 1923 novel, *The Spirit House*:

> It was close to New Year's Eve. The wind was blowing sand off the down-hill road and the wooden sandals of the passers-by clacked on the frozen ground. The sound made the very roots of one's hair shiver on this cold night. The wind carried the squeaking noise of the streetcars at the intersection into one's ears, and the rustle of the foliage near the Hachiman Temple mingled with the squeak. It sounded like a blind man's murmur from far away.

Memory landscapes and literary descriptions acquire a special poignancy in a city where evidence of the past is so quickly removed. The lack of monuments and monumentality, the absence of preserved zones, the scarcity of individual buildings hailing from the past, the importance of literature as remembrance, all underline the victory of the present over history. You do not have to be in Tokyo for very long (less than a decade will do) to look back on parts of the city that no longer exist. As Shimada Masahiko says in his novel, *Dream Messenger*:

> Tokyo itself is an amnesiac city set in a desert. Things that happened yesterday are already covered with shifting sand. And last month's events are completely hidden. The year before is twenty meters under, and things that happened five years ago are fossils.

Foreign writers who have lived for any time in Tokyo have defined it less in concrete terms than as a city of the imagination. Angela Carter certainly saw it this way: "…this city presents the foreigner with a mode of life that seems to him to have the enigmatic transparency, the indecipherable clarity, of dream. And it is a dream he could, himself, never have dreamed."

David Mitchell's 2001 novel, *number9dream*, has a Tokyo setting. Its main character, like Shimada's narrator, finds that time and space are fluid properties: "Yesterday and this afternoon seem weeks apart. This grid of narrow streets and bright shadows, and the pink quarter of last night, seem to be different cities." Mitchell's novel concludes with the report of a massive earthquake in the Tokyo region, the announcement of a state of emergency.

The mixture of stoicism and bravado that characterized the Edo era, mocking misfortune, laughing at the workings of fate, can still be found among Tokyo's inhabitants as they ponder imminent catastrophe. Seismologists and soothsayers agree on one thing: built optimistically above three crustal plates likely to jam at any moment, Tokyo is living on borrowed time. The easternmost of the Asian capitals, a sea-facing metropolis constructed on the planet's most geologically unstable landmass, it could all be gone in a matter of hours, or minutes. As cycles of seismic activity go, that hour is long overdue.

There is talk of cataclysm beyond imagination. Roads may be wider

Dissonance and unreality along the Shinjuku railway tracks

now than during the 1923 quake, but most are congested with traffic that will block them off as escape routes, and probably turn them, in the words of writer Peter Popham, "into rivers of gasoline, potential rivers of flame". A combination of toxic and flammable chemicals concentrated in the massive industrial strip of Tokyo-Yokohama, where there is also a nuclear reactor, with hundreds of small-scale manufacturing plants located in the crowded eastern residential areas will fuel the explosions. Rupturing gas mains will add to the liquid fire. Pedestrians not gassed by toxic emissions or cut down by squalls of razor-edged glass, collapsing air-conditioning boxes and utility poles will be buried alive or roasted in the fire storms that rage overhead or between the towers of scorched skyscrapers. Peter Hadfield explains the phenomenon is his book, *Sixty Seconds That Will Change the World: the Coming Tokyo Earthquake*:

> Fire has peculiar behavioral characteristics, one of which is that two separate fires will be drawn towards one another. A super-heated vacuum is formed in the air between and above them, creating a devastating wind that sucks the flames together and incinerates everything in its path.

A cataclysm is certain, but not the death of a city. Returning home from an inspection of Asakusa, the scorched wilderness where until only recently his beloved Opera House had stood, Nagai Kafu made the following entry in his diary for the year 1944: "I have been witness to it all, Tokyo going to ruin." Kafu, though he scarcely knew it at the time, was soon to bear witness once again to the rebuilding of a great city.

Further Reading

Ashihara, Yoshinobu, *The Hidden Order: Tokyo through the Twentieth Century*. Tokyo: Kodansha International, 1989.

Barr, Pat, *The Coming of the Barbarians*. London: Macmillan, 1967.

Becker de, J. E, *The Nightless City, or the History of the Yoshiwara Yukwaku*. Tokyo: ICG Muse, 1899.

Benfey, Christopher, *The Great Wave*. New York: Random House, 2003.

Bestro, Ted, *Neighborhood Tokyo*. Stanford CA: Stanford University Press, 1989.

Bird, Isabella, *Unbeaten Tracks in Japan*. New York: G. P. Putnam's, 1880.

Birnbaum, Phyllis, *Modern Girls, Shining Stars, The Skies of Tokyo*. New York: Columbia University Press, 1999.

Bodart-Bailey, Beatrice M., *The Dog Shogun: The Personality and Policies of Tokugawa Tsunayoshi*. Honolulu: University of Hawaii Press, 2006.

Buruma, Ian, *A Japanese Mirror: Heroes and Villains of Japanese Culture*. London: Penguin, 1985.

Buruma, Ian, *Inventing Japan*. New York: Modern Library, 2003.

Dunn, Charles J., *Everyday Life in Traditional Japan*. Tokyo: Tuttle, 1972.

Ernst, Earle, *The Kabuki Theater*. Honolulu: University of Hawaii Press, 1974.

Fowler, Edward, *San'ya Blues: Laboring Life in Contemporary Tokyo*. Ithaca NY: Cornell University Press, 1996.

Gerster, Robin, *Legless in Ginza: Orienting Japan*. Melbourne: Melbourne University Press, 1999.

Greenfeld, Karl Taro, *Speed Tribes: Days and Nights with Japan's Next Generation*. New York: Harper Perennial, 1994.

Guest, Harry, *Traveller's Literary Companion, Japan*. Chicago IL: Passport Books, 1995.

Guillain, Robert, *I Saw Tokyo Burning*. London: Murray, 1981.

Harvey, Robert, *American Shogun: MacArthur, Hirohitio and the American Duel with Japan*. London: John Murray, 2006.

Hibbett, Howard, *The Floating World in Japanese Fiction*. Oxford: Oxford University Press, 1959.

Ishiguro, Kazuo, *An Artist of the Floating World*. London: Faber and

Faber, 1986.

Ito, Ken K., *Visions of Desire: Tanizaki's Fictional Worlds*. Stanford CA: Stanford University Press, 1991.

Jinnai, Hidenobu, *Tokyo: A Spatial Anthology*. Berkeley CA: University of California Press, 1995.

Jones, H. J, *Live Machines: Hired Foreigners and Meiji Japan*. Vancouver: University of British Columbia Press, 1980.

Kawaguchi, Matsutaro, *Stories from a Tokyo Teahouse*. Tokyo: Tuttle, 2006.

Kern, Adam L., *Manga from the Floating World: Comic-book Culture and the Kibyoshi of Edo Japan*. Cambridge MA: Harvard University Asia Center, 2006.

McClain, James L., *Japan: A Modern History*. New York: W.W. Norton & Company, 2002.

Meech-Pekarik, Julia, *The World of the Meiji Print: Impressions of a New Civilization*. Tokyo: Weatherhill, 1986.

Mitchell, David, *Number9Dream*. London: Hodder and Stoughton, 2001.

Nakamura, Mitsuo, *Contemporary Japanese Fiction, 1926-1968*. Tokyo: Kokusai Bunka Shinkokai, 1969.

Nathan, John, *Mishima: A Biography*. New York: Da Capo Press, 1974.

Nishiyama, Matsunosuke, *Edo Culture: Daily Life and Diversions in Urban Japan, 1600-1868*. Honolulu: University of Hawaii Press, 1997.

Peace, David, *Tokyo Year Zero*. London: Faber & Faber, 2007.

Popham, Peter, *Tokyo: The City at the End of the World*. Tokyo: Kodansha International, 1985.

Richie, Donald, *A Hundred Years of Japanese Film*. Tokyo: Kodansha International, 2001.

Richie, Donald, *The Honorable Visitors*. Tokyo: ICG Muse, 2001.

Richie, Donald, *Tokyo: A View of the City*. London: Reaktion, 1999.

Rogers, Lawrence, *Tokyo Stories: A Literary Stroll*. Berkeley CA: University of California Press, 2002.

Sacchi, Livio, *Tokyo: City and Architecture*. Milan: Skira, 2004.

Saga, Junichi, *Confessions of a Yakuza*. Tokyo: Kodansha International, 1991.

Seidensticker, Edward, *Low City, High City*. Tokyo: Tuttle, 1983.

Seidensticker, Edward, *Tokyo Rising*. Tokyo: Tuttle, 1991.

Seidensticker, Edward, *Kafu the Scribbler: The Life and Writings of Nagai Kafu*, 1879-1959. Stanford CA: Stanford University Press, 1965.

Seigle, Segawa Cecilia *et al*, *A Courtesan's Day: Hour by Hour*. Amsterdam: Hotei, 2004.

Silverberg, Miriam, *Erotic, Grotesque, Nonsense: the Mass Culture of Japanese Modern Times*. Berkeley CA: University of California Press, 2006.

Smith, Martin Cruz, *December 6*. New York: Simon & Schuster, 2002.

Stokes, Henry Scott, *The Life and Death of Yukio Mishima*. New York: Farrar Straus Giroux, 1974.

Tanizaki, Junichiro, *Childhood Years*. Tokyo: Kodansha International, 1988.

Waley, Paul, *Fragments of a City*. Tokyo: The Japan Times, 1992.

Waley, Paul, *Tokyo: City of Stories*. Tokyo: Weatherhill, 1991.

Whiteney, Clara A. N., *Clara's Diary: An American Girl in Meiji Japan*. Tokyo: Kodansha International, 1979.

Whiting, Robert, *Tokyo Underworld*. New York: Vintage Books, 1999.

Index of Literary & Historical Names

Index of Places & Landmarks